Anti-Semitism
in America

ANTI-SEMITISM IN AMERICA

HAROLD E. QUINLEY AND

CHARLES Y. GLOCK

THE FREE PRESS
A Division of Macmillan Publishing Co., Inc.
NEW YORK

Collier Macmillan Publishers
LONDON

The Free Press
A Division of Macmillan Publishing Co.. Inc.
866 Third Avenue, New York, N.Y. 10022

Collier Macmillan Canada, Ltd.

Library of Congress Catalog Card Number: 78-20649

Printed in the United States of America

printing number
1 2 3 4 5 6 7 8 9 10

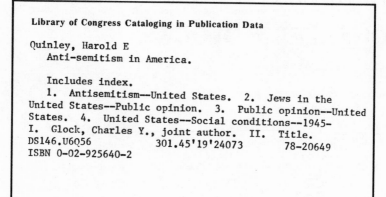

Library of Congress Cataloging in Publication Data

Quinley, Harold E
    Anti-semitism in America.

    Includes index.
    1. Antisemitism—United States. 2. Jews in the
United States—Public opinion. 3. Public opinion—United
States. 4. United States—Social conditions—1945-
I. Glock, Charles Y., joint author. II. Title.
DS146.U6Q56   301.45'19'24073   78-20649
ISBN 0-02-925640-2

Copyright
Acknowledgments

To Oscar Cohen
and to
Ann and Mickey

Contents

Preface

On Christmas Eve, 1959, a gang of German youths desecrated a Jewish synagogue in Cologne. Within days the Cologne incident was repeated in many other German cities. And that was only the beginning, for the waves spread beyond Germany, and then beyond Europe to the United States. By March 1960, barely two months after the first German incident, at least 643 similar incidents had occurred in the United States alone. Synagogues across the country suddenly bore the crude epithets of bigotry and the ubiquitous swastika. Not synagogues alone, but Jewish cemeteries, stores, and homes were smeared and shattered in the epidemic of nightly anti-Semitic vandalism. On occasion, Jews were personally tormented and beaten.

The mass media immediately reflected the outrage and alarm of millions of Americans shocked by the apparent durability of anti-Semitism. How could such feelings survive the grisly horrors of Nazism? Public shock increased as it became known that these acts were not a final spasm on the part of aged Nazis but were committed by youngsters reared and educated in supposedly enlightened postwar America.

In a few weeks the storm of incidents began to subside. The mass media turned to other sensations, and public interest waned. Soon, few Americans probably even remembered that such events had ever happened. But not everyone forgot. Victims did not, nor did the leaders of the Anti-Defamation League of B'nai B'rith. The ADL was founded in 1912 to fight anti-Semitism in the United States. In the beginning the task seemed nearly overwhelming, but slowly times changed, and by 1960 the ADL leaders had begun to feel that violence against Jewish persons and property had become a thing of the past. They had turned their main attention instead to more subtle processes, such as discrimination against Jews by social clubs, schools, and industry. The incidents of 1960 were a stunning and grievous contradiction to their hopes. And if such things were possible, what else was? Could anything about anti-Semitism in America be taken for granted?

Thus, the officials of the ADL began to ask some old and stubborn questions once again. What accounts for the persistence of anti-Semitism in our democratic society? How is it that in generation after generation there are Americans who seem to regard their Jewish countrymen with suspicion and even contempt? Is it possible that such sentiments might be incorporated into the political doctrine of new extremist movements in the United States? The questions assumed new urgency as a result of the incidents of 1960, but the ADL found that the answers were still by and large unknown.

Consequently, the ADL decided to commission a new social science investigation of the enduring phenomenon of anti-Semitism in the U.S. They conceived such an effort as contributing to knowledge about the extent, location, and character of contemporary anti-Semitism. But they also wanted to learn as much as possible about the root causes of anti-Jewish prejudice in order to find more effective ways to combat it.

Once decided on this course, the ADL invited a group of scholars associated with the Survey Research Center of the University of California at Berkeley to draw up a prospectus for such a comprehensive study. This proposal was submitted to the Anti-Defamation League through the Regents of the University of California in the fall of 1960; ADL committed itself to supplying the five hundred thousand dollars which the program called for beginning in the fall of 1961. Thus was born what came to be called the University of California Research Program on Patterns of American Prejudice.

The plans for the research program committed the Survey Research Center associates to conduct a series of interrelated projects, each designed to illuminate a different facet of the phenomenon of anti-Semitism. There had never before been a systematic effort to measure simply the amount and character of anti-Semitism in the United States. Accordingly, one of the projects was to be devoted to this descriptive purpose, having in mind that such measurement would also enable some specification of the relative distribution of anti-Semitism in different parts of the society as well as provide a benchmark against which to measure future changes in the level of anti-Semitism.

A second project, responsive to growing concern about black–Jewish relations in the society, was to address the attitudes of black Americans toward Jews, especially within the context of the civil rights movement. A third study was to explore the link between anti-Semitism and political extremism, with special interest in the ways in which political movements become anti-Semitic.

Three additional studies, later expanded to five, were to examine the role of three major institutions of the society—the churches, the schools, and the mass media—in the struggle to combat anti-Semitism. These studies were motivated by the initiating scholars' concern that the research program not only add to basic knowledge about anti-Semitism but also contribute suggestions of more effective means for dealing with it. If additional leverage is to be secured to help eliminate anti-Semitism as a cultural artifact, the schools, the churches, and the mass media appear to be major societal instruments for doing so.

Provision was also made to study immediate and ongoing events that had a special and immediate bearing on problems of anti-Semitism. A special "firehouse" fund was set aside to be used for research on events as they were happening.

The research plans called for technical, scholarly publication of the results of the various studies. They also called for what came to be called a "wrap-up" volume, a final volume in the series, written in a form that would attract a lay as well as a professional audience, summarizing what the research program had learned about anti-Semitism in America, and confronting the critical question of what the findings signify for future efforts to combat anti-Semitism and other forms of prejudice in our society. This is the "wrap-up" volume.

The studies reported upon are nine in number. They have been conducted over a period from January 1963, when the first project was launched, to August 1975, when the technical report on the last project was published. The present report gives principal attention to the findings of these studies rather than to the means adopted to produce them, that task having been attended to in detail in the technical documents. Some brief report here on how the studies were done seems nevertheless advisable in order to place the findings in proper context.

The means adopted to assess the character and extent of anti-Semitism in the country as a whole was a survey carried on by personal interviews of a sample of the U.S. adult population.[1] The sample was drawn to give all American adults an equal chance at being chosen as respondents, thus ensuring that the results from the survey can be projected to the population from which the sample was drawn. Sampling and interviewing were carried out on behalf of the Survey Research Center by the National Opinion Research Center of the University of Chicago, an organization that is specially equipped to pursue surveys of an academic nature on a nationwide level. The total number of persons interviewed was 1,976, of which 61 were Jewish. For obvious reasons the Jewish respondents have been omitted in the report, given later, of the results of this study.

It was intended originally that the special study of black attitudes toward Jews also be based on a national sample, this time, of course, of the black adult population.[2] It turned out, however, that there was no American research organization capable of conducting such a survey using exclusively or primarily black interviewers, a condition that had to be met in light of the subject matter of the interviews. The National Opinion Research Center, to which the Survey Research Center again called for assistance, was able to mount a survey, using black interviewers, of the black population living in metropolitan areas of the country outside of the South, and in the South to do so but only in large Southern cities. Given these limitations, it was decided to conduct one study of a sample representative of the adult black population living in metropolitan areas outside of the South. In addition to this metropolitan sample, four urban centers were chosen for special study, and a representative sample of blacks was interviewed in each, using the same research instrument as was used in the metropolitan sample. New York, Chicago, Atlanta, and Birmingham were selected as the most important centers of black population and because of the differences they offer in region and in history of intergroup relations. In all, 1,119 interviews were conducted with black adults, 492 of them with the metropolitan sample. In reporting on black attitudes, use was made also of data collected from black respondents in the aforementioned survey of the general U.S. population.

The study of political extremism and prejudice was largely historical, tracing the ways in which extremist movements throughout American history have sought to further their causes through utilizing appeals to bigotry.[3] The methodology, consequently, was historiographic, making use primarily of available documentary materials in the nation's libraries and historic survey materials archived at the Roper Public Opinion Library of Yale University and the University of Connecticut. In examining extremism in its contemporary manifestations, the study also made use of 115 interviews with persons who had written letters to a national Republican leader making evident their commitment to extremist causes.

The original study research plans called only for a single study on religion and anti-Semitism. As it turned out, three studies were in fact undertaken. The first, designed to test a theory that certain interpretations of the Christian faith may continue to be a source of contemporary anti-Semitism, was conducted through a survey of a probability sample of the church-member population of four counties along the western side of the San Francisco Bay Area: San Mateo, Santa Clara, San Francisco, and Marin.[4] This area proved to be the only one out of more than half a dozen tried where it was possible to gain necessary Diocesan authorization to undertake the project in Roman Catholic parishes.

In the study area all Protestant and Roman Catholic congregations were listed, and a sample of these congregations was then drawn. From the membership of the sampled churches, a sample of church members was then chosen. The sampling procedure followed made sure that each Protestant and Catholic church member had an equal chance of being selected, so that the resulting samples for both faiths would be representative of the population from which they were selected. In all, 3,000 completed questionnaires were received, 485 from Roman Catholics and the balance from Protestants.

Eighteen months after the data for this first study were collected, the opportunity arose to replicate the study on a national sample of the population through adding appropriate questions to the national study of anti-Semitism described above, which was then being launched.[5] This opportunity was seized upon since it allowed for assessing the extent to which the findings for the Northern California sample were parallel to the nation as a whole.

The third study on religion and prejudice resulted from an opportunity that arose to piggyback our questions on religious beliefs and anti-Semitism on a study of political attitudes being conducted by a colleague at Stanford University on a sample of Protestant clergy in California.[6] This opportunity promised to enable investigation of whether or not what had earlier been learned about the links between religious beliefs and anti-Semitism among laymen also applied to clergy. It seemed too good an opportunity to miss, and while by then even the half million dollars was beginning to look like not enough for all that was being done, the decision was made to go ahead. The sample size of this study was 1,580, representing all Protestant ministers serving parishes in the state of California.

The project on the schools and prejudice was concerned both with measuring the incidence of anti-Semitism among adolescent youths and with investigating its causes.[7] Special attention in the latter regard was given to examining the significance of a Jewish presence in a school on anti-Semitism. To this end, the study was undertaken in three school systems, all of them within a 200-mile radius of New York City but varying in the proportion of their students who were Jewish. In one of the school systems 42 percent of the students were Jewish, in another 23 percent, and in a third less than 1 percent. In these three school systems, *all* youngsters in the eighth, tenth, and twelfth grades were included in the study. Their participation called for their completing three intensive questionnaires administered in three settings over a three-week period. In all, 4,631 teenagers participated in the study.

A study of how the mass media may be contributing to or helping to contain anti-Semitism in America was promised in the initial prospectus for the research progran, but just how the investigation was to be done wasn't set forth in the prospectus. This was simply because no one at the time had a clear idea as to how such a project might be mounted effectively. The idea that came along as the research program unfolded was to do such a study on the mass media's treatment of the Eichmann trial and the trial's impact on attitudes toward Jews and toward Israel.[8] At the time, Eichmann's capture by Israelis in Argentina and the trial itself had been headline news for almost a year. If anything might serve to inform world opinion about the evils of anti-Semitism, the Eichmann trial seemed an ideal medium for that purpose. The study was based on 463 hour-long interviews with a representative sample of the population of Oakland, California.

It was decided to do the study in a single city rather than the nation as a whole to permit a focus on the mass media's treatment of the trial; a national population would have been exposed to too great a variety of local newspaper treatments for their different effects to be isolated effectively. The choice of Oakland also meant that the study could be done in greater depth and detail than would have been possible elsewhere because of its proximity to research headquarters and the investigators' familiarity with the city's characteristics and the mass media serving it.

The study of the Eichmann trial can be characterized as a "firehouse" project; that is, one taken up as the opportunity presented itself, with the investigation quickly organized and pursued while the event was still in progress. A second "firehouse" project, also undertaken during the research program's course, was stimulated by an anti-Semitic incident in the township of Wayne, New Jersey, which embroiled that community in internal conflict. Members of the research team quickly traveled to Wayne to study at first hand the unfolding of the controversy and its treatment by local and mass media. The mode of investigation in this instance was primarily open-ended interviewing of the principal antagonists in the controversy as well as a small number of local citizens from different walks of life. Representatives of the mass media covering the event were also interviewed.

Very briefly, then, that is how the series of studies were done. In the report on them which follows, studies on anti-Semitism done by others have been referred to where helpful in making the reporting as current as possible. Studies by others on racial prejudice are also cited to compare antiblack with anti-Jewish prejudice. Chapter 1 addresses the question of what constitutes anti-Semitism and summarizes what the research program learned about the present extent and character of anti-Semitism in American society. Evidence about changes in the level and form of anti-Semitic prejudice is also presented.

Chapter 2 takes up the question of what kinds of people are disposed to be anti-Semitic and what kinds are not. Chapter 3 considers alternative theories of anti-Semitism and most especially the question of why the uneducated are so much more inclined to anti-Semitism than the educated. Chapter 4 summarizes the research program's findings about anti-Semitism among black Americans. It compares the amount of anti-Semitism of blacks and whites, examines the relationship between black militancy and anti-Semitism, and explores how much anti-Semitic feelings among blacks are part of a more general hostility toward all whites. Chapter 5 turns to the study of the schools and prejudice and reports on the extent and sources of prejudice among America's youth. Chapter 6 summarizes the three studies of religion and anti-Semitism, and Chapter 7 is a report on the study done during the Eichmann trial. Chapter 8 compares anti-Semitism with racial prejudice and shows what was learned in the series about these two forms of prejudice. Chapter 9 reports on what was found in the area of political extremism and anti-Semitism.

The last chapter of the book is given to answering two questions: What have we learned about anti-Semitism that we didn't know before the studies began, and what do these findings imply for future efforts to combat anti-Semitism?

Acknowledgments

THIS BOOK has its origins in a grant from the Anti-Defamation League of B'nai B'rith to the University of California in support of an extended research program on anti-Semitism and other forms of prejudice in America. The book, the last in a series of eight produced under that grant, reports for the general reader what the research program has learned about anti-Semitism in contemporary America.

To the Anti-Defamation League we owe much more than the generous financing which made the project possible. At all times its officials have offered us friendship, assistance, and encouragement. In particular we are indebted to Oscar Cohen, Program Director Emeritus of the ADL. He conceived of the program and from the outset has been its most ardent supporter. He has been extraordinarily generous of his time and energy in initiating the program and in helping to bring it to its successful conclusion. Benjamin Epstein, National Director of the ADL, and Henry Schulz, former National Chairman, were instrumental in securing the resources enabling the program to be developed. Theodore Freedman, the present Program Director, and Eleanor Blumenberg, Stan Wexler, and Sam Elfert are among other Anti-Defamation League officers who have been especially helpful to us.

We are also indebted to Bruce Foster, Gertrude Jaeger, Seymour Martin Lipset, Gary Marx, Jane Allyn Piliavin, Earl Raab, Joe L. Spaeth, Metta Spencer, Stephen Steinberg, Rodney Stark, and Robert Wuthnow for graciously allowing us to draw upon and summarize the studies on prejudice they pursued as part of the research program. In drawing on the work of others, the general practice we have followed has been to paraphrase that work. Where we have drawn from previously published work, either our own or that of which one or the other of us was senior author, we have felt free, on occasion, to use sentences or paragraphs as they appeared in their original form without quotation marks.

The research reported upon was conducted at the Survey Research Center of the University of California, Berkeley, of which J. Merrill Shanks is Director and William L. Nicholls is Assistant Director. We want to thank them and the many members of the Center staff who helped make the research program possible. We have benefited immensely from the editorial and secretarial assistance of Ann Stannard. The fine editorial hand of Gladys Topkis of The Free Press is also very much appreciated.

Last but not least, the book owes much to the many thousand Americans who allowed us and the other investigators to study them. A sincere thanks to one and all of you.

H. E. Q.
C. Y. G.

CHAPTER 1

Anti-Semitism in Contemporary America

CONTRADICTORY STATEMENTS ARE OFTEN MADE about the anti-Semitism of Americans. On the one hand, there are many who consider anti-Semitism to be of declining significance in American society. Prejudice toward Jews is said to be a social reality, but one of sharply reduced proportions. Few Americans are seen as harboring the type of scurrilous attitudes toward Jews that once were prevalent, and fewer still as supporting blatant discrimination against Jews. Americans have become allegedly more enlightened in their beliefs about Jews and more sympathetic toward them. To the extent that prejudice and discrimination toward minority groups exists in America, blacks, it is argued, are considerably more likely than Jews to be the victims.[1]

On the other hand, there are many who feel that anti-Semitism in America is as prevalent as ever and may, in fact, be on the rise. From this perspective, anti-Semitism is viewed as a deeply embedded and pervasive element in American culture—passed on from generation to generation in the home, the churches, and even the schools. A number of observers, moreover, have expressed concern about a potential in contemporary events for the outbreak and growth of anti-Semitism. Cited are the increased tensions between blacks and Jews, concern over Arab oil, the poor state of the economy, and a possible backlash against American support of Israel.[2] Such observers, mindful of past history, point out that political attacks upon minorities have regularly been a concomitant of social and economic strains in American history.

This chapter examines the current state of anti-Semitism in America, as well as the changes in anti-Semitic attitudes that have occurred over the past forty years. Its principal source of information is the national survey of the adult population of the United States described in the Preface.[3] Findings

1

from this study are supplemented by the results of other national surveys conducted from the mid-1930s through the mid-1970s.

Two principal methods have been used to measure anti-Semitism in these studies. The first focuses upon negative images or stereotypes of Jews, and the second on the extent to which people support discriminatory actions directed against Jews.

Negative Images of Jews

How anti-Semitic are Americans? There is no simple or definitive way of answering this question. Anti-Semitism has a number of dimensions and can thus be measured through a variety of techniques. In most studies the principal procedure has been to identify anti-Semitism with holding negative beliefs or stereotypes about Jews. For example, an anti-Semite is someone who believes such things as: Jewish businessmen are more dishonest than others; Jews are pushy and aggressive; and Jews look out only for their own kind. Such a person is assigning negative traits to Jews solely on the basis of their membership in that group. This corresponds closely to what is commonly meant by "being prejudiced."

This procedure was one of several used to measure anti-Semitism in the national study. Statements were prepared associating Jews with various negative characteristics. The respondents were then asked to state their agreement or disagreement with each. In the following discussion, responses are considered under six headings or traditional images of Jews: as monied, as dishonest and unethical, as clannish, as prideful and conceited, as power-hungry, and as pushy and intrusive.

THE JEW AS MONIED

The view that Jews are money-oriented is an old and central part of anti-Semitic ideology. In the United States, a majority of Jews are in fact monied in the sense of having above-average incomes. This fact is acknowledged and apparently accepted by most non-Jews. When asked whether they think the average Jew has more, less, or the same money as most people, 60 percent of the respondents said more. When this last group was asked whether they were bothered by Jews having more money, 97 percent said no. Typical comments were: "They work for it and earn it, they're entitled to it." "If they're smart enough to get it, they deserve it." "It's their money. It doesn't bother me, wish I had some of it."

These remarks suggest that viewing Jews as monied need not be accompanied by hostility. Indeed, this was one of the most commonly accepted images among those ultimately classified as being unprejudiced. At the same time, the image of Jews as monied often goes beyond a simple recognition of this fact. Even the unprejudiced exaggerate the amount of Jewish wealth, while for the prejudiced this belief is an integral part of anti-Semitic ideology. For anti-Semites, Jewish wealth is conceived to be the result of economic chicanery and is cited as evidence that Jews are money-mad, unethical, and power-hungry.

Thus even factual or quasi-factual beliefs can have an anti-Semitic potential. The critical factor often is not the truthfulness of the stereotype but the manner in which it is interpreted. Anti-Semites characteristically believe firmly in various falsehoods and fantasies about Jews. Just as characteristically, they tend to explain real "facts" about Jews in perverse and malicious ways. The latter tendency often makes it difficult to distinguish between the prejudiced and the unprejudiced since the acceptance of the same "fact" will carry a different meaning to each group.

THE JEW AS DISHONEST AND UNETHICAL

The relationship between Jewish wealth and anti-Semitism is apparent in responses to statements pertaining to alleged Jewish business activities. The view that Jews engage in unethical economic practices dates back to at least the Middle Ages. At that time, such Jewish economic activities as money-lending at interest were forbidden to Christians and were carried out in an environment of extreme religious hostility. For this and other reasons, economic stereotypes of the unethical Jew became deeply embedded in European cultures and were carried over largely intact to the New World.

A substantial proportion of non-Jewish Americans conceive Jewish businessmen to be dishonest and unethical. Thirty-five percent agreed that "Jewish businessmen are so shrewd and tricky that other people don't have a chance in competition," while 42 percent agreed that "Jews are more willing than others to use shady practices to get what they want." A more stringent test is included in a statement worded positively: "Jewish businessmen are as honest as other businessmen." To go out of one's way to disagree with this statement would seem to represent an especially strong affirmation of one's position on this issue. Twenty-eight percent of the non-Jewish public did so.

From these responses, it appears that at least a quarter of the American public have negative views about Jewish business practices. This historic stereotype remains a prevalent one among contemporary Americans.

THE JEW AS CLANNISH

Another common stereotype of Jews is that they are clannish. This image also has its origins in medieval European practices. For centuries, European Jews were segregated from community life and lived by their own strict codes of separation. When Jews began to be freed from years of oppression and persecution, beginning around the middle of the eighteenth century, their self-segregation became more problematic. Once Jews were accepted as equal members of society, any tendency on their part to associate regularly with other Jews made them vulnerable to charges that they were clannish and self-segregating.

A considerable number of Americans think of Jews as being clannish. About half agreed that "Jews stick together too much" and that "Jewish employers go out of their way to hire other Jews." Two statements went farther, implying that Jews are selfishly clannish and distant. These gained less frequent but still significant acceptance—26 percent agreeing that "Jews don't care about anyone but their own kind" and 30 percent that "Jews are more loyal to Israel than to America."

The perception of Jews as clannish has some basis in fact and can thus be accepted without necessarily being a symptom of prejudice. The last two belief statements, however, represent rather harsh assessments of alleged Jewish behavior and cannot be dismissed as innocuous.

THE JEW AS PRIDEFUL AND CONCEITED

A related negative image of Jews is that they are prideful and conceited. Only one question was asked on this dimension, and it dealt with the issue somewhat indirectly. In an allusion to Jewish pride, Jews are often referred to scornfully in anti-Semitic propaganda as the Chosen People. For this reason, the statement was included that "Jews still think of themselves as God's Chosen People." It was accepted by 59 percent of the non-Jewish public, with 24 percent saying they didn't know.

Since this belief is a part of traditional Jewish religion, it can hardly be taken as an indicator of anti-Semitism. However, additional statements alleging Jewish pride and conceit were included in other surveys to be reported below. These show that a substantial minority of Americans associate Jews with this image.

THE JEW AS POWER-HUNGRY

Another traditional image of Jews is that they are preoccupied with the getting and holding of power. It follows that others should be wary of the political machinations of Jews—a fear used in the recent past to justify actions ranging from disfranchisement to mass genocide.

Five statements were included on this subject. The most widely accepted (by 54 percent) was that "Jews always like to be at the head of things." Forty-seven percent believed that Jews "pretty much" control the movie and television industries, and 30 percent that they control international banking. Two other questions were more direct: "Do you think Jews have too much power in the United States?" "How about the business world—do you think the Jews have too much power in the business world?" Eleven percent said yes to the former, 29 percent to the latter.

The image of Jews as power-hungry seems to be a continuing one for some Americans. To investigate the subject further, those who believe that Jews have too much power either in the country or in the business world were asked whether "something should be done to take power away from Jews." Twenty-eight percent of this group—or 8 percent of the total sample—replied in the affirmative. This 8 percent were next asked what should be done. About a third suggested restrictive laws or government action, but virtually no one mentioned violence. About half could offer no specific proposals at all.

The alarm over Jewish power is clearly not what it once was; this will become more apparent as additional information is presented below. Nevertheless, a reservoir of hostility and fear remains about Jewish power.

THE JEW AS PUSHY AND INTRUSIVE

A final traditional image of Jews is that they are pushy and aggressive. This stereotype bears some relation to the economic issues examined above; it is often associated with alleged Jewish business practices. However, it is a paradox of prejudice that the minority seeking to overcome discrimination is often perceived as being overly aggressive and intrusive. It is in this way that the repertory of prejudice is often expanded, and that the image of the "pushy" Jew becomes an element in anti-Semitic ideology.

Only 18 percent agreed that "Jews today are trying to push in where they are not wanted," suggesting that the image of Jews as pushy and aggressive is not as widespread among Americans as some other stereotypes. However, a less narrowly worded statement that "Jews have a lot of irritating faults" produced substantially greater agreement, with 40 percent answering that they do. Other studies to be reported below, framing the question somewhat differently, come up with higher estimates of the degree of acceptance of the "pushiness" stereotype.

How Anti-Semitic Are Americans?

The results cited so far reveal anti-Semitic beliefs to be fairly common among non-Jewish Americans. Such traditional images of Jews as dishonest, clannish, prideful, and pushy continue to be widely subscribed to in America. At the same time, the responses indicate that, while many people support these traditional shibboleths, it is proportionately only a minority of the population that does so. Indeed, the percentage of Americans expressing serious concern about Jewish power or Jewish money, to the extent of wanting something to be done about it, is less than 10 percent. The anti-Semitism that persists in America is not, for the most part, of the virulent, hate-inspired type. Such prejudice may survive within some extremist groups, but it is not practiced by large numbers of Americans.

Any determination of how many anti-Semites there are in the country must be arbitrary to a degree. It is possible, however, to use these responses to make a reasoned estimate. The procedure followed was to omit from consideration stereotypes such as "Jews still think of themselves as God's Chosen People," which are not unambiguously negative, and to examine only the pattern of acceptance scores of the outrightly negative stereotypes. The distribution of the population according to how many of these stereotypes were accepted is shown in Table 1-1. Sixteen percent did not agree with any of these statements, while 15 percent accepted one as being true. At the other extreme, 5 percent scored as anti-Semitic on nine belief statements, 3 percent on ten, and 2 percent on all eleven.

TABLE 1-1.   Distribution of American Respondents by Scores on Index of Anti-Semitism.

Index Score[a]	Percent	Number	
0	16	(316)	Least anti-Semitic third
1	15	(289)	(31 per cent)
2	12	(227)	
3	10	(183)	Middle anti-Semitic third
4	10	(192)	(32 per cent)
5	8	(156)	
6	6	(125)	
7	7	(130)	
8	6	(108)	Most anti-Semitic third
9	5	(95)	(37 per cent)
10	3	(58)	
11	2	(34)	
	100 (N) =	(1,913)	

Average score = 3.75

[a]The index scores and percentages refer to the number of anti-Semitic statements accepted by respondents as true.

SOURCE: Reproduced from Gertrude J. Selznick and Stephen Steinberg, *The Tenacity of Prejudice: Anti-Semitism in Contemporary America* (New York: Harper & Row, 1969), p. 26.

The exact point on this index where anti-Semites and non-anti-Semites may be distinguished is necessarily somewhat arbitrary, but score 5 is a reasonable place at which to decide that an individual ranks high in anti-Semitism. It is here that the acceptance rates begin to exceed acceptance rates for the population as a whole. (For example, 26 percent of all Americans agree that Jews care only about their own kind, but among those who score 5 on the index, 34 percent respond this way.) Adopting the standard that anti-Semitism is indicated when five or more of these negative stereotypes are subscribed to, then roughly a third of the American public—37 percent—is anti-Semitic.

Of the remaining respondents, most accepted at least some of the anti-Semitic stereotypes as true. Thus another third (those scoring between 2 and 4) might be considered to be moderately prejudiced toward Jews. The final "unprejudiced" third are those agreeing with none or only one of the statements.[4]

The specific beliefs of these three thirds are shown in Table 1-2. The table shows that a majority of the most anti-Semitic group accepts all but one of the items in the index of anti-Semitic belief. Most accept statements depicting Jews as clannish, dishonest, and unethical. The middle group shares many of these beliefs, but only the stereotype of Jews "always liking to be at the head of things" receives clear majority support. The final group largely rejects these and other negative images.

Trends in Anti-Semitic Belief

These results describe the incidence of anti-Semitism in America in the mid-1960s, when the national survey was done. The question may be raised legitimately as to whether the amount of anti-Semitism has since declined, risen, or remained the same. It will also be of some interest to know whether anti-Semitism in the mid-1960s was greater or less than it had been at earlier points in American history. It is not possible to go back earlier than the late 1930s, but since then questions about Jews have been periodically included in national public opinion polls. These questions, while not always asked in comparable form, are similar enough to indicate the general trends.

CONCERN OVER JEWISH POWER

The major changes to occur are in public images of Jewish power. During the 1930s and early 1940s, concern about Jewish power was widespread in this country. Jews were often blamed for the Depression or the growth in political extremism, and millions of Americans supported Father Coughlin's anti-Semitic Union for Social Justice. In a 1938 poll, for example, 41 percent of the public agreed that Jews had too much power in the United States. This figure rose during World War II, reaching a peak of 58 percent in 1945.[5]

TABLE 1-2.   Acceptance of Anti-Semitic Beliefs Among
Least, Middle, and Most Anti-Semitic Thirds of the
Population.

Statement	Least Anti-Semitic Third	Middle Anti-Semitic Third	Most Anti-Semitic Third
Jews always like to be at the head of things.	12%[a]	56%	88%
Jews stick together too much.	14	50	86
Jews are more willing than others to use shady practices to get ahead.	3	37	81
Jews have a lot of irritating faults.	6	36	72
The trouble with Jewish businessmen is that they are so shrewd and tricky that other people don't have a fair chance in competition.	2	20	77
International banking is pretty much controlled by Jews.	5	26	54
Jews are more loyal to Israel than to America.	2	23	60
Jews have too much power in the business world.	2	20	60
Jews are not as honest as other businessmen.	1	16	60
Jews don't care what happens to anyone but their own kind.	1	10	62
Jews have too much power in the United States.	0	2	27
100% equals	(605)	(602)	(706)

[a]Percentages show the acceptance by non-Jewish Americans of the eleven belief statements included in the index of anti-Semitic belief.
SOURCE: Adapted from Selznick and Steinberg, *Tenacity of Prejudice,* p. 28.

Concern about Jews' having too much power remains today but is not nearly so prevalent. In a 1962 survey, only 17 percent of the public agreed that Jews were too powerful;[6] in the 1964 survey the figure fell to 11 percent. The question about power has not been asked since that time, but other questions asked more recently reveal little tendency to blame Jews for the country's problems. In 1975 and 1976, for example, a negligible proportion (2 to 3 percent) held Jews accountable for the energy crisis, the troubles encountered by former President Richard Nixon, or the poor state of the economy.[7]

Prejudice remains in this area, and it is easy to envision circumstances under which this trend might reverse itself. A prolonged war in the Middle East, in particular, might serve as such a catalyst. In general, however, Americans today are much less likely than in the past to believe that Jews have too much power.

CONTROL OVER BANKING AND THE MASS MEDIA

A related stereotype about Jews is that they control banking and the mass media. In the mid-1960s, 47 percent of the public agreed that Jews pretty much controlled the movie and television industries, while 30 percent thought they controlled international banking. A 1975 Harris poll framed the questions somewhat differently. It found that only 18 percent of Americans believed the movie industry to be "controlled" by Jews, but 31 percent on top of that felt that Jews played an "important role in this area." Similarly, 14 percent saw Jews as controlling "big New York banks," but 30 percent in addition saw them as playing an "important role." In another section of the same survey, respondents were asked whether they agreed with a recent statement by General Brown that Jews "own the banks and newspapers in this country." Twenty percent replied in the affirmative.

The different wordings make comparisons difficult, and it is impossible to say for sure whether acceptance of these stereotypes has declined or remained about the same. It would appear, however, that acceptance of them has not increased over the last decade.

JEWS AS UNETHICAL, CLANNISH, DISLOYAL, AND PUSHY

There is some evidence of a decline in acceptance of other traditional anti-Jewish stereotypes, although the evidence is not entirely consistent, especially for the last decade. Polls show that there was a modest drop in acceptance of such negative stereotypes as Jews being dishonest in business, clannish, and disloyal to America between the 1930s and the early-to-mid-1960s. For example, a national sample was asked in 1940 and again in 1962 to name the "objectionable qualities" they believed to be associated with Jews. More listed these traits in the earlier interviews than in the later ones.[8] Similarly, in a 1938 survey 44 percent of Americans said Jews were less honest than other businessmen. When the same question was asked in 1964, the figure had dropped to 28 percent.[9]

Since the mid-1960s the existing evidence suggests that there may have been a decline in acceptance of the stereotype that Jews are dishonest and unethical in business dealings. A Harris poll conducted in 1975 reports that 18 percent of a national population sample subscribed to the view that "Jews are not as honest as other businessmen." This compares to the 28 percent acceptance of an almost identical statement in the 1964 survey. In 1975 the allegation that "Jewish businessmen will usually try to pull a shady deal on you" was accepted by 21 percent of Americans. In 1964 a similarly worded statement—"The trouble with Jewish businessmen is that they are so shrewd and tricky that other people don't have a fair chance in competition"—received 35 percent support.

This decline in the perception of Jews as dishonest and unethical is not matched by a similar decline in the view that they are clannish and of questionable loyalty. In 1964, 26 percent acknowledged a belief that "Jews don't care what happens to anyone but their own kind." In 1975, 27 percent subscribed to a statement that "Jews always stick to their own and never give an outsider a break." Similarly, the statement "Jews are more loyal to Israel than to America," phrased identically in the two surveys, gained 30 percent acceptance in 1964 and 33 percent in 1975.

Finally, two additional questions asked in the 1975 Harris poll show that a substantial minority of Americans continue to see Jews as pushy and intrusive and hold negative beliefs about Jewish money. Thirty-one percent agreed that "Jews are irritating because they are too aggressive"; 34 percent agreed that "when it comes to choosing between people and money, Jews will choose money."

All in all, the data allowing an assessment of trends are not as systematic or comprehensive as would be desired ideally. The most reasonable conclusions that can be drawn from the information that does exist is that there was an almost across-the-board decline in acceptance of traditional anti-Semitic shibboleths from the late 1930s to the mid 1960s. Since then, there appears to have been no increase in anti-Semitism, but the general decline in all stereotyping, which characterized the earlier period, has not continued. Some stereotypes, notably that Jews are clannish and less loyal to America than to Israel, continue to be as widely accepted now as they were a decade ago.

Positive Beliefs About Jews

Along with the negative images which non-Jewish Americans harbor about Jews, there are often positive qualities that are also acknowledged. Jews are frequently considered to be an especially friendly, religious, generous, and family-oriented people. They are also seen as being highly intelligent, ambitious, and successful in business. Such positive images have consistently been reported in studies dealing with anti-Semitism, but, even though more widely held than the negative ones described above, they have received less emphasis and attention.

That Americans hold favorable images of Jews has been revealed in surveys dating as far back as 1938. In national surveys conducted in 1938,

1940, and 1962, for example, Americans were asked to indicate what "admirable qualities" they believe Jews to possess more than others. In all three years, the most commonly mentioned traits were ability in business, religious loyalty, family loyalty, intellectual attainments, and ambition.[10] Similar traits predominated when in 1975 a national sample was asked what "two or three things" they liked about Jews as people.[11]

Statements describing Jews in positive terms almost consistently gain wide acceptance when they are included in studies of attitudes toward Jews. In the 1964 survey 75 percent of the public agreed that "Jews are a warm and friendly people" and 67 percent that "the more contact a person has with Jewish people, the more he gets to like them." Both positive statements were more widely endorsed than any of the negative ones included in this study. Similarly, in the 1975 Harris poll 85 percent agreed that "Jews raise their children to accomplish something in the world," while 58 percent agreed that "Jews have contributed much to the cultural life of America." Again, these beliefs gained greater acceptance than the negative ones.

It is not entirely clear what should be made of such findings. They would seem to indicate that Jews are widely admired and that a reservoir of good will exists toward them. At the same time, it is apparent that many of the positive responses were given by respondents scoring high in anti-Semitism. Indeed, it seems to be a characteristic of prejudice that certain "positive" stereotypes exist alongside the negative ones. Blacks are good athletes and musicians, Orientals are well disciplined, and Italians are spirited. Many Americans associate admirable traits with minorities even while denigrating them in other ways.

This tendency helps explain a common protestation among the anti-Semitic: that some of their best friends are Jews and that, as a consequence, they couldn't possibly be anti-Semitic themselves. Such behavior is not uncharacteristic of Americans. The anti-Semite may well have positive feelings about a Jewish friend or neighbor while holding derogatory beliefs about Jews generally.

All of these positive attitudes toward Jews, of course, cannot be dismissed in such a fashion. There are clearly Americans who are not anti-Semitic persons whose attitudes toward Jews are unambiguously positive.

Discrimination Against Jews

Another component of anti-Semitism is discrimination. In the past, Jews have been frequent victims of discriminatory acts. They have been prevented from entering certain lines of work and barred from living in many neighborhoods. They have been admitted to colleges in restricted numbers and on occasion not at all, refused admittance to prominent social clubs, and kept from occupying key political offices. Whether such practices are supported by Americans today is a question that was explored in some depth in the national study.

It was expected that modern Americans would be found considerably less discriminatory in their attitudes toward Jews than Americans of the past. Laws have been passed prohibiting many forms of discrimination, and Americans have become more critical toward many kinds of segregation. This expectation was largely borne out. Few respondents to the national survey supported anti-Jewish discrimination in such conventional areas as hiring and housing. Political discrimination against Jews also appears to have declined, although nowhere near to a point where it can be considered inconsequential. Similarly, while less prevalent than in the past, discriminatory attitudes persist on such issues as intermarriage, the right of social clubs to exclude Jews, and the singing of Christmas carols in the schools.

DISCRIMINATION IN HIRING

It was apparent during interviews conducted in preparation for the national study that few Americans still support such past discriminatory practices as denying hotel accommodations to Jews, refusing to patronize Jewish stores, and denying a person a job because he or she is Jewish. Other studies have likewise shown that support for such forms of discrimination against Jews is minimal.

For these reasons, only a few questions of this kind were included in the final study. One such inquiry dealt with discrimination in hiring. Respondents were offered four alternative policies that "big companies" should follow, and the vast majority (90 percent) chose the statement, "Hire the best people whether they are Jewish or not." Only 4 percent said "Hire Jews only when they are so good that no one else could do the job as well," and 2 percent "Hire no Jews at all." Persons ranking high in anti-Semitic belief tended to give the latter answers most often, but even those respondents largely rejected anti-Jewish discrimination in hiring.

RESIDENTIAL DISCRIMINATION

Similarly, there was little support for residential discrimination. Respondents were asked: "How do you feel about having Jews in your neighborhood? Would you like to have some Jewish neighbors, wouldn't it make any difference to you, or would you prefer not to have any Jewish neighbors?" Eighty-six percent said it would make no difference, 7 percent said that they would prefer having no Jewish neighbors, and 6 percent that they would like to have some Jews as neighbors.

Public attitudes toward Jews have not always been so tolerant in these and related areas. Table 1-3 shows the trends in public opinion that have taken place in discrimination in hiring, residence, and college admittance. By the mid-1960s, very few Americans supported discrimination against Jews in any of these areas, whereas around 1940 upwards of 25 percent of the population was doing so.

TABLE 1-3. Discriminatory Attitudes Toward Jews, 1940s to 1960s.

Item							
		Response					

If you were an employer hiring a new employee, would it make any difference to you if he were a Jew?

		1940	1942	1945	1962
Yes		43%	37%	42%	6%
No		51	57	50	94
No opinion		6	6	8	—

If you were moving to a new house and found that your next-door neighbor was Jewish, would it make any difference to you?

	1940	1950	1953	1956	1959	1962
Yes[a]	25%	30%	19%	12%	10%	3%

Do you think colleges should limit the number of Jews they admit?

	1938	1962
Yes	26%	4%
No	65	88
Don't know	9	8

[a]Slightly different wording and response alternatives were used in some of these years.

SOURCE: Adapted from Charles Herbert Stember *et al.*, *Jews in the Mind of America* (New York: Basic Books, 1966), pp. 92, 96, 104. Reprinted by permission.

POLITICAL DISCRIMINATION

Public support for political discrimination against Jews has also declined sharply, but not quite to the same extent as in other areas. The best indication comes from responses to a question asked repeatedly in Gallup polls over a thirty-year period. It asked respondents what they would do "if your party nominated a well-qualified man for President who happened to be a Jew." The percentage of Americans replying they would vote for such a candidate has risen sharply over the years. It was 46 percent in 1937, 62 percent in 1958, 80 percent in 1965, and 86 percent in 1969. In 1969, the last time the question was asked, only 8 percent of Americans said they would definitely not vote for a qualified Jew running for President.[12]

In the 1964 study the following question was asked: "Suppose your political party wanted to nominate a Jew for President of the United States—

that is, a religious Jew who would go to synagogue every week the way a Christian goes to church every Sunday. Would this disturb you very much, somewhat, very little, or not at all?'' Such wording made it much easier to acknowledge one's reluctance to support a Jew for President. Even so, a substantial majority of Americans gave nondiscriminatory responses. Sixty-nine percent said they would be disturbed little or not at all, 17 percent would be somewhat disturbed, and 12 percent very disturbed. Even the most extreme anti-Semites were as likely to accept a Jewish presidential candidate as to reject one.

What would happen if a Jew were to be nominated by one of the major parties may well be different. Undoubtedly such a candidacy would trigger an outbreak of anti-Semitic demogoguery, which might find support among those already oriented toward anti-Semitism. Overt resistance to the idea of a Jew as President, however, has declined sharply in recent decades.

INTERMARRIAGE

The responses described to this point make it evident that there is very little support for more blatant forms of anti-Semitic discrimination. Such is not the case, however, where discrimination assumes a more subtle character and where competing values come into play. Then, even the otherwise unprejudiced show some willingness to exclude Jews.

Intermarriage is one such area. Respondents were asked: ''Suppose you had a child who wanted to marry a Jew who had a good education and came from a good family. How would you feel about this—would you object strongly, somewhat, a little, or not at all?'' A majority (55 percent) answered ''a little'' or ''not at all'' but 42 percent said they would object strongly or somewhat. Many non-Jews are hesitant to extend their tolerance to intermarriage.[13]

Anti-Semitic respondents are more opposed to intermarriage, but this tendency is not strong. Even among the highest scorers on the index of anti-Semitic belief, there were a substantial minority—28 percent—who would not object if their child elected to marry a Jew. That other values enter in to allow this to happen is illustrated by the case of a retired truck driver from South Carolina. He gave anti-Semitic responses to every one of the eleven questions included in the index of anti-Semitic belief and, in addition, favored action to take power away from Jews because they ''take advantage of the unlearned people—they get in second-class goods and sell them to people who don't know better than to buy them.'' Nevertheless, on intermarriage he replied: ''I'd leave this up to the child. If he or she wanted it, I would not object.'' Similar comments were made by other individuals who scored high in anti-Semitism.

The majority of those who scored as unprejudiced on the index of anti-Semitic belief were unopposed to intermarriage, but the majority was not an overwhelming one. Twelve percent of this group indicated that they would object "strongly" to their child's marrying a Jew, and 19 percent "somewhat." An important finding emerges when the responses to this question are placed next to those concerning a Jewish president. The unprejudiced make a sharp distinction between the two areas—31 percent disapprove of intermarriage, but only 13 percent oppose a Jewish president. The prejudiced make no such distinction—55 percent and 53 percent, respectively, oppose the two propositions. The unprejudiced, in other words, tend to limit their intolerance to the *private* area of intermarriage. The prejudiced, in contrast, are more willing to discriminate against Jews in the *public* as well as the private realm.

SOCIAL CLUB DISCRIMINATION

That other considerations, in addition to prejudice, affect a person's attitudes toward private forms of discrimination is illustrated in another question—one involving the right of social clubs to exclude Jews from membership. A majority of respondents felt that it is wrong to exclude Jews from social clubs. At the same time, a majority also believed Christians have a right to their own clubs. The two positions are not necessarily contradictory—few would deny Christians the right to exclude Jews from religious organizations. The problem comes in deciding which kinds of organizations have a legitimate right to exclude individuals solely because they are Jews, and which do not.

The ambiguous nature of public attitudes toward social club discrimination was exhibited on a battery of questions dealing with this issue. They involved a hypothetical attempt by "Mr. Smith" to get "Mr. Cohen" into his exclusionary club. The majority replies on these questions are revealing. Most Americans did not think that the club's members had a right to keep Cohen out because he was Jewish (68 percent) and most felt that other members had no right to be angry with Smith for trying to get Cohen in (61 percent). Yet at the same time a majority would acquiesce to a club's decision to keep Cohen out. Fifty-one percent counseled Smith to "stay in and forget the whole thing" (only 10 percent thought he should quit), and 74 percent felt that Smith should not be angry but "should realize that Christians have a right to their own clubs."

It is instructive to group these responses into four categories: (1) defenders of social club discrimination—those who said that a social club has a right to exclude Jews; (2) token opponents—those who denied this right but said that Smith should stay in and forget the whole thing; (3) militant opponents—those who in addition to denying the right to exclude Jews said that Smith should either quit the club or stay in and keep trying; and (4) the opinionless. Twenty-eight percent of the public were defenders, 29 percent token opponents, and 36 percent militant opponents.

These categories are related to the index of anti-Semitic belief. The extreme anti-Semites tend to be defenders, and the unprejudiced, militant opponents, but the relationship is not strong. There are sources of discrimination other than prejudice, and social club exclusion is another example of this.

CHRISTMAS CAROLS

The singing of Christmas carols in public schools raises even more ambiguous questions about discrimination. On the one hand, Christmas carols have been sung in the schools traditionally, and it has been argued that they are little more than the cultural expression of the religion of most Americans. On the other hand, the Constitution forbids the state to give preference to one religion over another, and it can be argued that the singing of Christmas carols in public schools constitutes just that.

A number of questions were asked to explore the nuances of public attitudes toward the singing of carols. Most respondents approved of the practice and expressed little support for those who would oppose the inclusion of carols in the school program. Eighty-three percent agreed, first of all, that a public school teacher should "teach Christmas carols even if some of the children are Jewish"; only 5 percent disagreed. When asked how they would feel if the parents of some Jewish children requested that the carols not be sung, very few—5 percent—were strongly sympathetic. Fifteen percent said they were "somewhat" sympathetic, 21 percent said they would sympathize "a little," and 56 percent "not at all." This last question was meant, in part, to remind respondents that the singing of Christmas carols might offend Jews. Following it, respondents were asked once again what should be done about the singing of Christmas carols in school. Almost as many people (74 percent) said that they should continue to be sung as had subscribed to this view (82 percent) before being reminded that Jewish parents might be upset.

Most Americans clearly support the singing of Christmas carols in the schools and are unsympathetic to charges that this constitutes discrimination against Jews. Such positions would seem to be only vaguely motivated by anti-Semitism. The responses of the unprejudiced and the extreme anti-Semites varied little on these questions. The main differences occurred when respondents were asked to restate their positions after being reminded of possible Jewish objections.

That support for Christmas carols is not inspired predominantly by prejudice is also illustrated in the responses of Jews to these questions: 54 percent began and 44 percent ended by saying that carols should be sung. Further, while 38 percent said they would be very sympathetic to the Jewish parents, 48 percent said they would not be sympathetic at all.

POLITICAL ANTI-SEMITISM

The previous questions dealt with the extent to which Americans are tolerant of Jews; two other questions dealt with the extent to which Americans are tolerant of anti-Semitism. They were:

If a candidate for Congress should declare himself as being against the Jews, would this influence you to vote for him or to vote against him?

If the United States government wanted to pass a law to stop more Jews from immigrating to this country, would you be in favor of this or against it?

Neither of these events at present appears likely to happen, and judging from previous responses few Americans would be expected to support either an anti-Jewish candidate or a restrictive immigration law. Also important, however, is whether Americans are concerned about or indifferent to the fate of Jews. Most Americans may not advocate political anti-Semitism, but they may be apathetic to such actions if they were to arise. Political attacks upon Jews and other minorities have been a recurring feature in American politics and have only infrequently been opposed by those outside the Jewish community.

Table 1-4 shows the responses to the first of these questions, as well as responses to the same inquiry asked of a national population sample in 1945. Consistent with other trends in anti-Semitism, the proportion of Americans who would vote for an anti-Semitic candidate has dropped sharply, while the proportion who would vote against him has almost doubled. Along with the decline in concern about Jewish power, charted earlier, has come a decline in support for political anti-Semitism.

TABLE 1-4.   Political Anti-Semitism, Mid-1940s to Mid-1960s.

Reply to: "If a candidate for Congress should declare himself as being against the Jews, would this influence you to vote for him or to vote against him?"[a]	1945	1964[b]
"Vote for him"	23%	5%
"Vote against him"	31	58
"Would make no difference"	35	33
"Don't know"	10	4
No answer	1	0
100% (N) =	(2,444)	(1,651)

[a]The exact wording in the 1945 survey was as follows: "If a candidate for Congress in this state should declare himself as being against the Jews, would this influence you to vote for him or against him?"

[b]Figures are for whites only, in order to make them comparable to the 1945 data. The responses of blacks were virtually identical to those of white, and these are combined in subsequent discussions of this question.

SOURCE: Reproduced from Selznick and Steinberg, *Tenacity of Prejudice*, p. 54.

Of some interest, however, is the fact that a third of the respondents in both the 1945 and 1964 surveys were indifferent to the candidate's anti-Semitism—being a proclaimed anti-Semite "would make no difference" in how they voted. Such a failure to declare oneself opposed to an anti-Semitic candidate might signify weak resistance to possible future anti-Semitic movements. Those answering in this way, furthermore, tended to be among the "opinionless" (with respect to either Jews or issues in general) or among those high in anti-Semitic belief.

On the second question—that pertaining to restrictions upon Jewish immigrants—fairly similar patterns were uncovered. Fifty-five percent opposed the hypothetical law, 20 percent favored it, and 19 percent volunteered the no-difference response. Again, failure to oppose the immigration law had two sources, anti-Semitic prejudice and indifference.

SYMPATHY WITH THE JEWISH PLIGHT

One problem in eliminating prejudice is that its very existence provides a rationale not to sympathize with its victims: The assignment of undesirable traits to a group is a built-in justification for mistreating its members. Moreover, the members of the majority group are often not personally aware of the harmful effects of prejudice upon its victims. Certainly this has been the case with respect to American blacks, and it was true as well with respect to Jews in Germany during the 1930s and 1940s.[14]

The following question was asked in the 1964 survey: "Some people say that Jews have suffered a great deal in the past. Which of these statements comes closest to your own feelings about this? The Jews have suffered no more than anybody else; the Jews have suffered but they generally brought it on themselves; the Jews have suffered through no fault of their own." One-third of the respondents replied that Jews had not suffered more than others, 17 percent felt that Jews had generally brought such problems on themselves, and 43 percent chose the unequivocally sympathetic response. Responses to another question indicated that many Americans do not wish to be reminded of the holocaust: 43 percent agreed with the statement that Jews should stop complaining about what happened to them in Nazi Germany.

These findings should be evaluated in proper perspective. As a matter of objective reality, many Americans may believe that blacks or some other group have suffered more than Jews; most Americans, as seen, recognize Jews to be among the more wealthy. Further, as many as a third of the Jewish respondents in this survey agreed that Jews should stop complaining.

Nevertheless, it was again the most anti-Semitic Americans who were least sympathetic to Jewish suffering. Forty percent of the extreme anti-Semites blamed Jews for bringing their past suffering on themselves, while

58 percent said that Jews should stop complaining about what happened in Nazi Germany. As above, lack of special sympathy for Jews is often but not always grounded in anti-Semitism.

Summary

Two forms of prejudice were examined in this chapter: the holding of negative beliefs or stereotypes about Jews and the approval of discrimination directed against Jews. The first of these dimensions involves the assigning of negative traits to individuals solely because of their being "Jews." Such an act represents what is commonly meant by the term "prejudice." The second form deals with the social and political consequences of anti-Semitism—the extent to which non-Jews refuse to associate with Jews and the extent to which they tolerate or engage in discriminatory acts against them. These things may happen in private areas or in public ways, in politics or in social affairs.

Anti-Semitic stereotypes were found to be common in contemporary America. Many Americans think of Jews as unethical, dishonest, aggressive, pushy, clannish, and conceited. On the basis of such beliefs, more than a third of the public were classified as anti-Semitic. Another third were found to hold moderately anti-Semitic beliefs, with the remaining third consistently rejecting all negative stereotypes of Jews.

These figures represent a decline from the 1930s and 1940s, when anti-Semitic feelings were more widespread in the country. This decline in anti-Semitism largely took place between the mid-1940s and mid-1960s. The evidence since then is not conclusive but suggests that there has either been a reduction in the rate of decline or that no changes have occurred in the amount of anti-Semitic stereotyping since the mid-1960s.

Americans were not as prejudiced on the second measure of anti-Semitism—support for discriminatory actions against Jews. Very few Americans today approve of discrimination against Jews in such areas as housing, employment, and the use of public facilities. Few would vote against a Jew for president simply because he is Jewish. All of these attitudes constitute a major change in sentiment from the more anti-Semitic 1930s and 1940s. Part of the change reflects the relative liberalization in attitudes taking place over this period. Americans today hold less discriminatory attitudes toward most minorities, and many acts of discrimination are now prohibited by law. Part of it also reflects the relative affluence of Jews as a group. Support for discrimination is much higher when the minority is poor.

Jews are, however, the object of discriminatory attitudes in some realms. A significant minority of Americans would be upset if their child were to marry a Jew, and most Americans either approve of or acquiesce to social club discrimination. Further, resistance to political anti-Semitism is not as firm as it might be. A third of the public is indifferent to a congressional candidate who openly opposes Jews—not an insignificant number given the tendency of Americans to support extremist political movements.

In sum, a mixed picture of contemporary anti-Semitism emerges from these findings. On the one hand, there is evidence showing that anti-Semitism remains prevalent in this country. Americans are particularly prone to associate negative images with Jews, to see Jews as pushy and aggressive, money-oriented, shady in business dealings, and clannish. More than a third of the public can be classified as anti-Semitic on this basis. On the other hand, it is clear that few Americans today support anti-Semitism in its more virulent and malicious forms. Few are alarmed at the power of Jews in the country or blame Jews for the nation's problems. Few favor discrimination against Jews in housing, employment, or running for office.

Such findings, of course, represent the broad spectrum of opinion in America—not the views of specific groups or kinds of individuals. The anti-Semitism of various subgroups in the population is examined in subsequent chapters. A more complete assessment of contemporary anti-Semitism follows the presentation of this information.

CHAPTER 2

The Social Location of Anti-Semitism

ANTI-SEMITISM, WHILE WIDELY PREVALENT in American society, is not a trait possessed by everybody. As has been demonstrated in the previous chapter, some Americans show strong dispositions to anti-Semitism and others appear to harbor virtually none. Just why should this be? What is it that produces anti-Semitism in some Americans? Then again, what makes other Americans free of this societal disease? To begin to answer these questions, it is necessary first to know just who the anti-Semites are and how they are different from persons who are not anti-Semites. In the present chapter examination is made of the incidence of anti-Semitic prejudice among Americans of different class status, religious affiliation, age, sex, residence, and ethnicity. Attention is given to determining which social and personal characteristics are most closely linked with being prejudiced toward Jews.

Both of these undertakings are important steps in the analysis of anti-Semitism. Knowledge about who the anti-Semites are and where they tend to be located socially affords a more complete description of American attitudes toward Jews. Such knowledge is also helpful in the process of identifying the causes of prejudice. To learn, for example, that anti-Semitism is more common among the less educated or within certain religious groups indicates where further inquiry might be fruitfully directed—namely, to finding out why education and religion have this effect. Knowledge about the social location of prejudice is also useful to efforts to combat anti-Semitism, since it helps pinpoint just who should be the target of such efforts.

Information concerning the social location of anti-Semitism is again drawn from the national survey. This source is supplemented by other studies where appropriate. Generally speaking, however, the findings from the

21

national study are consistent with what other studies conducted before and since have learned about the social location of anti-Semitic prejudice.

Class Differences in Anti-Semitism

Much speculation about anti-Semitism has conceived of it as being rooted in particular social classes in American society. One prominent view is that anti-Semitism is primarily a middle-class phenomenon, brought about because middle-class Americans are especially likely to be in direct competition with Jews for status and money. Working-class Americans, in contrast, compete more directly with blacks and other poor minorities and are thus more likely to be racially prejudiced.[1] Supporters of this view cite as evidence the discrimination against Jews practiced by resort hotels, by social clubs, and in the past by many of the nation's prestigious colleges and universities. Such exclusionary practices are engaged in only by those able to afford such privileges themselves.

An opposing view associates anti-Semitism and other forms of prejudice especially with the working class. Two theories have been advanced as to why this should be the case. The first conceives of prejudice as being psychologically caused.[2] Prejudice is seen as a means to relieve emotional frustrations through hostility directed against others. According to this theory, working-class Americans, being economically and socially deprived, are more disposed than other class groups to such frustration and to seeking the relief that prejudice is said to provide.

A second theory argues that prejudice is grounded more in cognitive failure than psychological malfunctioning.[3] Anti-Semitism thus is seen as a sign of intellectual deficiencies: cultural ignorance, social insensitivity, and failure of comprehension. Because of their relative lack of education and restricted social experiences, it is argued, working-class Americans are more likely to have such intellectual deficiencies and therefore to be prejudiced.

SOCIAL CLASS AND ANTI-SEMITISM

Class differences are assumed commonly to be indicated by such factors as occupation and amount of education and income. Those with college educations, high incomes, and white-collar jobs are considered to be middle class; those ranking low on these criteria are seen as working class. Table 2-1 shows the distribution of anti-Semitism on these three indicators of social class. On each, anti-Semitism is seen to be more prevalent among Americans of working-class status. It is greatest among those with no more than grade-school educations, those earning less than $5,000 annually, and those working in blue-collar jobs. The one exception to this pattern was among the highest income group, where anti-Semitism showed a slight increase from the next lower level.

TABLE 2-1.   Anti-Semitism Among Americans, by Education, Income, and Occupational Status.

	Percentage Scoring as Anti-Semitic[a]
Education	
grade school	52%
high school	36
some college	24
college graduates	15
Income	
Less than $5,000	54%
$5,000–$9,999	37
$10,000–$14,999	30
$15,000 or more	31
Occupation[b]	
blue collar	56%
semiskilled workers (mostly machine operators)	63
farmers (mostly small proprietors)	60
skilled workers (craftsmen, foremen, etc.)	52
service workers (barbers, policemen, etc.)	51
laborers (lumbermen, fishermen, etc.)	50
white collar	31%
managers, officials, and proprietors (shop owners, executives, etc.)	35
sales workers (insurance agents, sales clerks, etc.)	33
semiprofessional workers (technicians, nurses, etc.)	34
clerical workers (secretaries, clerks, etc.)	34
professionals (teachers, doctors, etc.)	19

[a]Percentages show proportion scoring high in the index of anti-Semitic belief.
[b]Refers to present occupation of the respondents or past occupation if retired or unemployed; housewives are excluded.
SOURCE: Adapted from Gertrude J. Selznick and Stephen Steinberg, *The Tenacity of Prejudice: Anti-Semitism in Contemporary America* (New York: Harper & Row, 1969), pp. 72, 75, 79.

Anti-Semitic prejudice is thus more common among working-class than middle-class Americans. This difference can best be summarized by combining the three status measures into a single index of "socio-economic status" (SES). When this is done, the proportion of anti-Semites is found to be 62 percent among those lowest in SES, 38 percent among those in the middle group, and 23 percent among those of the highest SES. Another recent survey has likewise found prejudice toward Jews to be more prevalent within the working class.[4]

These findings clearly disconfirm the theory that economic competition is an important source of anti-Semitic prejudice. Some anti-Semitic beliefs may develop from it, but Americans most directly in contention with Jews for economic rewards show less rather than greater prejudice as compared to Americans not in contention. Such a finding, of course, does not mean necessarily that all forms of anti-Semitism are more prevalent among the working class. Some forms of prejudice, such as social club discrimination, are available only to the middle class and can be practiced, consequently, only by them. Further, these findings show that prejudice toward Jews is not absent from the middle class. In many ways, this class's domination of leadership roles and greater control of resources make its members' anti-Semitism a more serious issue of concern.

EDUCATION THE KEY FACTOR

It is possible to carry the analysis of these class-related factors a step farther: to determine which of the three social factors—education, income, or occupation—is the most strongly related to anti-Semitism. Such an analysis finds education to be the key factor. The less-educated virtually always emerge as the most anti-Semitic group, even when they occupy the same income and occupational levels. The converse, however, does not hold true. Among those with similar years of schooling, it makes little difference whether an individual has a high or low income or is a factory worker or businessman. Those with similar levels of education score the same in anti-Semitism irrespective of their incomes or occupations.

Education, it is to be noted, is a multifaceted phenomenon and might affect anti-Semitism in a variety of ways. First of all, it is a learning process. Education teaches people to develop their rational capabilities and to think in an independent and critical manner. It introduces them to new values, ideas, and forms of knowledge. Second, attending school is a social process. It exposes students to other people and places them in an environment that is more liberal and tolerant than most others. Education, finally, is also a ticket of admission into the middle class. It is necessary to have a good education to aspire to most positions of responsibility in the business and professional worlds and to be accepted in many social settings. Education thus may influence anti-Semitism by placing individuals in settings in which prejudice is less acceptable or less likely.

Such factors may work singly or together in producing lower levels of anti-Semitism among the more educated. Various aspects of the impact of education upon prejudice are explored throughout this book and especially in Chapter 3.

THE MIDDLE CLASS AND SOCIAL CLUB DISCRIMINATION

While this study shows anti-Semitism to occur most regularly among working-class Americans, it is also found within the middle class. Even among college graduates, one of seven score high on the index of anti-Semitic belief. More important, some forms of anti-Jewish discrimination are available only or largely to the more affluent, and consequently receive most support from middle-class people. During the 1940s, for example, high-income Americans were more reluctant that those with low income to have Jews as neighbors—this was a time when residential discrimination against Jews was more prevalent than now.[5]

A more contemporary example of this pattern was found on the question dealing with social club discrimination. Fifty-two percent of those in the highest income and educational category support social club discrimination, as compared with 30 percent of those in the lowest.

The import of this finding would seem clear. The educated and the wealthy are most often social joiners and belong to the type of organizations most attractive to the predominantly middle-class Jewish population. They are also the people with whom middle-class Jews most commonly come into contact in their communities and in their work. The exclusionary policies of the middle class are thus most visible to many Jews. This is undoubtedly one reason anti-Semitism is sometimes thought to be more prevalent among middle-class than among working-class Americans. It is where some forms of discrimination are most directly experienced.

As a whole, however, it is among those low in education and social status generally that anti-Semitism in America is predominantly located. This is true of anti-Semitic beliefs as well as all other forms of discrimination examined in this study. Of particular concern is the greater political anti-Semitism of the working class. Lower-status Americans are more likely to oppose a Jew for the presidency and less likely to deny their votes to an anti-Semitic candidate. They thus remain a potential base of support for extremist movements using anti-Semitic appeals.

Religious Differences in Anti-Semitism

Another factor often linked with anti-Semitism is religion. That Jews are a member of a competing religious faith and profess to different doctrinal truths would seem to create a strong potential for conflict with non-Jewish churchgoers. Indeed, Christianity has been a major historical force in the development and promulgation of anti-Semitic prejudice. In the past Jews were often seen not just as disbelievers but as heretics of the worst kind.

They had turned their backs on the Christian God and rejected the Christian Savior. According to the Bible, furthermore, the Jewish multitude had demanded Jesus' crucifixion and brought down upon themselves a curse for all time. Thus Jews for centuries have been branded as "Christ-killers."

Religious conflicts between Jews and non-Jews have been less severe in this country than in many others. Part of the reason is the early establishment of freedom of religion. This constitutional guarantee did not prevent religious hostilities from developing, but it narrowed the scope and impact of their effects. In addition, Jews are relative newcomers to the United States, not entering the country in large numbers until the late 1890s and early 1900s. Christian–Jewish relations thus developed during a relatively more tolerant period in the nation's religious history.

The relationship between American religion and anti-Semitism has been the subject of intense speculation but little empirical investigation. Among respondents to the national study, Protestants as a whole showed a slightly greater disposition to anti-Semitism than Roman Catholics. Thirty-six percent of Protestants scored high on the index of anti-Semitic beliefs as against 32 percent of the Catholics. The Protestant figures mask considerable variation by denomination, however. Members of more "conservative" denominations emerge as considerably more anti-Semitic (38 percent) than members of more "liberal" ones (23 percent).

Both of these patterns are interesting. That Protestants are more anti-Semitic than Catholics, first of all, was found on almost all measures of prejudice used in this study. The only exception was on resistance to political anti-Semitism, where both religious groups scored about the same.

Other studies as well have shown Catholics to be less anti-Semitic than Protestants.[6] Despite this fact, Catholics are often perceived by Jews as the more prejudiced group.[7] It is likely that such notions have carried over from historical times when Catholicism was a major source of anti-Semitism and from contemporary perceptions of the Catholic Church as authoritarian in its structures and theological dogmas. It may also result from the early history of Catholic–Jewish relations in this country. Both groups lived in the same urban centers, and what prejudice Jews experienced came largely at the hands of Catholics.

Whatever the source of such misperceptions, Catholics today are somewhat less prejudiced toward Jews than Protestants. The difference is not large, but it is consistent across a number of measures of anti-Semitism.

The second pattern—that conservative Protestants are more anti-Semitic than liberal ones—remains strong even when adjustments are made for the relatively lower educational levels of conservative Protestants. Conservative Protestants scored higher in anti-Semitism at all educational levels except among the college-educated, where no differences were found.

This pattern suggests that doctrinal differences may contribute to the anti-Semitism of Christian Americans. Indeed, it has often been said that certain Christian teachings promote anti-Jewish beliefs and hatreds—that Jews cannot be saved until they accept Jesus as Savior, that they cannot be forgiven for crucifying Jesus, and that they have been eternally damned by God. Such religious beliefs evoke hostile images in themselves that might be considered another form of prejudice. They might also facilitate the acceptance of secular stereotypes of Jews as dishonest, pushy, clannish, and power hungry. This matter was considered to be of sufficient importance that it was made the subject of special intensive study. The results are presented in Chapter 6.

Age Differences in Anti-Semitism

A third important social correlate of anti-Semitism is age. The incidence of anti-Semitic prejudice was found to be considerably higher among older Americans than among the young. This was a consistent finding on all questions pertaining to anti-Jewish beliefs and discrimination.

On the index of anti-Semitic belief, 31 percent of the young (thirty-four years of age and under) scored as anti-Semitic, as compared to 40 percent of the middle-aged (thirty-five to fifty-four) and 59 percent of older respondents. In the older group, more than half (52 percent) would not oppose a candidate running for office as an avowed anti-Semite, as compared with 35 percent of the youngest group. Older people were also significantly more likely to say that they would be very much disturbed if their party nominated a Jew for the presidency and to endorse social club discrimination.

It is evident that much of the generational difference is caused by rising levels of education. Fewer than half of the respondents in their mid-fifties and beyond had more than a grade-school education. Among the youngest group, in contrast, 91 percent had at least attended high school and a third had gone on to college. Adjusting for these educational differences, the effect of age is not eliminated entirely, but it is considerably reduced.[8] One reason, then, that older Americans are more anti-Semitic is that as a group they are far less educated.

The age-related differences that remain after education is taken into account can be due to a number of factors. One is the changing quality of education over the past thirty to forty years. Two generations ago it was widely taught that social differences are caused by innate biological traits. Such a view is still being advanced today but has been widely repudiated. The modernization of education would thus seem to be one reason why older Americans, even when they have had the same amount of schooling, are more anti-Semitic. A second possibility is that the aging process produces greater anti-Semitic tendencies. It may lead to greater insecurity, rigidity, and withdrawal, and thus to greater ethnocentrism, intolerance, and prejudice.

Third, Americans may grow more anti-Semitic with age because of their greater exposure to anti-Semitic ideology. They may have had more time to come in contact with negative imagery and to learn the full repertory of anti-Semitic beliefs. Finally, it is also possible that the greater anti-Semitism of the older generation is a carryover from youth. It may be traceable to the older respondents' having spent their formative years in a more outspokenly anti-Semitic era than our own.

None of these theories could be tested with the type of information collected in this survey. To do so, it would have been necessary to carry out "longitudinal" research—to study the same individuals over their lifetimes. One piece of indirect evidence, however, is the finding that the largest generational difference occurs on the most outdated of anti-Semitic stereotypes: that Jews control international banking. Twenty-nine percentage points separated the responses of the youngest and oldest generational groups on this measure. This difference remained almost as strong (25 percent) when the effect of education was controlled. Indeed, this was the only belief statement in the index whose acceptance was almost exclusively a function of age.

The most logical explanation is that the elderly acquired this belief in their younger years. If that is true, they may have acquired other of their anti-Semitic beliefs during that period as well. The greater anti-Semitism of older Americans, then, may result from their greater exposure to anti-Jewish stereotypes during their youth.

This line of reasoning is speculative, of course. Nevertheless, there would seem to be some grounds for optimism in these figures. Anti-Semitism appears likely to decline as more of the population is exposed to higher education and as the schools do a better job teaching about minorities. It may also decline as the percentage of Americans brought up during earlier periods of anti-Semitism shrinks.

Other Social Correlates of Anti-Semitism

A number of other possible social correlates of prejudice were examined— sex, region, place of residence, nativity, and ethnicity. None of these factors produced strong differences in anti-Semitism. The results, however, were sufficiently illuminating to warrant their being reported upon briefly.

SEX

Men and women, first of all, hold much the same attitudes toward Jews. They score similarly on the index of anti-Semitic belief, and their approval or disapproval of different forms of discrimination is about the same.

Where differences occur, however, it is women who are usually the less prejudiced. This tendency corresponds with other survey findings as well.[9]

Women, on the average, are more likely than men to say "I don't know" when asked about their images of Jews. Among those with an opinion, however, the relative acceptance of different stereotypes is in virtually all cases the same. The only negative image on which substantial sex-related differences occurred was on the belief that Jews control international banking. It was accepted by 38 percent of the men and only 22 percent of the women. On issues of discrimination, women continue to be less anti-Semitic, but the differences are not substantial. On only one measure did this pattern reverse itself. Women were slightly more likely to disapprove of intermarriage; 45 percent of the women and 38 percent of the men would object strongly or somewhat if their child were to marry a Jew.

As a whole, then, men and women do not differ much with respect to either anti-Semitic beliefs or discriminatory attitudes. While women are somewhat less prejudiced, the differences are so small that no importance can be attached to them.

REGION

Somewhat larger differences were found in the regional distribution of anti-Semitism. Anti-Semitism is most prevalent in the South, where 49 percent score as prejudiced, and the Midwest, where the figure is 44 percent. The least anti-Semitic region of the country is the Northeast—33 percent prejudiced—with the West following closely behind—36 percent. Attitudes toward anti-Jewish discrimination are distributed similarly. The proportion of whites who would be disturbed if their party nominated a Jew for the presidency, for example, was 41 percent in the South, 31 percent in the Midwest, 26 percent in the Northwest, and 19 percent in the Northeast.

Identical regional variations have been discovered in other surveys of anti-Semitism.[10] Residents of the South and the Midwest consistently score as the most anti-Semitic; residents of the West and East as the least. These patterns hold only for whites, however. As will be seen, black anti-Semitism is greater in the urban North than the urban South.

URBAN-RURAL RESIDENCE

Anti-Semitism has sometimes been viewed as an urban phenomenon and sometimes as a feature of rural life. On the one hand, the cities are where most Jews live and where the greatest potential for Jewish–non-Jewish conflict exists. On the other hand, rural dwellers may base their attitudes toward Jews more on what they imagine Jews must be like than on actual experience.

Prejudice toward Jews was found to be more common in rural than urban areas, but only in two sections of the country: the South and the Midwest. Indeed, it turns out that the regional variations noted earlier were caused largely by the greater anti-Semitism of rural residents. Urban Southerners and Midwesterners were only slightly more prejudiced than urban dwellers in the remainder of the country.[11]

This information is shown in Table 2-2. Much the same rates of anti-Semitism are seen to exist in the rural West and rural Northeast as in urban areas throughout the country. In all cases, anti-Semitism ran at one-third or slightly higher. In contrast, the percentage of anti-Semites in the rural South was 60 percent and in the rural Midwest 52 percent.

TABLE 2-2.   Anti-Semitism by Residence and Region.

Rural–Urban Residence[b]	Percent anti-Semitic, whites only[a]			
	South	Midwest	Northwest	Northeast
Rural	60% (176)	52% (179)	33% (61)	35% (85)
Urban	38% (194)	38% (263)	36% (171)	33% (273)
Total	48% (371)	44% (444)	36% (247)	33% (366)

[a]Percentages show the degree scoring high on the index of anti-Semitic belief, excluding the opinionless.

[b]The 1960 Census classification of urban and rural is used. "Urban" includes small communities that are within a standard metropolitan statistical area. "Rural" refers to counties outside metropolitan areas.

SOURCE: Adapted from Selznick and Steinberg, *Tenacity of Prejudice*, p. 114.

Thus it is not rural living in general that is associated with anti-Semitism but living in rural areas of the South and Midwest. The gap between these residents and the rest of the country can be illustrated on two of the questions dealing with political anti-Semitism. The proportion of respondents who would vote against an anti-Semitic candidate was 47 percent in the rural South and 50 percent in the rural Midwest, but 62 percent in the remainder of the country. The proportion who would be disturbed if their party nominated a Jew for the presidency was 45 percent in the rural South, 38 percent in the rural Midwest, and between 10 and 25 percentage points lower elsewhere.

NATIVITY AND ETHNICITY

The last social correlates to be examined are nativity and ethnicity—both of which have often been associated with anti-Semitism. The foreign-born often are said to have brought over their prejudices from Europe, where many countries have had long histories of virulent anti-Semitism. Ethnicity has been linked with anti-Semitism in a variety of different ways. It has sometimes been said to be more prevalent among older-generation Americans and sometimes among those of certain other ethnic backgrounds.

The foreign-born were found to be more anti-Semitic in their beliefs than native Americans. Fifty-seven percent of the former group and 42 percent of the latter score as prejudiced on the index of anti-Semitic belief. However, the foreign-born also tended to be disproportionately old and disproportionately uneducated. When these factors were taken into account, there appeared to be little difference in the anti-Semitism of foreign-born and the native-born.

The relative proclivity toward anti-Semitism of different ethnic groups could not be measured using the data from the national study, because there were not enough cases to represent the different groups. However, other studies have discovered some variations in prejudice among ethnic groups. The Irish have been shown to be among those low in anti-Semitic prejudice; the Italians and Poles among those higher.[12]

Summary

Through reporting on the social distribution of anti-Semitic prejudice, this chapter sought to present a more complete picture of anti-Semitism in contemporary America and to explore some of the possible causes of prejudice toward Jews. The findings reported also serve to introduce several subjects to be explored in greater detail in subsequent chapters.

Three principal social patterns in anti-Semitism were found. First, anti-Semitism is more prevalent among Americans of lower than higher SES, that is, among those with relatively little education, low incomes, and employed in blue-collar jobs. Middle-class Americans are not free of prejudice, and certain forms of anti-Semitism are found to predominate in the middle class. Nevertheless, it is among the more socially deprived—the working class—that prejudice toward Jews is most common.

This finding runs counter to theories linking anti-Semitism with economic competition. It is not those in most direct competition with Jews for income and status—middle-class businessmen and professionals—who are most anti-Semitic, but those lower in SES. The most important class-related finding, however, was that involving education. Education was found to be the main social factor accounting for class differences; it is not the fact that working-class Americans earn less or work in different occupations that makes them more anti-Semitic, but their lesser exposure to schooling. What it is in education that produces the differences is the subject of the next chapter.

A second social pattern in anti-Semitism involves religion. Prejudice toward Jews was found to be higher among Protestants than Catholics and higher among the members of conservative than among members of liberal Protestant denominations. The first finding is interesting in that Catholics are often viewed as being the more anti-Semitic. Jews themselves have consistently named Catholics as the more discriminatory in opinion surveys. More theoretically significant, however, was the large difference found between conservative and liberal Protestants. This pattern suggests that certain doctrinal beliefs may serve as a source of anti-Semitic prejudice, a suggestion examined in some detail in Chapter 6.

The third major social correlate of anti-Semitism is age. Anti-Semitism was found to rise with age, with older Americans especially high in prejudice. This is a result, in part, of the fact that more recent generations are better educated than older generations. It seems also to be the result of older generations' having had greater exposure to anti-Semitism when they were young. It may also be the case that people become more anti-Semitic as they move through the life cycle, but this possibility could not be checked with the available data. All in all, these findings suggest that anti-Semitism may decline somewhat as a higher percentage of Americans are educated and exposed to less virulent forms of anti-Semitism.

Other social differences were found to have little or no relation to anti-Semitic prejudice. The most pronounced were the regional urban–rural patterns. Prejudice toward Jews is more prevalent in the rural areas of the South and Midwest than in the rest of the country.

CHAPTER 3

Education and Anti-Semitism

EDUCATION, AS REPORTED IN the last chapter, is a powerful indicator of anti-Semitic prejudice in America. Americans with grade-school educations, for example, are more than three times as likely to hold anti-Semitic beliefs as the college educated and are more frequent supporters of discrimination against Jews. Discovering why those education-related differences occur was one of the main objectives of this research series. An understanding of this relationship should help explain why anti-Semitism remains so prevalent in America. It should indicate which theory or theories of prejudice best account for contemporary anti-Semitism. It should suggest, finally, what kinds of actions might be taken to reduce the incidence of prejudice toward Jews.

What is it about education that leads to a decrease in anti-Semitic prejudice? Alternatively, why should a lack of education be associated with greater anti-Semitic tendencies? These questions received prominent attention in two of the research projects in this series—the national study of public attitudes and the three-community study of adolescent prejudice. The results of the national study are reported in this chapter; those of the adolescent study (which are similar) are presented in Chapter 5.

To understand what it is that might cause the association between education and anti-Semitism, it is necessary to turn to existing theories of prejudice. Two such theories, in particular, offer thoughtful and insightful explanations of the relationship. The first conceives of prejudice as evidence of intellectual impairment, rooted in the cognitive deficiencies of the less-educated. The second views prejudice as an emotional response and a reflection of the psychological frustrations of the less privileged and less-educated.

33

This chapter begins by reviewing these two theoretical approaches to the study of prejudice. It then presents the findings of the national study as they support or disconfirm these two competing explanations of anti-Semitism.

Cognitive Theories

Cognitive theories constitute the first approach to the study of anti-Semitic prejudice.[1] Cognitive theories conceive of prejudice as a form of intellectual unenlightenment—a deficiency in reasoning, logic, and information—and seek to explain its existence in these terms. They offer a highly plausible explanation for why education might serve as an antidote to anti-Semitism.

Cognitive theories begin by noting the prevalence of anti-Semitic imagery in the culture at large. Most Americans are likely to be exposed to frequent negative stereotyping of Jews. Some of the stereotypes are such gross distortions of reality that they will be rejected out of hand by all but the most bigoted. More commonly, however, the ideology of prejudice is intricate and insidious. It is based upon half-truths, false inferences, and misrepresentations. The distortions are so subtle and beguiling that they can be easily overlooked and accepted as true. Most of the stereotypes associated with contemporary anti-Semitism appear to be of this nature. They contain elements of truth that are interpreted in such a way as to cast negative aspersions on Jews. Jews, for example, can be business-oriented without being deceitful, monied without being money-hungry, or ethnic-oriented without being unfair to others.

To detect beliefs of this nature and to judge them for what they are, according to cognitive theories, requires considerable knowledge and intellectual ability. One must be aware of the dangers involved in generalizing from the behavior of a few people to that of an entire group. One must be sensitive to differences that exist in cultural values and traditions. One must, finally, have some knowledge of the historical, economic, and social forces that created group differences in the first place. Without such sophistication, it is difficult to distinguish true from false differences and to reject common cultural stereotypes.

Having the cognitive capacity to do all of these things is not, of course, a guarantee against prejudice. Social stereotypes may be so strongly held—and reinforced through peer pressures or other factors—that even the most intellectually sophisticated will succumb to them. Nevertheless, intellectual ability is believed to be a primary safeguard against anti-Semitism and other forms of prejudice. The cognitively sophisticated will be more informed about minorities and better able to separate the false from the true.

Cognitive theories ask what it is that is likely to produce greater intellectual sophistication among some people as opposed to others. It is recognized that a variety of factors may be involved and that to some degree intellectual ability is an inherited rather than a learned trait. In general, however, exposure to the educational process is seen as the principal factor creating greater intellectual sophistication and lower levels of prejudice and intolerance. This effect is said to occur in a variety of ways. Education helps to develop one's cognitive abilities to reason and to make critical, independent judgments about the social world. It introduces one to the cultural diversities of American society and the differences existing among people. It imparts the rules of evidence and inference. Finally, it teaches about the dangers of holding overly simplified and prejudiced beliefs about others. In short, education develops intellectual abilities that might counteract prejudiced thinking by exposing the distortions and half-truths of anti-Semitic ideology and by providing reasons to reject them.

The educational process is sometimes said to reduce anti-Semitic prejudice in still another way: by teaching norms of tolerance, democracy, equality, and civil liberties. Such norms are thought to produce values that militate against the development of prejudiced and intolerant beliefs. They are taught in most schools but are not nearly so prevalent in the broader culture. Americans with more schooling, accordingly, should have more enlightened and tolerant beliefs generally, including lower levels of prejudice.

To illustrate this latter point, a distinction is sometimes made between the official or "ideal" norms of American society and the unofficial or "common" norms. In this country, the ideal norms tend to be democratic and egalitarian. They stress such values as equality, fair play, mutual respect, individuality, tolerance, and civil rights; they exclude prejudice and discrimination toward minority groups. In contrast, the common norms are not so tolerant. They are the values and practices transmitted socially from one generation to the next. They are often based on folklore, parochialism, and narrowly prescribed perspectives; they tend to be predemocratic, prescientific, and intolerant. Greater exposure to the "ideal" culture should thus be associated with lower levels of prejudice; greater exposure to the "common" culture with higher rates of anti-Semitism.

Cognitive theories view the schools as the principal purveyors of the enlightened values of the official culture. Thus education, in addition to developing one's intellectual abilities, also introduces people to more enlightened and less prejudiced beliefs. In both of these ways, cognitive theories predict, educated Americans will become the least anti-Semitic.

The strong association found between education and anti-Semitism would seem to support the cognitive explanation of prejudice. That the less-educated would be more prejudiced, however, is not inconsistent with emotive theories of prejudice. These too locate anti-Semitic sentiments largely among the educationally deprived segments of the population, but for different reasons.

Emotive Theories

Emotive theories emphasize the negative feelings or emotions associated with anti-Semitism. They point out that anti-Semitic ideology is pejorative, derogatory, and sometimes inciting, and that it provides reasons for disliking Jews and avoiding contact with them. Emotive theories locate the source of anti-Semitic ideology in psychological rather than cognitive processes. They focus on the psychological "needs" that hostile attitudes and feelings fulfill in an individual's personality make-up, rather than on the intellectual deficiencies such attitudes and feelings display.

Emotive theories are usually based upon a "frustration–aggression" model of human behavior.[2] Frustration is said to develop as a result of such factors as a repressed childhood, economic failure, and deprivation in relation to others. Such frustrations are seen as building up like steam in a boiler until they must find some outlet. By venting their pent-up feelings on minorities, such individuals are able to live with their frustrations and the anxieties that accompany them.

Emotive theory originally grew out of efforts to understand why the German people supported the policies of Hitler—including Hitler's extermination policies toward Jews—and to determine whether similar tendencies existed in this country. It was articulated in its most comprehensive and celebrated form in *The Authoritarian Personality*, first published in 1950.[3]

According to this theory prejudice, specifically anti-Semitism, is closely related to a personality configuration labeled "authoritarian." Authoritarian personalities are characterized, among other things, by dispositions to *conventionalism*, to *authoritarian submission*, and, at the same time, to *authoritarian aggression*. The disposition to conventionalism is manifested by rigid adherence to middle-class values and by high responsiveness to social pressures to conform to such values. Authoritarian submissiveness comprises an exaggerated emotional need to submit to external authority. Authoritarian aggression is characterized by hostility toward what is described as "ingroup authority," especially toward one's parents.

According to this theory, what makes such individuals prone to anti-Semitism is a need to find an outlet for their aggressive tendencies. Authoritarian personalities tend to project onto outgroups the feelings of hostility they feel toward ingroup authorities, but against whom they find it psychologically impossible to rebel. That outgroups (minorities) become the target of such aggression is because they are perceived as not conforming to conventional norms. They are deviants who deserve to be shunned and treated differently from others. The tendency toward authoritarian submission, it should be noted, is not inherently related to being prejudiced. However, where the external authorities to whom the authoritarian personality submits advocate scapegoating, as the Nazis did, the authoritarian personality is ill equipped not to go along. Such personality types are thus highly susceptible to the use of prejudiced appeals by political leaders.

According to *The Authoritarian Personality*, such personality predispositions develop out of a strict, harsh, and repressive upbringing characterized by highly ambivalent feelings toward one's parents. Other emotive theories associate these tendencies with additional kinds of material, social, or psychological deprivations.[4] What emotive theories share in common is the postulate of some psychological need to be hostile and the assertion that aggression toward minority groups is an important mechanism to release the inner hostilities.

That anti-Semitic beliefs are morally and intellectually benighted is not overlooked by emotive theories. Rather, the acceptance of such beliefs is conceived as possible only where a person is driven by emotional conflict of a serious kind, including deep feelings of frustration. Thus there is a recognition in emotive theory that an element of cognitive failure exists in the acceptance of anti-Semitic beliefs. The emotive element, however, is seen to dominate the cognitive one.

Emotive theories are not in agreement entirely as to the mechanism producing the association found between education and anti-Semitism. "Frustration–aggression" theory would allow for the frustration's being a product of a lack of education. The less-educated might feel frustrated because of the greater rewards that accrue to the educated and thus might turn to prejudice as a form of relief. The alternative model, inferred from *The Authoritarian Personality*, is that the psychological processes leading to the development of authoritarian personalities begin early in childhood, well before formal education actually begins. From this viewpoint, the negative association between level of education and anti-Semitism is not to be understood as a consequence of education effecting a reduction in anti-Semitism. Rather, the fact that the two are associated is an artifact of personality both influencing the amount of education obtained (authoritarian personalities obtain less) and the amount of prejudice exhibited (authoritarian personalities exhibit more).

Education and Unenlightenment

Cognitive and emotive theories of prejudice are thus similar in some respects and different in others. They are similar in that both theories postulate that anti-Semitism is unlikely to be found as a unique or isolated phenomenon. Instead it will usually be accompanied by a related set of beliefs or attitudinal orientations. The two approaches differ fundamentally, however, in how they conceptualize prejudice and explain this hypothesized syndrome of beliefs. Cognitive theories view anti-Semitic beliefs as distortions and simplifications of reality and as a sign of intellectual unenlightenment. They see intellectual unenlightenment arising from many sources, but principally from a limited or poor education. Emotive theories, in contrast, view anti-Semitic prejudice as aggressive and hostile behavior in response to some psychological need. They see such a need developing among those unable to cope with their own inner anxieties and frustrations.

Anti-Semitic beliefs undoubtedly have both cognitive and emotive sources. Especially among more extreme anti-Semites, it is difficult to separate these two dimensions of prejudice. Which factor is *primarily* responsible for prejudiced beliefs, however, is a matter of considerable importance. It carries serious implications for the understanding of contemporary anti-Semitism, for its probable course in the future, and for the steps to be taken to reduce its incidence.

These contrasting theories were examined in the national study in a number of different ways. Respondents were judged as to their general tendency toward simplistic thinking, and this was compared with their rate of anti-Semitism. They were asked about their knowledge of and support for democratic norms. They were queried on their use of the mass media and tested on their knowledge of current events. They were evaluated, finally, on their intolerance of cultural diversity and their holding of anomic beliefs. These procedures turned up evidence that supported both cognitive and emotive explanations of anti-Semitism. Their general effect, however, was to confirm the central role of education in reducing anti-Semitism and thus the cognitive approach to the understanding of prejudice.

SIMPLISM

The first procedure undertaken was to determine whether the anti-Semitism of the less-educated was a part of a more general tendency toward simplistic thinking. The concept of simplism, it will be seen, is closely connected with both cognitive and emotive theories.

The idea behind "simplism" is that some people respond to social reality in primitive and nonrational ways. They are uneasy when confronted with complexity and quick to give singular answers to difficult questions. They are often superstitious and moralistic and tend to think in dichotomous categories of "good" and "bad" or "right" and "wrong." People possessing such characteristics are also inclined to explain human behavior in terms of such external or uncontrollable forces as "fate," "luck," or "the stars." They are distrustful of education or "book learning'' and of the advice offered by supposed experts and those with advanced degrees.

The interview schedule used in the national study included a number of questions designed to measure the relative disposition of Americans toward simplistic thinking. As Table 3-1 shows, more-educated Americans hold considerably less simplistic attitudes than the less-educated. The grade-school-educated, in particular, are prone to accept many simplistic statements as true. They frequently believe in the efficacy of will power, admit to a dislike of contrary arguments, and agree that "practical experience is worth more than all the books put together." On an index derived from these measures, 51 percent of the grade-school-educated scored high in simplism, as compared with 34 percent of those who had attended high school, 15 percent of those with some college, and only 9 percent of college graduates.[5]

It is also found that simplism and anti-Semitism are highly related. Among respondents scoring highest in simplism, 64 percent also scored high in anti-Semitism. Among the middle group, the proportion of anti-Semites dropped to 39 percent; among the least simplistic group, it fell further to 17 percent. Americans with simplistic beliefs thus tend to hold anti-Semitic beliefs as well.

Both of these findings lend support to cognitive explanations of prejudice. They indicate that anti-Semitic stereotyping is an element in a more general tendency to simplistic thinking. They also indicate that it is the least-educated who most frequently exhibit this general orientation. If education has any effect, of course, it ought to lead people away from thinking too simplistically about the world.

What gives some pause in drawing such conclusions is the fact that the first five items in Table 3-1 were taken from the so-called F scale, developed by the authors of *The Authoritarian Personality* to measure a disposition to authoritarianism.[6] These items, in addition to being strongly related to education, are also related to anti-Semitism. Moreover, they are related to anti-Semitism independently of level of education. That is to say, at each level of education, those who accept the F items are more likely to be anti-Semitic than those who reject them. It is also true that level of education is strongly related to anti-Semitism, independently of whether the F items are accepted or rejected; the less-educated are more prejudiced regardless of their F scores. These results, consequently, do not deny cognitive theories of prejudice. However, interpreting the F items as measures of personality rather than as indicators of simplistic thinking, emotive theory is confirmed as well.

It is not possible, with these questions alone, to say for sure whether the F items are measuring personality type or level of cognitive ability. Critics of *The Authoritarian Personality* have suggested that the strong association

TABLE 3-1. Acceptance of Simplistic Views of Social Reality, by Level of Education.

	Grade School	High School	Some College	College Graduate	Total
1. No weakness or difficulty can hold us back if we have enough will power.	80%[a]	80%	70%	66%	78%
2. Sex crimes, such as rape and attacks on children, deserve more than mere imprisonment; such criminals ought to be publicly whipped, or worse.	70	58	42	38	57
3. People can be divided into two distinct classes—the weak and the strong.	68	50	28	20	50
4. Much of our lives is controlled by plots hatched in secret places.	33	24	20	15	25
5. Reading the stars can tell us a great deal about the future.	26	16	5	5	16
6. I don't like to hear a lot of arguments I disagree with.	76	64	53	40	64
7. A little practical experience is worth more than all the books put together.	74	58	42	29	58
8. The answers to this country's problems are much simpler than the experts would have us think.	37	27	19	16	28
9. Getting to the top is more a matter of luck than ability.	33	11	9	7	17
100% (N) =	(536)	(957)	(226)	(193)	(1,913)

[a]Percentages show the degree of acceptance of each statement.

SOURCE: Reproduced from Gertrude J. Selznick and Stephen Steinberg, *The Tenacity of Prejudice: Anti-Semitism in Contemporary America* (New York: Harper & Row, 1969), p. 140.

between lack of education and a high score on F occurs because F beliefs resemble other unenlightened beliefs characteristic of the less-educated, hence these beliefs are not necessarily indicators of personality. In effect, F beliefs are alleged to be indicators of cognitive weaknesses rather than of emotional state.

Fortunately, it is not necessary to rely on these results alone to settle the issue. Other questions asked in the national study allow further assessment of these alternative theories.

KNOWLEDGE AND SUPPORT OF DEMOCRATIC NORMS

Another area of disagreement between cognitive and emotive theories is the role that the internalization of democratic norms and values plays in prejudice reduction. Both theories agree that prejudice will probably be less in evidence where such norms and values are subscribed to. The two theories disagree, however, about the process by which internalization may come about.

From a cognitive perspective, democratic principles are abstract and complex and require a high degree of intellectual sophistication to be properly understood. Not only is such sophistication most fully nurtured in the schools, but educational institutions themselves devote considerable efforts to socializing students in the norms of democracy. Modern education would be judged a failure if the educated were not better able to understand and appreciate the importance of democratic ideals. Emotive theories, in contrast, view antidemocratic beliefs as a salient example of authoritarian tendencies. Such beliefs are said to develop early in life as a result of a strict upbringing and repressed childhood. They are thus expressions of a deep-seated emotional need, *not a product of a limited education.*

To explore this issue, respondents were asked two sets of questions about their knowledge and support of democratic norms. The first involved the constitutional guarantee of free speech and association, reading as follows:

> Suppose Congress wanted to pass a law saying that groups who disagree with our form of government could not hold public meetings or make speeches. As far as you know, would Congress have a right under the Constitution to pass such a law?

A majority of respondents (65 percent) responded correctly that Congress did not have such a right. As cognitive theories predict, the percentage of Americans responding correctly varied substantially by education. Eighty-seven percent of college graduates said Congress had no such right, as compared with 67 percent of the high-school-educated and 48 percent of the grade-school-educated. The second question asked whether Congress has a right to pass a law requiring the president to believe in God. Again the percentage replying that Congress had no such right varied by education—from a high of 72 percent among college graduates to a low of 33 percent among the grade-school-educated.

Educational differences thus loom large in the extent of knowledge Americans possess concerning democratic principles. To measure support for those principles, respondents were also asked whether they favored each of these restrictive laws.[7] The less-educated again gave the more nonliberal answers. Nineteen percent of college graduates favored restrictions on free speech, as compared with 39 percent of the grade-school-educated. Support for requiring a president to believe in God was higher but similarly patterned, with 46 percent of college graduates and 76 percent of grade-schoolers approving. These two response patterns were closely related. Americans who correctly understood constitutional principles usually supported them as well. In both instances, it was the more-educated who most frequently answered correctly.

These findings are consistent with cognitive theories in demonstrating a strong relation between education and intellectual enlightenment. They also add another dimension to understanding the intellectual sources of prejudice. Knowledge and support of democratic norms are found to be strongly related to the attitudes of respondents toward Jews. Americans with more knowledge of democratic norms—and who gave support to them—showed relatively few anti-Semitic tendencies. Americans who were ignorant and nonsupportive of democratic principles held pronounced anti-Semitic views. The democratic values of Americans would thus seem to be a preventative to the holding of anti-Semitic beliefs.

There are undoubtedly many reasons for this effect. A principal one is likely to be the weak resistance to prejudice among Americans with little understanding of democratic principles. When it is not known that the Constitution protects minority views and rights, there will be fewer intellectual reasons to believe that minorities are equal and should be treated as equal. Americans with little knowledge or appreciation of democratic norms can thus easily fall under the sway of popular prejudices. They will have less respect for ethnic or cultural differences and less reason to believe that the rights of Jews ought to be protected.

These findings, while supporting cognitive theory, do not disallow the possibility that personality factors also play some role in determining whether democratic norms and values are accepted. Some support for this theory is provided by the fact that respondents who score high on the F scale are less likely than low scorers to be knowledgeable about and to support constitutional norms. F does not affect the strong relation between education and knowledgeability and support. Thus the evidence for cognitive theory holds firm. At the same time, however, F is related to knowledge and support of constitutional norms, independent of education, suggesting that emotive factors may also be at work in producing these results. At issue, once again, is whether the items making up the F scale are truly measures of personality or, as the aforementioned critics insist, really measures of cognitive sophistication.

EXPOSURE TO MASS MEDIA

It has been seen that education contributes to tolerance by bringing people into contact with what is sometimes called the "official" or ideal norms of society. Better-educated Americans hold less simplistic views of social problems and exhibit a fuller appreciation and acceptance of democratic norms.

It is possible that there are other ways besides education that Americans might be exposed to norms of tolerance and minority rights. A leading candidate for such a role is the mass media (newspapers, television, magazines). The media disseminate a wide range of information of relevance to minority group prejudice. They provide news about what minority group members are like and what they think. They often investigate the conditions under which poorer minorities live and champion the cause of civil rights. Most important, they publicize the objectives of government policy and the views of prominent national leaders. Such leaders are likely to emphasize the official norms of tolerance, equality, and civil rights in most, though not all, cases.

For the media to provide such information, they must have an audience. If newspapers and television are to be a substitute source of knowledge for less-educated Americans, they must be used by them. Data from the national study show, however, that it is precisely the less-educated who are the *least* likely to pay attention to the media. Daily reading of a newspaper, for example, was reported by 91 percent of the college graduates in this survey, as compared with 81 percent of those with some college, 74 percent of high schoolers, and 57 percent of the grade-school-educated. Similar patterns were found with respect to the reading of "serious" magazines. Presented with a list of nine such publications, only 11 percent of college graduates indicated that they never read any of them—a figure that rose with each drop in educational level and reached a high of 65 percent among those with grade school educations. Only with respect to the number of hours spent watching television was there no difference between the highly educated and the less-educated.

Merely reading a newspaper or magazine, of course, is not the same as learning information from those media sources. Some "readers" may avoid the news sections and thus have little or no knowledge about current events or personalities. To determine to what extent this was true, respondents were presented with a list of prominent Americans and asked to identify each as a politician, entertainer, or sports figure. As might be expected, it was the better-educated who were best able to identify the politicians named in the test. Ninety-five percent of the college graduates, for example, correctly identified three or four of the political personalities, as compared with only 47 percent of the grade-school-educated.[8] It is possible that these differences reflect the greater attention middle-class Americans give to politics and political news. Working-class Americans, it might be argued, have other cultural interests and are likely to do better at identifying personalities in these fields. Such apparently is not the case. Differences almost as large are found in the respondents' identification of sports and entertainment figures.[9] Among the college-educated, 87 percent correctly identified a majority of the athletes and 75 percent a majority of the entertainers. Among the grade-school-educated, the comparable figures were 40 percent and 33 percent, respectively.

There is thus little doubt that better-educated Americans are far more knowledgeable than less-educated Americans and that this disparity extends over a wide range of public issues. The information gap exists, moreover, irrespective of the media usage of the two groups. Even when the less-educated read newspapers, they are less able to identify personalities than college-educated Americans who are not regular readers. The educated apparently have other sources of information besides the media from which to learn about the political, sports, and entertainment worlds.

What these findings suggest is that being poorly educated is a double handicap. First, it leaves individuals with relatively few intellectual resources and with relatively little knowledge about the social world. They have been exposed to less information and have less ability to seek out and comprehend that which is available to them. Second, such disabilities are reinforced by the experiences of adulthood. Uneducated Americans are likely to occupy less privileged positions in society and thus have few reasons to identify with the larger society or to acquire information about it. A limited education thus makes for the cumulative isolation of such individuals from the official norms of society.

Given these patterns, it is not surprising to find that newspaper reading has little direct relation to the anti-Semitic beliefs of Americans. Among the most-educated (those with at least some college), no difference is found in the level of anti-Semitism between readers and nonreaders; among the less-educated, only a slight tendency existed for nonreaders to be more anti-Semitic. This is not to say that the media are completely ineffective as an antidote to prejudice. They may create a climate of tolerance in society as a whole or may influence the resolution of a specific issue of prejudice. These are possibilities addressed in greater detail in Chapter 7. Insofar as anti-Semitic beliefs are concerned, however, the media apparently do not overcome the handicaps imposed by a lack of education.

These findings thus again demonstrate the importance of education as a preventative to anti-Semitism. They show that more-educated Americans go to greater lengths to keep themselves informed about current events, further arming themselves against simplistic thinking. As such, these results provide additional evidence supporting cognitive explanations of prejudice.

INTOLERANCE OF CULTURAL DIVERSITY

The relative strength of cognitive and emotive approaches to prejudice was also explored by examining these respondents' tolerance of cultural diversity. From both cognitive and emotive points of view, it would be expected that persons who are anti-Semitic would also be disposed to intolerance generally. According to cognitive theory, this is because intolerance of any kind is a sign of intellectual unenlightenment. According to emotive theory, it is because personality needs create antagonisms not only toward Jews but toward members of other outgroups as well.

The cultural intolerance of Americans was measured by examining their reactions to three culturally "different" groups—atheists, immigrants, and persons wearing beards. Responses to various questions on these matters, broken down by educational level, are shown in Table 3-2. Perhaps the most striking findings are those related to public tolerance of atheists. Many Americans are only nominal church members, but most profess to a belief in God.[10] As Table 3-2 shows, most Americans are also intolerant of those who publicly believe otherwise. In all, 60 percent of these respondents would not allow an atheist to teach in a public high school, 54 percent would keep an atheist from holding public office, and 34 percent would remove an atheist's books from the public library. Such responses are consistent with others obtained in questioning of this nature.[11] It should be noted that these responses probably represent broad sentiments as much as policy positions. All of these actions are unconstitutional and would undoubtedly receive less backing if they were actually initiated. Nevertheless, the responses demonstrate the extent of intolerance among Americans and again show the prevalence of such tendencies among the less-educated. Intolerance of atheists can be found at all educational levels but is considerably greater among Americans with grade school or high school educations.

The other items in Table 3-2 tell a similar story. Americans hold intolerant attitudes toward immigrants and toward teachers who "insist on wearing beards." (This last question was included because teachers were being dismissed for this reason at the time of this survey.) In each instance, such positions were most often taken by Americans with little formal education.

The responses to five items were combined to form a summary index of intolerance of cultural diversity.[12] Respondents scoring high on this index were largely drawn from the ranks of the less-educated. Americans with grade school educations, for example, were more than three and a half times as likely to score high in intolerance than college graduates. More important, Americans who are intolerant of cultural diversity are also found

TABLE 3-2. Intolerance of Cultural Diversity, by Level of Education.

Intolerance of Cultural Diversity	Grade School	High School	Some College	College Graduate	Total
Intolerance of Atheists					
Suppose a man admitted in public that he did not believe in God:					
1. Should he be allowed to teach in a public high school? (no)	78%[a]	58%	46%	38%	60%
2. Should he be allowed to hold public office? (no)	70	54	42	30	54
3. Do you think a book he wrote should be removed from a public library? (yes)	55	30	20	12	34
Intolerance of Immigrants					
4. America owes a great deal to the immigrants who came here. (disagree)	30	26	16	12	24
5. It bothers me to see immigrants succeeding more than Americans who were born here. (agree)	28	18	9	6	18
6. Foreigners who come to live in America should give up their foreign ways and learn to be like other Americans. (agree)	86	66	56	39	67
7. Nothing in other countries can beat the American way of life. (agree)	86	71	54	41	70
Intolerance of Wearing Beards					
8. Persons who insist on wearing beards should not be allowed to teach in public schools. (agree)	39	23	16	12	25
Percent high on index of intolerance of cultural diversity[b]	70	46	34	19	49
100% (N) =	(531)	(945)	(223)	(193)	(1,892)

[a]Percentages show the proportion giving the intolerant responses indicated in the parentheses after each item.
[b]Index consists of five items: the two described earlier to measure support of the Constitution and 1, 6, and 8 in the above table; scores of 3 or more are designated as high.
SOURCE: Adapted from Selznick and Steinberg, *Tenacity of Prejudice*, p. 153.

to be disproportionately anti-Semitic in their beliefs. Among those high in intolerance, 69 percent scored high in anti-Semitism. Among the middle group, the comparable figure was 45 percent, while among the least intolerant it was 20 percent.

As presented thus far, these results give strong support to cognitive theories of prejudice. Once again, however, when F is entered into the analysis, it is found to be related to tolerance of cultural diversity, independently of education. At each level of education, the high scorers on the F scale are more likely to be intolerant than the low scorers. This is not to deny cognitive theory, since education continues to be related to tolerance, independently of F. Rather, what is suggested once again is that both theories are true. Such a conclusion, however, makes the assumption that F is a valid measure of personality. In light of all of the evidence, what can be concluded about this assumption?

The Question of F

It has been shown that Americans who hold anti-Semitic beliefs tend to hold other unenlightened attitudes as well. They have simplistic conceptions of social reality, are ignorant of democratic norms, reject civil libertarian principles, and are intolerant of cultural diversity. All of these attitudes are highly related to one another as well as to education. In effect, what is involved is a syndrome of unenlightened beliefs—a syndrome that encompasses all of these diverse elements of cognitive sophistication. Closely associated with this syndrome is a relative lack of education. Less-educated Americans hold less enlightened beliefs generally, including negative stereotypes toward Jews.

The point at issue between cognitive and emotive theories of prejudice is how this syndrome comes about. Cognitive theory suggests that the process is rooted in education. Less-educated Americans hold certain beliefs because they don't know any better; they haven't developed the cognitive abilities—or been exposed to the proper values—to believe otherwise. Emotive theory, as presented in *The Authoritarian Personality*, suggests that authoritarian personalities, created by repressive childrearing practices, are the source of this syndrome. Such personalities are said to be acting out of deeply felt psychological needs in seeking out and embracing authoritarian beliefs and rejecting enlightened values.

The evidence gathered in the national study provides strong and unambiguous support for the cognitive approach to explaining prejudice. A lack of education is strongly related to all of the elements in this syndrome of unenlightenment. The evidence also suggests, however, that two processes may be at work—that alongside of a cognitive process, personality factors may also be generating not only the acceptance of anti-Semitic beliefs but other unenlightened values as well. The principal evidence in support of this position is the finding that high F scores are correlated with each of these indicators of intellectual unenlightenment, independently of education. Americans scoring high on the F scale tend to reject democratic norms and to be culturally intolerant, even when they have had similar educations.

Does this mean, then, that emotive theories account for some of the differences among Americans with respect to anti-Semitism? If the F scale is taken as a valid measure of authoritarian personality, this would seem to be the conclusion. But there are reasons to suspect, as the critics argue, that the F scale is less a measure of personality than a measure of cognitive sophistication. The strong tendency for high F scorers to hold unenlightened attitudes on all of these measures of cognitive sophistication would suggest as much, as would the strong relation between F scores and education. Further, the items in the F scale, upon closer examination, allow for such an interpretation. The existence of a primitive cognitive style would seem to be indicated by such beliefs as "no weakness or difficulty can hold us back if we have enough will power," "people can be divided into two distinct classes—the weak and the strong," or "much of our lives is controlled by plots hatched in secret places." Beliefs of this nature are cognitively unsophisticated, and so are the people who accept them.

Acceptance of F beliefs, then, is not necessarily a sign of authoritarian personality, nor is it proof that such personality characteristics antedate or "determine" these orientations. It is true that F beliefs, once accepted, can be integrated into an individual's underlying personality structure and serve perverse emotional functions. But this process must be distinguished from a lack of cognitive sophistication that enters into their initial acceptance.

Where emotive theory would seem to err is in its implicit assumptions that enlightened and unenlightened values are equally available to all and that personality determines the acceptance of one set of values in preference to the other. In effect, authoritarian personalities are said to choose unenlightened values over enlightened ones because such values satisfy otherwise unmet psychological needs. On logical grounds, however, it is difficult to believe that enlightened values are equally accessible to all, available to be selected or rejected like entrees on a menu. It would seem apparent that some Americans are more fully exposed to the "ideal" values of the culture than others. The assumption of equal access is also in contradiction to the empirical evidence that it is principally the uneducated who choose unenlightened values. More-educated Americans, the evidence suggests, are more fully introduced to the ideal norms and values of American society. Given the rewards that accrue to being educated, such Americans would also have greater reason to conform to these norms.

One final piece of evidence exists that also casts doubt upon an emotive interpretation of the relation between F scores and anti-Semitism. According to *The Authoritarian Personality*, the authoritarian tendencies measured by the F scale are a result of childhood rather than adult experiences. This inference, however, was drawn from research on adults, not children. Since the national survey was likewise conducted among adults rather than children, it too is unsuitable for establishing whether authoritarian personalities develop early in life. This study can be used, however, to inquire into the degree to which the acceptance of F beliefs is a function of family background over and above an individual's own educational exposure. This can be done by comparing the F scores of those who come from highly educated families with the F scores of those from less-educated families, holding the respondents' own education constant. If authoritarian personalities are developed in childhood, Americans from less-educated and presumably more authoritarian backgrounds will score higher on the F scale.

These procedures show that the respondents' position on F is determined by their own education level, not that of their parents. Only among the grade-school-educated is there any sign of possible parental influence on authoritarian personality: Grade schoolers from grade school backgrounds are especially high on F. However, no differences in F scores exist between grade schoolers whose parents have high school and college educations, nor between the high-school- and college-educated who come from different educational backgrounds.

Such findings suggest that an individual's own education determines whether F beliefs are accepted or rejected and that family background has little or no independent effect upon the holding of such beliefs. They thus lend further support to the critics' contention that F beliefs are more measures of cognitive sophistication than of personality. It is possible that more refined measures of personality—or research conducted among children and carried into their later years—would provide greater support for the thesis advanced in *The Authoritarian Personality*. The results of this study, however, cast doubt upon an emotive interpretation of the F scale or emotive explanations of the origins of prejudice. This question was explored again in research conducted among adolescents, with similar results. The additional evidence is reported in Chapter 5.

In sum, the findings from the national study strongly confirm the cognitive approach to prejudice. While it does not show emotive theories to be patently false, it lends little support to theories that explain prejudice in psychological terms. This conclusion is reinforced from other evidence, which remains to be reviewed.

Education and Anomie

A final attitudinal disposition examined in the national study is "anomie." Anomie refers to feelings of bewilderment, anxiety, and normlessness; it is a state of mind in which the individual feels adrift in life without a sense of purpose or meaning. According to many observers, anomie is a common response to modern social conditions. In the past, most people grew up and worked within the same communities all their lives. Relations with their families and other community members served to define their positions in society and to give them a sense of purpose and belonging. The process of industrialization, however, acted to break down those traditional ties by requiring occupational mobility and specialization. As a result, modern men and women are often socially and psychologically uprooted, and in extreme cases they experience anomic tendencies.

Anomie has sometimes been linked with being prejudiced toward minorities. Americans who suffer from anxiety and bewilderment, it is reasoned, can easily impute their own normlessness to others. They can easily accept stereotypes that impugn the characteristics of minorities because it is their general tendency to view human nature in these terms. As with several previous concepts, anomie has both cognitive and psychological aspects.

A widely used scale of anomie—the A scale—has been developed to measure this dimension. Three questions from this five-item scale were included in the national study. Respondents were asked whether they agreed or disagreed with the following:

> Most people in government are not really interested in the problems of the average man.

> You sometimes can't help wondering whether anything is worthwhile any more.

> Nowadays, a person has to live pretty much for today and let tomorrow take care of itself.

Responses to these items provide a rough indication of the anomic tendencies of Americans. The second and third statements, in particular, seem to represent extreme assertions of normlessness and frustration.

Respondents who agreed with two or all three of these statements were regarded as having anomic tendencies. About two out of every five Americans fell into this category. It might be thought that these measures involve a psychological dimension absent and independent from previous measures The anomic are not merely accepting one set of "common" norms over another, but find themselves questioning the very existence of social norms and values. What was found, however, was that Americans scoring high in anomie also score high in anti-Semitism and in the other attitudinal dimensions examined in this chapter—simplism, a lack of knowledge of the Constitution, and cultural intolerance. Most significantly, it was again education that was found to underlie the holding of anomic attitudes. It was the less-educated who most often scored high in anomie and the most-educated who most often scored low.

While the measures are crude, this analysis of anomie would seem to complement the previous discussion. It is easy to understand why less-educated Americans would also score high in anomie. Those who are ignorant of the Constitution—and who believe that sex criminals should be publicly whipped—are bound to be bewildered by the official practices of American society. Instead of viewing governmental actions as examples of due process, such individuals are likely to view them as an abdication of social responsibility altogether. Similarly, those who maintain simplistic either/or conceptions of social reality are apt to confuse norms imperfectly applied with the absence of norms altogether. Since such individuals do not understand the ambiguities of social and political life, they can easily conclude that the future is unpredictable. Finally, it is not surprising to find that Americans who are intolerant of cultural diversity often interpret dissent and disagreement as signs of normative disintegration. The failure to tolerate diversity is often tantamount to not understanding it.

Anomic beliefs are thus logical extensions of the beliefs examined in the previous pages. As noted, however, anomie introduces an additional dimension to the analysis. Anomic beliefs would seem to represent not merely a failure to accept ideal norms but also an intellectual incapacity to understand them—a failure to grasp the complex, subtle, higher-order considerations involved in these norms. Lack of education would thus appear to contribute to feelings of anomie in several ways. First, it leaves an individual in an intellectually disadvantaged position to participate in the larger society. The uneducated are likely to be less skilled in the use of reason and deduction and therefore less able to grasp the world around them. Second, a lack of education places an individual at the periphery of society. Even when the less-educated are able to comprehend social norms, they are not in a position to observe them in operation. Finally, the less-educated have fewer reasons to take part in the official culture. Hard work and social conformity may benefit the educated, but for the uneducated the payoffs are much less. It is a small step for those who do not benefit from society's norms to conclude that these norms are nonexistent and illusory.

Thus for at least three reasons—a lack of cognitive sophistication, social isolation, and a paucity of rewards—the uneducated have fewer reasons to understand or to identify with the norms of the larger society. Being uneducated does not merely mean that one is less familiar with and less socialized into the official norms. For the adult, the effects of being uneducated are cumulative, leaving the individual in a state where he finds the outside world itself confusing and can see few reasons to participate in it.

These patterns help explain the strong relation found between anomie and anti-Semitism: Among those scoring high in anomie, 63 percent likewise scored high in anti-Semitism; in the middle group, 39 percent scored as anti-Semitic; in the lowest group, 20 percent were anti-Semitic. To a large degree, being prejudiced involves the imputing of normlessness—or a lack of ethics—to minority groups. To hold that Jews are dishonest in business or that they conspire to gain power over others is, in effect, to accuse Jews of being normless in their dealings with others. Much the same can be said about prejudiced stereotypes about other minorities—assertions that blacks are naturally promiscuous or that confession leaves Catholics free to sin with impunity. Prejudiced beliefs are also anomic in the sense that they provide reasons for suspending the normative protections generally accorded others. The belief that minority groups are violators of basic human values has often provided the justification for the worst crimes against them.

Summary

These findings show that Americans who hold anti-Semitic beliefs usually hold other unenlightened attitudes as well. They distrust experts, don't like to hear contrary arguments, and look to conspiracies, the stars, or just plain luck for the explanation of life's vicissitudes. They know little about the Constitution and give little support to the First Amendment protections of the Constitution. They follow the media less than most people, know less about the world around them, and are often social isolates. They are intolerant of cultural diversities and of social deviance. They are bewildered and confused by the world around them and frequently feel that life has little rhyme or reason to it.

Underlying such attitudes are low levels of educational exposure. Less-educated Americans are found to hold less enlightened beliefs in general. This finding supports the cognitive rather than the emotive approach to prejudice. In the latter, the question asked is why people *accept* anti-Semitic beliefs, and the answer given is in psychoanalytic terms. In a culture in which anti-Semitic ideology is deeply embedded, however, no such elaborate theory would seem to be necessary: People are anti-Semitic because they learn such attitudes through the normal process of socialization. For those enmeshed in such a cultural milieu, it is easy to pick up negative beliefs about Jews. Thus a more pertinent question would seem to be why in such a society some people *reject* anti-Semitic stereotypes. The primary answer seems to be that many people are taught otherwise in the educational process. They are taught to understand prejudiced beliefs for what they are and to reject them. They have been trained in the rules of evidence and inference, introduced to the customs and practices of minority groups, and taught to make independent, critical judgments about societal norms and practices. Educated Americans have also been more fully exposed to the "ideal" norms of the society. They more often support constitutional guarantees of minority rights and better understand the importance of social and political equality. More-educated Americans, finally, receive a greater share of society's rewards. They have more reason to accept the official norms of the culture and to abide by them.

A lack of education is thus a primary source of anti-Semitic prejudice in America. Having less education produces a syndrome of unenlightened beliefs, of which anti-Semitic prejudice is one part. Cognitive theories, in their emphasis upon education as an antidote to prejudice, are strongly confirmed by such findings. Emotive theories, in their emphasis upon psychological sources of prejudice, are not.

A lack of education, of course, is not the only source of prejudice in America. Other factors also contribute to the holding of anti-Semitic beliefs and to other forms of prejudice toward Jews. These factors were examined in other studies, to which our attention will now turn.

CHAPTER 4

Anti-Semitism Among Black Americans

A GREAT DEAL HAS BEEN SAID and written in recent years about how black Americans feel toward Jews, most of it leading to the conclusion that blacks dislike Jews. Even black leaders have sometimes acknowledged the existence of widespread anti-Semitic feeling among blacks, though they attribute this largely to the economic role that Jews have played in the ghetto economy. For example, James Baldwin once wrote:

> Jews in Harlem are small tradesmen, rent collectors, real estate agents, and pawnbrokers; they operate in accordance with the American business tradition of exploiting Negroes, and they are therefore identified with oppression and are hated for it. I remember meeting no Negro in the years of my growing up, in my family or out of it, who would really ever trust a Jew, and few who did not, indeed, exhibit for them the blackest contempt.[1]

Other black writers and spokesmen have made similar statements. It was during the civil disorders of the mid-1960s, however, that the question of black anti-Semitism first reached public visibility. There were some press reports claiming that rioters were deliberately singling out Jewish stores as targets for looting and destruction and that cries of "Let's get the Jews" were often heard. A number of black militants took up the charge and attacked Jews for what they saw as the deliberate exploitation of ghetto residents. In more recent years conflicts have frequently developed between blacks and Jews over self-help programs in black neighborhoods. Blacks in charge of such programs have sometimes attacked Jews in anti-Semitic language.

This chapter examines what black Americans actually think about Jews. Black and non-Jewish white beliefs about Jews are compared, the economic basis of black anti-Semitism is assessed, and signs of positive ties between blacks and Jews are reported. Similarities between black dislike of Jews and of whites generally are also examined.

To understand these findings properly, it is necessary to know a few basic facts about black–Jewish relations in this country. Viewed broadly, they have been characterized by both unique enmities and unique empathies. In this first respect, there is no question but that relations between the two groups have been carried out within a framework of black economic dependency. In part, this situation reflects the commercial tradition that Jewish immigrants brought with them to America. Many Jews began working in this country as peddlers or small tradesmen. Their business beliefs (and perhaps their own positions as a persecuted minority) encouraged them to do business with blacks at a time when many others would not.

More generally, this pattern is also an accident of urban history. The nation's cities have absorbed a long line of impoverished minorities—with each successive wave of migrants moving into neighborhoods vacated by the previous group. In many sections of the country, blacks moved into areas being left by upwardly mobile Jews. Jews thus owned the homes, the stores, and the businesses; blacks were tenants, employees, and customers. Such economic relations in themselves would seem cause for black dislike of Jews.

Viewed from a different perspective, however, there have also been elements in black–Jewish relations drawing the two minorities together. Both groups have been the object of widespread prejudice and discrimination in American society. Both have also worked together in civil rights efforts as well as in other liberal causes. For these reasons, it is possible that special bonds of sympathy and mutual identification may exist between blacks and Jews. Instead of being especially hostile toward Jews, many blacks may feel especially drawn to them.

Black and White Anti-Semitism Compared

One way to evaluate black anti-Semitism is to compare the attitudes of blacks and whites toward Jews. This can be done by examining how black and white respondents in the national survey answered questions about their images of Jews and about their tolerance of discrimination against Jews.

ANTI-SEMITIC BELIEFS

Judged simply by their scores on the index of anti-Semitic belief, blacks are more disposed than whites to be prejudiced against Jews. Forty-seven percent of blacks and 35 percent of whites scored high. These overall figures, however, mask an important distinction in the content of black as compared to white anti-Semitism—revealed when all eleven items making up the index are examined separately, as is done in Table 4-1.

TABLE 4-1.   Negative Economic Images of Jews, by Race.

Statement	Percentage Giving Anti-Semitic Response[a]		Percentage Point Difference, Blacks Minus Whites
	Blacks	Whites	
Jews are more willing than others to use shady practices to get ahead.	58%	40%	+ 18
The trouble with Jewish businessmen is that they are so shrewd and tricky that other people don't have a fair chance in competition.	46	34	+ 12
International banking is pretty much controlled by Jews.	40	28	+ 12
Jews are [not] as honest as other businessmen.	35	27	+ 8
Jews don't care what happens to anyone but their own kind.[b]	43	24	+ 19
Jews always like to be at the head of things.	60	53	+ 7
Jews have a lot of irritating faults.	44	40	+ 4
Jews stick together too much.	48	53	− 5
Jews are more loyal to Israel than to America.	32	30	+ 2
Jews have too much power in the United States.	9	11	− 2
Jews have too much power in the business world.	19	31	− 12

[a]Percentages show the degree of acceptance among blacks and whites of the eleven items included in the index of anti-Semitic belief.
[b]This stereotype is consistent with the image of Jews as economically exploitative.
SOURCE: Adapted from Gertrude J. Selznick and Stephen Steinberg, *The Tenacity of Prejudice: Anti-Semitism in Contemporary America* (New York: Harper & Row, 1969), p. 119.

On items that have to do directly or indirectly with Jewish business practices—the first five items in the table—blacks were consistently and substantially more likely than whites to subscribe to negative attributions of such practices. Fifty-eight percent of blacks as compared to 40 percent of whites, for example, endorsed the belief that "Jews are more willing than others to use shady practices to get ahead." The item "The trouble with Jewish businessmen is that they are so shrewd and tricky that other people don't have a fair chance in competition" received 46 percent support from blacks as compared to 34 percent from whites. On items in which Jewish business practices are not an issue—the last six items in Table 4-1—the differences between the proportion of blacks and whites subscribing to these views is either small or reversed. Thus there are actually more whites than blacks who subscribe to the view that Jews "stick together too much" and that they have too much power in the U.S. generally and in the business world in particular.

Averaging of the scores for the economic and the noneconomic items reveals that an average of 44 percent blacks subscribe to the economic items, as compared to 31 percent of the whites. On the noneconomic items the average acceptance rate for blacks is 35 percent and for whites 36 percent. Blacks, then, are distinguished from whites only by their more widespread feelings of economic hostility toward Jews. They show no significantly greater tendency than whites to perceive Jews as aggressive, clannish, prideful, and conceited; they are somewhat less fearful than whites of Jewish power.

These differences are partly the result of the fact that whites, on the average, are more educated than blacks. When education is taken into account, black–white differences on economic stereotypes are somewhat reduced. On noneconomic stereotypes, however, the differences are increased, with blacks at each educational level showing less noneconomic prejudice than whites.

These findings are consistent with a theory that black anti-Semitism is economically based. Further support for this view was found when the effects of having business contacts with Jews were examined. Among white respondents, those having such contacts were *less* anti-Semitic than those without them in both their economic and their noneconomic beliefs. Knowing Jews leads evidently to a lessening in anti-Semitic tendency among whites. Among black respondents, having business contacts with Jews was also associated with a lessening in noneconomic prejudice, but on the economic issues it was associated with a sharp rise in anti-Semitic responses. Blacks who reported having business contacts with Jews were the ones who were the most critical of Jewish economic behavior.[2]

DISCRIMINATION AGAINST JEWS

While blacks are more prejudiced in their economic beliefs about Jews, they might be expected to be less anti-Jewish in their attitudes toward discrimination. Black Americans have been frequent victims of discrimination themselves and have often worked with Jews in opposition to such practices.

This expectation was borne out. Black respondents are more opposed than whites to political anti-Semitism, and to other forms of discrimination against Jews as well. For example, almost all blacks—91 percent—oppose social club discrimination, while twice as many blacks as whites (68 percent versus 31 percent) were willing to combat such discrimination in practice as well as in principle. Likewise a larger proportion of blacks than whites said that they would not be disturbed at all if their party were to nominate a Jew for the presidency (68 percent versus 51 percent).

Black Americans are thus found to be more anti-Semitic on some measures, white Americans on others. This is apparently because black anti-Semitism and white anti-Semitism are influenced by different factors. A negative factor is the kind of economic relations existing between blacks and Jews; a positive factor is the experience of blacks themselves as an excluded minority.

SOCIAL LOCATION OF BLACK ANTI-SEMITISM

The number of black respondents in the national study was too small to make an extensive analysis of the social location of black anti-Semitism. However, insofar as analysis was possible, two important configurations emerged. On one, black anti-Semitism followed the same pattern as white anti-Semitism; on the other, it ran opposite to white anti-Semitism.

Among both blacks and whites education was the main social correlate of prejudice. Within both racial groups, anti-Semitism was greatest among those with eighth-grade educations or less and declined at each higher educational level. A relative lack of education thus appears to be a principal source of anti-Semitic prejudice for both black and white Americans.

In Chapter 3 it was reported that younger adults are less anti-Semitic than the elderly. While this is true for whites, the pattern is somewhat different for blacks. Middle-aged blacks are less anti-Semitic than older blacks, but younger blacks (under thirty-five) score almost as high on anti-Semitism as older blacks. This difference can be illustrated by referring to economic anti-Semitism. The proportion of young blacks who were anti-Semitic on a measure of economic anti-Semitism was 49 percent, almost as much as for older blacks—53 percent. The figure for middle-aged blacks was 34 percent.

This finding suggests that anti-Semitism among black youth may be on the rise. It is also possible that what is reflected here is greater hostility among black youth toward all whites, Jewish and non-Jewish. There will be an occasion later for further examination of these two possibilities.

TRENDS IN BLACK ANTI-SEMITISM

It has been seen that the anti-Semitic beliefs of Americans have changed little over the past ten years or so; Americans hold much the same attitudes toward Jews now as they did in the mid-1960s. For blacks, however, the 1960s were a time of heightened racial consciousness and black–white tensions. Times have changed, and it is possible that black Americans have come to hold less negative attitudes toward Jews or Jewish business practices.

Table 4-2 shows the racial breakdown of responses given in a 1975 survey of the national population conducted by Louis Harris. The patterns are virtually identical to those obtained in the survey conducted a decade earlier. Blacks again more frequently accept stereotypes reflecting negatively on Jewish economic practices. They again respond similarly to whites on items dealing with noneconomic beliefs. Thus the economic anti-Semitism of blacks is not merely a reflection of the racial turbulence of the 1960s but is of continuing endurance. Given this fact, attention is now turned to an investigation of anti-Semitism within a specially selected sample of urban blacks.

Anti-Semitism Among Urban Blacks

It is in the nation's cities that the greatest potential for black anti-Semitism exists. It is there that blacks and Jews most regularly come into contact with one another and that Jews usually occupy positions of economic superiority. Urban blacks regularly shop at Jewish-owned stores and have Jews as bosses, landlords, and creditors. Such economic conditions are often said to produce black anti-Semitism.

The anti-Semitic prejudices of urban blacks were examined in a survey using representative samples of blacks living in Northern metropolitan areas and in four major cities—New York, Chicago, Atlanta, and Birmingham.[3] This investigation was the first of its kind to be conducted with such a large cross-section of the black population in America. Its findings are discussed in the balance of this chapter.

ANTI-SEMITIC BELIEFS

As in the national study, a concerted effort was made to examine the anti-Semitic beliefs of the urban blacks in the samples. In this instance, responses to seven negative belief statements were used to assess the incidence of anti-Semitism. These statements were identical to those used in the national study, making possible direct comparisons between urban blacks and whites nationally.

TABLE 4-2. Negative Economic Images of Jews, by Race, 1975 Harris Survey.

Statement	Percentage Giving Anti-Semitic Response		Percentage Point Difference, Blacks Minus Whites
	Blacks	Whites	
When it comes to choosing between people and money, Jews will choose money.	48%	32%	+ 16
Jewish businessmen will usually try to pull a shady deal on you.	33	19	+ 14
Jews are not as honest as other businessmen.	24	17	+ 7
Jews always stick to their own and never give an outsider a break.	32	26	+ 6
Jews are more loyal to Israel than to the United States.	34	33	+ 1
Jews feel superior to other groups.	30	33	− 3
Jews are too ambitious for their own good.	14	18	− 4
Jews are irritating because they are too aggressive.	25	32	− 7

SOURCE: National poll conducted by Louis Harris & Associates.

Table 4-3 compares the responses of urban blacks and of the national sample of whites on these seven items. The results are consistent with the patterns reported above. The city-dwelling blacks, like blacks nationally, were distinguished from whites largely by their greater economic anti-Semitism. Jews were associated with "shady practices" and viewed as caring "only about their own kind," and Jewish businessmen were perceived as "shrewd and tricky." All of these negative economic images were more frequently accepted by urban blacks than by whites nationally.

The economic grounding of black anti-Semitism is revealed here once again. Also indicated again is that black Americans were not more anti-Semitic than whites on other dimensions of prejudice. It is only in their economic beliefs that urban blacks hold more negative images of Jews. On the noneconomic items reported upon in Table 4-3, blacks are no more or less likely than whites to give a prejudiced response.

TABLE 4-3. Economic Anti-Semitism of Urban Blacks and Whites.

Statement	Percentage Giving Anti-Semitic Response[a]		Percentage Point Difference, Blacks Minus Whites
	Blacks	Whites[b]	
Jews are more willing than others to use shady practices to get what they want	59%	40%	+ 19
Jewish businessmen are so shrewd and tricky that other people don't have a fair chance in competition.	44	34	+ 10
Jews don't care what happens to anyone but their own kind.	38	24	+ 14
Jews are not as honest as other businessmen.	29	27	+ 2
Jews have too much power in the United States.	12	11	+ 1
Jews have too much power in the business world.	26	31	- 5
Jews stick together too much.	43	53	- 10

[a]Percentages show the degree of acceptance.
[b]These figures are from the 1964 national survey and are identical to those in Table 4-1.
SOURCE: Adapted from Gary T. Marx, *Protest and Prejudice: A Study of Belief in the Black Community* (New York: Harper & Row, 1967), pp. 128–129; and from Selznick and Steinberg, *Tenacity of Prejudice*, p. 119.

Of particular interest are the regional variations in black anti-Semitism. Prejudice toward Jews was found to be considerably higher in the urban North—where most Jews reside—than in the South. On the average, 40 percent of Chicago blacks accepted the seven negative stereotypes of Jews and 41 percent of New Yorkers did so. In the two Southern cities—Atlanta and Birmingham—the figures were 28 and 29 percent. These regional patterns are comparable to those found for black respondents in the national study as well. They again suggest that black anti-Semitism is associated with the Jewish economic presence in ghetto life.

The initial results of this urban study thus confirm those of the national study. Black Americans are not significantly more anti-Semitic than whites but are clearly more critical of Jewish business practices. Attention will be given shortly to an examination of the bases of these negative evaluations of Jews. Before doing so, however, mention needs to be made of positive evaluations of Jews, else it be assumed that black attitudes were predominantly negative.

Positive Elements in Black–Jewish Relations

When anti-Semitism is made the focus of research, there is a danger that positive elements in black attitudes toward Jews could be overlooked. There is a built-in tendency to report how many blacks show anti-Semitic leanings while neglecting to stress that in most instances the majority do not respond in an anti-Semitic way. For example, the information that 40 percent of Chicago blacks on the average accepted negative stereotypes of Jews does not make explicit the fact that 60 percent on the average did not do so.

Positive black feelings toward Jews were expressed not only in the disavowal of negative descriptions but also in support for positive evaluations. Thus, for example, 81 percent of urban blacks agreed that "Jews are a warm and friendly people," and 75 percent of urban blacks agreed that "the more contact a person has with Jewish people, the more he gets to like them." These percentages were slightly above those found for whites in the national study.

These positive feelings result in part from the experience of both blacks and Jews as principal victims of prejudice and discrimination in American society, giving them a common understanding of what it means to be stigmatized and rejected. Thrity-seven percent of the blacks in the sample agreed that Jews have suffered more than others "through no fault of their own," and just over half expressed the belief that Jews are being discriminated against today.[4]

The special identification which many blacks feel with Jews is best illustrated in comments volunteered during the course of the interviews:

I think of Jews as almost being black.

They are like us. We blacks suffer through no fault of our own.

They know how it feels to be mistreated. Their hearts go out to black people.

Deep down inside they are not as prejudiced as other whites because they are discriminated against themselves.

They will socialize with you when the Italians and Irish and others will not.

Positive feelings also stem from black recognition of the extent to which the black struggle has received Jewish support. As a whole, white Americans have done relatively little to help the plight of the black minority, and in recent years the role of the white liberal in the black movement has become controversial. Nevertheless, Jews have been disproportionately active on behalf of many black causes. Jewish philanthropists helped found and fund the Urban League and the NAACP in the early 1900s, and Jews over the years have given strong personal support and financial assistance to those and other such organizations. Similarly, large numbers of Jews were active in the civil rights movement in the 1960s, including the two Jewish youths murdered in Mississippi during the summer of 1964; Jewish defense agencies have often cooperated with black groups in securing mutually beneficial legislation; and such predominantly Jewish unions as the International Ladies Garment Workers have played pioneering roles in involving blacks in the labor movement. Rank-and-file Jewish voters, finally, have supported liberal candidates and civil rights causes to a far greater extent than have other white ethnic groups.

Black Americans are aware of these facts and perceive Jews to be more supportive of civil rights and to be less discriminatory than other whites. When asked: "On the whole, do you think that Jews are more in favor of civil rights for Negroes than other white people are, less in favor, or is there no difference?" 45 percent replied "more in favor," only 3 percent said "less," and 35 percent said "the same."⁵ Similarly, when asked whether it was true that Jews were better than other whites about hiring Negroes, 69 percent said it was true and only 15 percent that it was false.

Thus many blacks see Jews as especially supportive of civil rights, and those who do are consistently more disposed than those who do not to reject negative sterotypes of Jews and to condemn discriminatory behavior against them. For example, blacks who perceived Jews as not supportive of civil rights were almost twice as likely to be anti-Semitic as those who viewed Jews as highly supportive.

Economic Bases of Black Anti-Semitism

While certain features of the black–Jewish relationship contribute to favorable black feelings about Jews, others have the opposite effect. Foremost among these, as has already been seen, are the economic associations existing between these groups. The study of urban blacks gave considerable attention to examining the nature of black–Jewish economic relations and to black responses to them.

ECONOMIC RELATIONS

Jews in the past have had substantial economic interests in black residential areas. The urban black study leaves little doubt that this pattern remains common today and that black–Jewish relations are largely economic in nature. In total, 70 percent of urban blacks reported having Jewish-owned stores in their neighborhoods, and 93 percent of this group said they shopped at Jewish stores. Similarly, 12 percent reported that they were working for a Jewish person at the time of the survey, while an additional 53 percent had done so in the past. Twenty-five percent had a Jewish doctor or dentist.

In the North, where black anti-Semitism tends most to be, such economic interactions are especially prevalent. In New York City, for example, 78 percent of the black respondents reported having Jewish stores in their area, and where there were such stores 98 percent of New York blacks said they patronized them. Eighty-one percent of New York blacks either currently worked for a Jew or had done so in the past, and 43 percent had a Jewish doctor or dentist. The figures for Chicago blacks are somewhat lower than for the New Yorkers, and lower still are the figures for Atlanta and Birmingham blacks. However, even in Birmingham, where black–Jewish economic relations are least frequent, 60 percent reported that they had Jewish stores in their areas, 90 percent with such stores patronized them, and 44 percent were working or had worked for a Jewish employer.

These impersonal economic associations were not matched by more intimate social forms of contact. In the North, for example, four of ten blacks report having had a Jewish friend at some time in their lives, while the figures for Atlanta and Birmingham are considerably less—28 and 19 percent respectively. Moreover, when asked whether or not they had contacts with Jews in any clubs or organizations to which they belonged, only 14 percent of Northern blacks, 7 percent in Atlanta, and 2 percent in Birmingham said that they had.

The relationships between blacks and Jews are thus more economic than social in nature, and the economic relationships are largely of a kind that makes blacks dependent on Jews—as customers to merchant, employees to employer, and tenants to landlord.

It is often charged that Jews, along with other white businessmen, deliberately exploit the residents of black ghettos. Whether Jews are any more or any less guilty than other whites in this respect is not known; that ghetto residents are often exploited has been amply documented.[6] Among the most common such practices are misleading advertising, high-pressure sales tactics, misrepresentations in price, the substitution of reconditioned or inferior merchandise for new or high-quality goods, and the charging of exorbitant prices for shoddy products. Such practices occur in many places, but they are more easily carried out among victims of poverty and discrimination.[7] Ghetto residents cannot as easily shop outside of their neighborhoods or take their business elsewhere. In a variety of ways, they are highly dependent upon local merchants for service and credit.

There is thus ample cause for urban blacks to distrust and dislike white merchants. One question in this survey sought to tap the anti-Jewish component of this dimension. It asked respondents whether they felt that Jewish store owners had treated them unfairly. In total, 16 percent replied that they had; 82 percent said that they had not; and 2 percent said they did not know. As in other such replies, the anti-Jewish response was more prevalent in the North than in the South. The portion of blacks reporting unfair treatment was 25 percent in Chicago, 21 percent in New York, 12 percent in Atlanta, and 7 percent in Birmingham. Such responses are thus more common where there are more Jews and more Jewish–black contacts.

Different assessments can be made of these figures. On the one hand, the percentage of blacks reporting unfair treatment is lower than many popular accounts suggest. On the other hand, one out of every four or five blacks living in Northern cities reports having been mistreated by Jewish businessmen—a sum translating into several million people. Furthermore, blacks who feel this way are three times as likely to score high in anti-Semitic belief as those who do not.

The personal feelings associated with alleged mistreatment are reflected in the comments of a number of these respondents. When asked how they believed they had been treated unfairly, they cited numerous concrete examples. Here are some of them:

> I have bought merchandise on credit, and picked it out in the store. I got seconds or damaged goods when it was delivered. They added more money to my bill than what I owed. When I send children to the store, the Jew sends tainted meat and damaged milk containers and canned goods.

> I got a rotten deal. He was pretty nasty about this money. I was behind in my payments, $10 a week, and I missed a week and he wanted to take stuff out. Furniture store. I told him I'd get a gun.

> They made me pay for goods twice. They didn't give receipts so I had to pay twice.

> He charged me more money for a plain television. I could get a colored television for the $500 I paid for this small one. They charge too much for the products they sell you.

> The price is higher than in Harlem where I used to live because he puts his hand on the scale to make the number of pounds more to charge me more money.

> I sold a car for a Jew once for $800. My share was to be $250. The guy paid the Jew with a thousand dollar bill. The Jew gave me $25. . . . I walked away to keep from shooting him.

In at least some ghetto areas, the word "Jew" is used to refer to all white people. Thus, to some unknown extent, such reports reflect generalized resentments toward whites rather than hostility toward Jews. Nevertheless, these examples do illustrate the likely economic foundation of much black anti-Semitism.

CREDIT PRACTICES

Credit practices are often said to be a prominent source of conflict between blacks and Jews or other whites. Low-income blacks are not much different from anyone else in desiring the material comforts of life. To purchase many items, however, they are forced to take out credit and often to rely upon those specializing in such matters. Empirical studies have shown that this is one of the principal areas in which blacks are exploited. They often end up paying exorbitant prices for inferior goods.[8]

The inquiries made on this subject were somewhat different from those above. They were designed not to measure anti-Jewish feelings exclusively, but to compare the attitudes that blacks hold toward Jewish and other white businessmen. One question asked respondents to indicate whether it was easier to obtain credit in a Jewish store or in a non-Jewish white-owned store. Sixty-two percent said the Jewish store, 9 percent selected the non-Jewish white store, while the remainder saw no difference or didn't offer an opinion. A second question asked whether Jewish merchants were harder or easier than other white merchants on people falling behind in their payments. Again Jewish businessmen were better perceived. Forty-nine percent said that Jewish store owners were easier on people, 16 percent said they were harder.

Most urban blacks thus have more favorable attitudes toward the credit practices of Jews than those of other whites. This pattern is further evidence of the positive dimension of black attitudes toward Jews.

For the moment, however, attention should be given to those blacks who are more distrustful of Jews than other whites. This group constitutes the hard core of black anti-Semitism. Its members report having many economic contacts with Jews and frequently being mistreated by Jewish store owners. To a considerable degree, these economic-related factors are found to be cumulative, or causally related. As blacks have more economic associations with Jews, they tend to respond more negatively to Jewish business practices.

ECONOMIC-BASED ANTI-SEMITISM

It is possible now to make a general estimate of the extent to which anti-Semitism, as expressed in hostile beliefs about Jews, has economic origins. Among respondents who have had little or no economic contact with Jews, and who neither thought they had been treated unfairly by Jewish businessmen nor believed that Jewish credit practices were worse than those of other whites, only 13 percent score as anti-Semitic in belief. From this beginning point, the percentage of anti-Semites gradually rises as economic discontent with and criticism of Jews becomes more frequent. It reaches a peak of 70 percent among blacks having the most contact and the most criticisms. These results can be seen in Table 4-4, which reports the amount of anti-Semitism exhibited according to the respondents' degree of contact with and criticism of Jewish business practices.[9]

TABLE 4-4.   Black Anti-Semitism, by Amount of Economic Contact with Jews.

| | Score on Index of Predisposition to Economically Based Anti-Semitism[a] | | | | | | |
	Low 0	1	2	3	4	5	High 6
Percent anti-Semit-ic (including those very high)	13%	16%	29%	36%	50%	67%	70%
Percent very high in anti-Semitism	3	2	7	16	12	24	31
Number	(279)	(231)	(200)	(81)	(52)	(21)	(13)

[a]Those low, medium, and high in impersonal economic contact were scored 0, 1, and 2, respectively. Those who felt that Jews compared unfavorably with other whites with respect to credit practices were scored 2, while those not feeling this way received a score of 0. Respondents who reported being treated unfairly by a Jewish merchant were scored 2, while those who had never shopped at a Jewish store or those who did shop and had not been treated unfairly were scored 0, as were those who said "don't know."
SOURCE: Adapted from Marx, *Protest and Prejudice*, p. 166.

Some caution must be exercised before concluding that the economic contacts come first and cause the anti-Semitism. It is possible that some persons are anti-Semitic first and because of this evaluate Jewish economic behavior negatively. Some theories would predict this result, namely those which associate anti-Semitism with certain personality traits. No evidence was found, however, to support this explanation of prejudice.

It would thus appear that economic factors are an important ingredient in black anti-Semitism. They are not necessarily the central cause of black anti-Semitism, but they are a prime source of such feelings. This is not to suggest that all Jewish merchants are grasping Shylocks or that Jews are less honest than other businessmen in black neighborhoods. How widespread dishonesty is among ghetto merchants and whether Jewish merchants are worse than others are questions that lie beyond the bounds of this research. Further, it is to be recognized that relations between merchants and customers are not always exploitative. Much of the evidence indicates that the opposite is also true. A passage from Dick Gregory's book, *Nigger,* illustrates the mixture of exploitation and altruism often involved in such relationships. Gregory, describing how the local Jewish merchant treated his family, notes that they were sold three-day-old bread (which was always given to credit book customers), that the peaches were rotten, that the butter was sometimes green, and adds that he himself once broke into the store for petty thievery. But, he writes:

When it came down to the nitty-gritty you could always go to Mister Ben. Before a Jewish holiday he'd take all that food that was going to spoil while the store was shut and bring it over to our house. Before Christmas he'd send over some meat even though he knew it was going on the tablet and he might never see his money. When the push came to the shove and every hungry belly in the house was beginning to eat on itself, Momma could go to Mister Ben and always get enough for some dinner.[10]

This study indicates that urban blacks often have the type of mixed experiences reported by Dick Gregory.

Economic relations between blacks and Jews thus have two sides to them. They often lead to conflict and prejudice, but they frequently produce positive feelings as well. These two predispositions don't quite balance out one another, since negative evaluations are the more common and powerful. Black Americans, however, would be a great deal more anti-Semitic if it were not for the positive side of their relations with Jews.

JEWISH VERSUS OTHER WHITE BUSINESSMEN

The existence of such cross-cutting sentiments helps explain another important finding. When asked to compare Jews with other white businessmen, most black respondents saw little difference. Those who did choose, however, favored the Jewish businessmen by a wide margin. Thirty-four percent, for example, said it was better to work for a Jew, 19 percent for a non-Jewish white. Twenty percent thought Jewish store owners were better than other white store owners, while 7 percent said they were worse. Twenty-four percent, finally, preferred having a Jewish landlord, compared with 7 percent preferring a non-Jewish white landlord.

These responses are similar to those above dealing with credit practices. They show that urban blacks—whatever their other feelings toward Jews—would rather carry out their economic transactions with Jews than with other whites. What is perhaps most striking is that this pattern holds up even among anti-Semitic respondents. Even among blacks who stereotype Jews in highly negative ways, there is a tendency to prefer Jews to other white businessmen.

This finding would seem to contradict one widely held theory of black anti-Semitism—that Jews are a scapegoat for black discontent. According to this notion, anti-Semitism represents a displacement of hostilities felt toward more powerful whites; Jews are made the scapegoat because, as a minority, they can more easily be attacked. Contrary to this theory, an array of evidence has been presented showing that blacks are in many ways drawn to Jews. It is possible that for some black Americans Jews *are* a scapegoat for more general discontents. The number of such blacks, however, could not be very large.

It is instructive to read some of the reasons given by these city-dwelling blacks for preferring Jewish businessmen. They are similar to the story told by Dick Gregory.

A Jew will give you an advance in your pay quicker than a cracker will. A Jew seems to feel that the people who work for him is part of his responsibility. If you need medical care, a Jew sees that you get that and holds your job for you. A cracker lets you go when you get sick. A Jew sticks by you for the good you have been. I know several Jews who still pay rent, buy groceries, helping people who used to work for them, but now they are sick.

I felt he was a relative. I could go to him with my problems and he would help me. Moneywise, he goes out of his way to help.

They treat Negro customers better. They will serve you just as fast as they serve anybody else. They will donate money faster to the Negro causes.

He will give you a better chance to pay bills—just call him when you don't have the money and he will give you time to pay and talk very courteous to you. He will show you all qualities of goods for your selection. The other race will show you goods depending on how you look and are dressed. The Jew will always put a handle on your name and not just call you Mary or Susie. They call you Mrs. or Miss and they also address you properly on their mail that is sent to you.

Jewish landlords are one hundred percent better. They are more lenient if you are behind in recent payments. They are better about fixing repairs. I would rather have a Jewish landlord than a white one.

The Jew automatically kind of gives you a chance to pay. Even if he has a white man collecting. The white man will want to put you out the minute you don't pay or get behind, but the Jew, you can call him, and he will make the white man extend you time. This is better when you're poor like I am and other Negroes.

They are very considerate. They would be giving us something every time when we paid the rent. They always gave us some clothes and goodies. If it weren't for the Jews, I wouldn't be here today. It was hard to get along with no father.

Not all respondents felt this way; examples could also be cited from the interviews with blacks preferring to do business with non-Jewish whites. To understand what blacks really think about Jews, however, it is necessary to take into account favorable as well as unfavorable attitudes. Black Americans have both uniquely positive and uniquely negative attitudes toward Jews.

Anti-Semitism and Anti-White Attitudes

One final area of investigation remains to be discussed. It is possible that black hostility toward Jews is largely a reflection of their dislike of whites generally. Black Americans may not be responding to having a Jew as a landlord or boss as much as to finding a white person in a position of superiority over them. That this is often the case is suggested by the results that most blacks see little difference between having a Jew and having another white as an employer, store owner, or landlord.

The same possibility is suggested by the survey of urban blacks' attitudes toward whites. Not surprisingly, many black respondents were found to distrust and dislike whites. One question, for example, asked how many white store owners took advantage of black customers. Twenty percent said "almost all of them," 16 percent "many," and 41 percent "a few"; only 13 percent said none or almost none. Similarly, 73 percent of this sample agreed that "most whites want to keep Negroes down as much as they can."

These and other questions were asked not to examine antiwhite feelings in depth—this would have required another study—but to build a rough index of antiwhite attitudes. Significantly, a close correspondence was found between the respondents' positions on this index and their anti-Semitism. Those scoring high on one measure usually scored high on the other; those unprejudiced toward one group were almost always unprejudiced toward the other. In total, only 4 percent of these city-dwelling blacks scored as anti-Semitic but not antiwhite, while another 4 percent were antiwhite but not anti-Semitic.

While the measures used were rough, they suggest that to a degree black anti-Semitism has similar origins with black hostility toward whites generally. This interpretation is reinforced by the social patterns associated with the two forms of prejudice. Both are found among the same kinds of blacks, most notably among the less-educated. At the same time, of course, anti-Jewish and antiwhite attitudes are distinguishable in important ways. Their ideological content is not identical but reflects different prevailing cultural myths and stereotypes. Moreover, black attitudes toward Jews have been shaped by the unique kinds of social and economic relations described above.

AGE, ANTI-SEMITISM, AND RACIAL MILITANCY

One distinctive feature of anti-Semitism noted above is its greater prevalence among the young. Among whites, prejudice toward Jews is most common among the oldest generation; among blacks, the youngest generation is disproportionately anti-Semitic. The question was raised as to whether these figures reflect a unique rise among younger blacks in hostility specifically toward Jews or an increase in hostility to all whites, Jewish and non-Jewish.

The urban black study affords more evidence for the second than the first of these interpretations. Among urban blacks, younger respondents were the most antiwhite, the most impatient with the pace of social change, and the most militant in their political views.[11] The greater anti-Semitism of the young would thus seem to represent one aspect of a more generally heightened racial consciousness.

This rise in black consciousness helps explain the growth in black–Jewish tensions over the past fifteen years. As blacks have sought to gain greater control over their own affairs, they have invariably come into conflict with white authorities—some of whom are Jews. This has been especially true of programs of self-help and community control. The effort to start black businesses and to patronize black stores often means *not* shopping at white-owned or Jewish stores. It is because of this that such programs have often taken on anti-Semitic tones. It is not necessarily their intention to be anti-Semitic; but in order to build up black independence, it is often necessary to tear down black dependencies.[12]

Summary

This chapter has provided an extensive look at the anti-Semitism of black Americans. It generally confirms popular notions about the economic basis of black anti-Semitism but shows that other factors also shape black attitudes toward Jews.

The economic foundations of black anti-Semitism were substantiated in a number of ways. Urban blacks indeed frequently patronize Jewish-owned stores, work for Jewish employers, and have Jewish landlords. Such relations, moreover, were found to be associated with higher levels of anti-Semitism. Blacks having such economic contacts held considerably more negative attitudes toward Jews.

It could not be determined from this research whether these negative feelings resulted from the inferior positions in which blacks found themselves or from outright economic exploitation. Many blacks, however, feel that they have been personally abused by Jewish businessmen. About a quarter (in the North) reported that they had been treated unfairly by Jewish store owners, while smaller percentages were critical of Jews as employers, landlords, and creditors. Those feeling this way scored especially high in anti-Semitism.

These findings also show that there is a more positive side to black–Jewish relations. Many blacks identify with Jews as fellow victims of discrimination. Many also see Jews as strong supporters of equal rights and of the civil rights movement generally. Significantly, attitudes of this kind were found associated with lower rates of anti-Semitism. Such positive orientations thus serve to reduce anti-Semitic tendencies among blacks, just as economic dependencies serve to promote them. Taken together, these two orientations have the result that the overall level of black anti-Semitism is about the same as for whites. Blacks are more anti-Semitic in their economic attitudes toward Jews. However, they hold about the same beliefs on other anti-Semitic stereotypes and give considerably less support to anti-Jewish discrimination.

There are thus important similarities and important differences in the anti-Semitic prejudices of whites and blacks. For most whites, anti-Semitism exists as a hearsay phenomenon. It bears little or no relation to actually knowing Jews, but is picked up through contact with the anti-Semitic imagery of the larger culture. White anti-Semitism, as a result, largely develops among those who are most susceptible to the simplifications and distortions of prejudice principally among the less-educated. Among blacks, a similar process is at work. Education is again a principal social correlate and cause of anti-Semitism. In addition, however, black attitudes toward Jews are shaped by the kinds of economic and social relations existing between the two groups. These associations affect both the ideological content of black anti-Semitism and its pervasiveness.

A final subject explored in this chapter was the relation between black attitudes toward Jews and toward whites generally. A close correspondence was found to exist between the two. Few blacks hold negative beliefs toward Jews who do not also hold them toward whites; few were antiwhite who were not also anti-Semitic. While the measures involved are crude, it appears that black anti-Semitism is to a large degree a racially induced response. Blacks who respond negatively to Jews do so more because Jews are white than because of other perceived traits.

This is not to suggest that anti-Semitism is nothing but an expression of antiwhite feelings. Black anti-Semitism draws upon prevailing cultural stereotypes and has been shaped by unique socio-economic relations with Jews. Nevertheless, it is largely as members of the oppressive white majority that blacks seem to react to Jews. Such a response helps explain the disproportionately greater anti-Semitism found within the youngest generation of blacks. Younger blacks are also the most antiwhite, the most impatient with social change, and the most militant politically. It has thus been within the younger generation that racial consciousness has grown in recent years and that antiwhite and anti-Jewish feelings have increased most sharply.

These last remarks should not be taken as an apology for black anti-Semitism or hostility toward whites. Prejudice should be deplored wherever it exists and for whatever reason. At the same time, prejudice toward the oppressor is not to be equated with prejudice toward the oppressed. The prejudice of blacks is in part a response to circumstances which white-dominated culture has imposed on them. The opposite does not apply with respect to the prejudice of whites.

CHAPTER 5

Anti-Semitism Among the Young

ANTI-SEMITISM IS WIDESPREAD among adult Americans, as the previous chapters demonstrate. Many anti-Semites, however, undoubtedly acquired their prejudices as youths rather than as adults. The anti-Semitism examined in other chapters may thus have first developed in childhood or the adolescent years. No fixed age seems to exist when prejudice first appears, but research shows that it can develop among the very young. When circumstances are there to nourish it, prejudice can appear as early as age four and, according to some observers, even earlier than that.[1]

This research program included a study of anti-Semitism among one important preadult group—adolescents. It was the first time such a systematic investigation had been made of the anti-Semitism of young Americans. Adolescents were chosen for study because the teenage years constitute an important formative period in life. Adolescence is a time when complex social and political beliefs are first developed and when ideological conceptions of social reality are constructed. In addition, it is a period during which the experience of prejudice, social ostracism, and outgroup hostility can be very painful. Teenagers are highly vulnerable to the disapprobation and rejection of their peers, and those who experience them often bear the scars for many years afterward.

Studying adolescent prejudice also allowed for additional testing of various theories associated with anti-Semitism. Most especially, it provided another opportunity to examine the cognitive and emotive theories discussed in Chapter 3. Of particular interest was whether those cognitively linked factors found to produce adult anti-Semitism are also operative among teenagers. The fact that the subjects were all attending school made it possible to examine, in more detail, the relation between academic achievement and anti-Semitism.

Such a research undertaking, finally, recommended itself because its results might contribute to the formulation of more effective means to combat anti-Semitism. Most teenagers remain exposed to the socializing influence of schooling. The study's results, it was felt, might suggest how the schools could do a better job of controlling anti-Semitism and other forms of prejudice.

The study of adolescent prejudice was carried out in three communities in the Eastern part of the United states.[2] These communities were specially chosen to examine the relation between the number of Jews in a setting and the amount and nature of teenage anti-Semitism. In one of the communities, Commutertown, 43 percent of the school population was Jewish. In a second, Oceanville, it was 23 percent, while in the third, Central City, there were virtually no Jews (less than one-half of one percent). The number of black youths was roughly the same in all three communities, ranging from 14 to 16 percent. In the three communities—for which pseudonyms are used here at the request of school officials—a series of questionnaires dealing with the subject matter under study were administered to all youths enrolled in the eighth, tenth, and twelfth grades.

In this report on the results, attention is given first to describing how much anti-Semitism was found and second to setting forth what was learned about where it was found. Reported next are the study's findings about the causes of adolescent prejudice. Finally, the results pertaining to the effects of a Jewish presence upon anti-Semitism are presented.

The Nature and Extent of Adolescent Anti-Semitism

Three approaches were used to detect anti-Semitism among teenagers. The first was to ask youngsters what they believed Jews to be like and then to judge their anti-Semitism according to the number of negative beliefs subscribed to. This method was similar to the one used to measure anti-Semitic beliefs among adults. A second approach was to ask the teenagers how they felt about associating with Jewish adolescents and to define anti-Semitism as an unwillingness to engage in such interactions. The third approach called for assessing actual friendship choices, and distinguishing non-Jewish teenagers according to whether or not they had Jewish friends. This approach was appropriate only in Commutertown and Oceanville, since in Central City there was no opportunity for non-Jewish youngsters to have Jewish friends.

BELIEFS ABOUT JEWS AMONG WHITE NON-JEWISH TEENAGERS

Ask adolescents to express themselves about Jews, it was discovered in preliminary interviews, and all sorts of imagery quickly pours forth. Sometimes negative and sometimes positive, the comments are almost always articulate. Only rarely do youths respond that they don't know anything about Jews. It doesn't matter much whether a youngster has never met anyone who is Jewish. He or she still has something to say.

The content of adolescent imagery is influenced markedly by the time-worn shibboleths of the past. Indeed, the traditional stereotypes virtually set the boundaries for these teenagers' remarks about what they know about Jews, what they imagine them to be like, and how they feel about them. The familiarity of adolescents with old saws about Jews—either pro or con—is testimony to how deeply these images have become embedded in American culture.

Because such traditional stereotyping dominated the preliminary interviews, the format adopted in the full study was to confront the youngsters with such stereotypes and ask them whether they agreed or disagreed with them. Some of the stereotypes used were culled out of the preliminary interviews, and some were adopted from other studies of anti-Semitism. A final set were added that had not been especially associated with anti-Semitism in the past. Examples of such atypical items are that "Jews are often sloppy and unconcerned about their personal appearance," or "Jews are rather loose in their moral standards and behavior." They were included to determine whether those with negative imagery tend to extend it unreservedly to the acceptance of anything "bad" that might be said about Jews.

In all, teenage respondents were asked to express their relative agreement or disagreement with twenty statements purporting to express what Jewish teenagers are like. Table 5-1 reports the responses of white non-Jewish teenagers to several of the positive and negative stereotypes included in the study.[3] (The beliefs of black students are considered separately below.)

TABLE 5-1. Teenagers' Acceptance of Stereotypes About Jews.

	Commuter-town	Ocean-ville	Central City
Positive Stereotypes			
Jewish teenagers are quite intelligent and well informed; think clearly about things. (Intelligent)	77%[a]	82%	75%

TABLE 5-1.   (Continued)

	Commuter-town	Ocean-ville	Central City
Jewish teenagers have a lot of school spirit; know what's going on around school and take part in activities. (School spirit)	76	69	76
Jewish teenagers are very concerned with getting good grades; are always working for A's. (Ambitious)	74	79	67
Negative Stereotypes			
Jewish teenagers have too much to say about what goes on in school; run pretty much everything. (Powerful)	70	55	26
Jewish teenagers think they are better than other students; easily develop a superiority complex. (Conceited)	70	61	35
Jewish teenagers are loud and show-offy; will do almost anything to gain recognition or draw attention to themselves. (Vain)	66	58	33
Jewish teenagers are likely to be selfish; concerned only for themselves or their own group. (Selfish)	60	55	32
Jewish teenagers often try to "get ahead" by "buttering up" the teachers. (Sly)	58	60	31
Jewish teenagers avoid forcing their beliefs and wishes on other students; are not bossy. (Bossy, if disagree)	52	48	33
Jewish teenagers are unfriendly; do not mix with others; go around with their own group. (Unfriendly)	50	39	25
Jewish teenagers often dress in a loud and flashy way. (Gaudy)	49	38	29
Jewish teenagers are rather loose in their moral standards and behavior. (Immoral)	48	33	28
Jewish teenagers try to push into groups where they are not really wanted. (Pushy)	42	44	32
Jewish teenagers are frequently in trouble with school authorities and the police; often break rules and laws. (Trouble-makers)	25	13	24
N =	(388)	(301)	(667)

^aPercentages indicate the proportion of white non-Jewish students agreeing with these statements.

SOURCE: Based upon Table 2 in Charles Y. Glock, Robert Wuthnow, Jane Allyn Piliavin, and Metta Spencer, *Adolescent Prejudice* (New York: Harper & Row, 1975), p. 7.

The teenagers in all three communities, it is seen, frequently held positive images of Jews. Seventy-seven percent of white non-Jewish students in Commutertown, for example, thought of Jewish teenagers as intelligent, as did 82 percent in Oceanville and 75 percent in Central City. Similarly high proportions viewed Jews as being ambitious and having a considerable amount of school spirit. As was true for adults, there is more support for these positive descriptions than for any negative ones. The acknowledgment of positive traits, of course, cannot be assumed necessarily to signal the absence of prejudice. Positively perceived traits can be and often are interpreted invidiously; for example, the ambition of Jews might be attributed to their being self-serving and ruthless. Nevertheless, that positive traits are acknowledged, even by youngsters who in other ways show hostility to Jews, is indicative once again of the ambivalence that characterizes many people's images of Jews.

As with adults, positive characterizations of Jews by teenagers were often accompanied by highly prejudiced ones. In Commutertown, 70 percent thought of Jewish teenagers as too powerful and as conceited, 66 percent thought of them as vain, 60 percent as selfish, 58 percent as sly, 52 percent as bossy, and 50 percent as unfriendly. Somewhat less acceptance of those negative stereotypes occurs in Oceanville, but a majority of the students accept all of the stereotypes just mentioned except bossy and unfriendly, which received respectively 48 percent and 39 percent acceptance.

In Central City, the community where there were virtually no Jewish students, there was considerably less anti-Jewish stereotyping: No single negative stereotype was accepted by as many as 50 percent of the students. About a third of this community's teenagers, however, saw Jews as being conceited, vain, bossy, selfish, and sly. Overall, an average of 43 percent of the students in Commutertown accepted negative stereotypes, followed by 37 percent in Oceanville and 26 percent in Central City.

Where comparisons can be drawn, the percentage of teenagers agreeing with such traditional anti-Semitic stereotypes is greater than was the percentage for adults in the national study. The teenagers in the three communities cannot be assumed to be representative of teenagers in the country as a whole, of course. Nevertheless, these communities are located within presumably more enlightened parts of the country, and there is little reason to expect the national figures for adolescents, were they available, to be better.

The community-by-community distribution of negative stereotyping, it should be noted, was wholly unexpected. Common wisdom, as well as some previous research, has it that prejudice will be reduced, not increased, through greater association between the members of different ethnic, religious, and social groups.[4] This will occur, it is believed, through the creation of new friendships and through greater exposure to accurate knowledge of what others are like. In the process, norms of tolerance will be generated and negative beliefs won't survive. It had been anticipated, consequently, that the amount of anti-Semitic stereotyping would be found to be lowest in the community with the most Jewish teenagers, Commutertown, and highest in the community without a Jewish presence, Central City. That the opposite occurs suggests that intergroup contact may not automatically result in a reduction of prejudice. Indeed, it has already been seen that when such contacts are one-sided and impersonal in nature—as is generally true between blacks and Jews—they often produce hostile feelings. Perhaps some similar process is at work among teenagers, causing their prejudice to rise with greater contact. This possibility is explored later in this chapter.

BLACK TEENAGERS' BELIEFS ABOUT JEWS

Like white youngsters, a majority of black teenagers endorsed positive stereotypes. In all communities, proportions ranging upwards of 68 percent think of Jewish teenagers as intelligent, ambitious, and school-spirited. By and large, positive imagery is about the same for both black and non-Jewish white teenagers.

As to negative stereotyping, there were no dramatic or significant differences in the proportion of black and non-Jewish white teenagers subscribing to negative descriptions of Jews. The slight differences that did occur saw blacks showing somewhat less hostility than whites in Commutertown and Oceanville and a hair more hostility in Central City. In Commutertown, 43 percent of the white students on the average subscribed to the outrightly negative stereotypes, as compared to 37 percent of black students. In Oceanville, the equivalent figures were 37 percent for whites and 34 percent for blacks, and in Central City they were 26 percent for whites and 28 percent for blacks. As with whites, then, black hostility toward Jews is more common where there are more Jewish youngsters in the school system.

SOCIAL DISTANCE

Another approach used to assess adolescent anti-Semitism was based on a version of the well-known Social Distance Scale.[5] The Social Distance Scale is a measure designed to gauge the extent to which members of one group feel open to interacting with members of an outgroup; for example, would they be willing to sit next to a member of the outgroup in class, eat lunch with that person, have the outgroup member as a friend, or have the outgroup member date a sibling. The usual way of tapping social distance was amended by asking respondents first how they would respond to a successful Jewish teenager (a student in the college preparatory program who is white, Jewish, and getting B's). Then they were asked how they would respond to an unsuccessful Jewish teenager (a student in the vocational program who is white, Jewish, and getting failing grades).

The results for non-Jewish students are presented in Table 5-2. Several significant findings emerge. First, these teenagers clearly felt more "social distance" from Jews in some situations than in others. Relatively few objected to sitting next to a Jewish student in a classroom; but more would be unwilling to be in a social club with a Jew, and still more to having a Jewish student date his sibling. It is thus in situations of a more personal or intimate nature that anti-Jewish feelings were most common. Responses were about the same in all three communities studied.

Table 5-2 also reveals that the social distance expressed toward an unsuccessful Jewish student is considerably greater than toward a successful one. For example, in Commutertown, 54 percent would be unwilling to have a successful Jewish student date a sibling, whereas 74 percent would not want a sibling to date an unsuccessful Jew. Similar differences prevail on each social distance item in each of these three communities. These results indicate just how status-conscious teenage students can be. Indeed, this difference extended even to the feelings held by the Jewish students in the three communities. When asked the same questions, they expressed complete openness to interacting with a successful Jewish student in all of the situations asked about. When it came to the unsuccessful student, however, a significant number of Jewish teenagers expressed an unwillingness to interact. For example, in Commutertown 58 percent would not want to have an unsuccessful Jewish student date a sibling and 44 percent would not want him or her as a close friend. On the whole, Jewish teenagers were more open to interaction with an unsuccessful Jewish student than non-Jewish adolescents. Still, in both groups a considerable amount of class prejudice is revealed.

Given this class prejudice, it seems better to rely on the social distance expressed to the successful than to the unsuccessful student in estimating anti-Semitism. Doing so, it is seen that on the most intimate form of contact asked about—having a sibling date a successful Jewish student—upwards of 50 percent objected in all three communities. Likewise, between a third and a quarter would not want to have a successful Jewish student as a close friend or to their house for dinner. On less intimate forms of contact, however, fewer than 20 percent in all instances expressed an unwillingness to interact. There is no way to decide which of these figures best indicates how anti-Semitic these teenagers tend to be. It is enough, perhaps, to conclude that there is considerably more adolescent prejudice than is consistent with American principles of freedom and tolerance.

It is also difficult to decide, given the disparate nature of the questions, whether more prejudice is indicated by the teenagers' feelings of social distance from Jews or by their acceptance of anti-Semitic beliefs. From a crude comparison of Table 5-2 with Table 5-1, however, it appears that the young respondents tend less to reject having social or economic contacts with Jews than to accept traditional anti-Semitic imagery. This difference, of course,

TABLE 5-2. Teenagers' Willingness to Interact in Personal Situations with Successful and Unsuccessful Jews.

	Social Distance to Successful Jewish Student			Social Distance to Unsuccessful Jewish Student		
Percentage *Unwilling* to Have Jewish Student:	Commutertown	Oceanville	Central City	Commutertown	Oceanville	Central City
Date sibling	54%[a]	57%	58%	74%	76%	78%
Home to dinner	32	25	31	57	55	58
As close friend	32	27	26	52	51	55
Member of social club	28	26	19	50	54	49
To lunch	20	11	13	28	27	28
At party	18	15	19	23	21	32
On same committee	18	10	9	50	54	58
As speaking acquaintance	14	8	12	18	22	38
Sit beside in class	10	5	5	26	24	25
Mean percent	25%	20%	21%	43%	43%	47%
N =	(388)	(301)	(667)	(388)	(301)	(667)

[a]Percentages indicate the proportion of white non-Jewish students saying they would be unwilling to engage in these activities with a successful and unsuccessful Jewish student. A successful student was defined as "a student in the college preparatory program who is white, Jewish, and is getting B's"; an unsuccessful student as "a student in the vocational program who is white, Jewish, and is getting failing grades."
SOURCE: Computed from Tables 8 and 9 in Glock et al., *Adolescent Prejudice*, pp. 18–19.

is analogous to that found among adults. Americans of all ages thus tend to be more anti-Semitic in their beliefs about Jews than in their attitudes toward interacting with them.

This conclusion is reinforced by an additional question asked on this subject: how the teenagers would react in meeting a person about whom the only known fact was that he or she was Jewish. The responses to this inquiry were firmly on the positive side. More than two-thirds of the students said they would be "a little" or "quite" friendly, while about a quarter said "nothing either way." The portion reporting that they would react in an "unfriendly" manner ranged from 16 percent in Commutertown to 10 percent in Oceanville and 9 percent in Central City.

In sum, these students expressed some unwillingness to interact with Jews, but their prejudice on this dimension is not as high as when anti-Semitism is measured by the acceptance of negative stereotypes. The responses of black students to social distance questions did not differ significantly from the responses of non-Jewish white students. The black teenagers were somewhat more hesitant to interact with upper-status Jewish students but somewhat less hesitant to interact with lower-status Jews. On balance, however, their preference, as among white students, was always for the successful student. On the friendship question, black students responded to meeting a Jew in a slightly more favorable way than did the white students.

INTERGROUP FRIENDSHIPS

A final measure involves the extent of friendships between Jewish and non-Jewish students. Friendship between members of different social or religious groups is not an absolute sign of the absence of prejudice. Indeed, the claim of friendship is a mask that the prejudiced sometimes adopt. Other things being equal, however, it seems reasonable to infer that prejudice will be less prevalent where friendship exists.

Friendship is partly a matter of opportunity, of course, and the opportunity for Jewish and non-Jewish students to become friends was virtually nil in Central City, with only a handful of Jews in the student body. In both Commutertown and Oceanville, however, the substantial number of Jewish students provided ample opportunity for the formation of friendships.

To obtain information on friendships, each student was asked to name those other students in their grade with whom they went around most often. Boys were asked to name only boys, girls to name girls, and a limit of five was set on the number to be named. Since all students in the grade participated in the study, it was possible to determine for each non-Jewish teenager how many of his or her friends were Jewish. In turn, for Jewish teenagers the number of their friends who were Jewish and non-Jewish could also be determined.

The chances of a non-Jewish teenager's having a Jewish friend in Commutertown were considerably greater than in Oceanville, simply because there was almost twice the proportion of Jews in the former community. Consequently, in looking at friendship patterns, a measure was used that takes into account the difference in opportunity to make Jewish friends.[6] This measure ranges from $+1$ to -1. A score of 0 means that a teenager is as likely to choose a Jew as a non-Jew as a friend. Positive scores indicate a tendency to prefer Jewish over non-Jewish friends, with a score of $+1$ signifying that the teenager has only Jewish friends. Negative scores indicated a tendency to prefer non-Jewish to Jewish friends, with a score of -1 meaning that a teenager has only non-Jewish friends.

The scores for non-Jewish whites were identical in Commutertown and Oceanville, $-.41$, signifying a tendency to avoid Jews as friends. The scores for black students were considerably more negative, $-.82$ in Commutertown and $-.89$ in Oceanville. Black scores, however, reflect the more general tendency of black students not to have white friends, whether Jewish or non-Jewish. Looking at the Jewish students, they show a decided propensity, as might be expected, to choose Jews as friends. Their score in Commutertown was $+.68$ and in Oceanville $+.55$.

These results are perhaps more revealing of the results of prejudice than of its incidence. Making friends with others who are different religiously from oneself is a choice that anti-Semitism militates against among its victims as well as among its purveyors.

This study thus explored several different dimensions of teenage anti-Semitism. The main findings thus far can be summarized as follows: (a) Teenagers are highly prejudiced in their beliefs about Jews. (b) They are less prejudiced in their attitudes toward interacting with Jewish students. (c) They tend to have relatively few close relationships with their Jewish classmates.

Though black students were found to be somewhat less anti-Semitic than white teenagers, on the whole, the level of prejudice among the two groups was about the same.

AN INDEX OF TEENAGE ANTI-SEMITISM

As in the other studies, an index was created to serve as a measure of teenage anti-Semitism. This index was built on teenagers' responses to eight of the twenty questions asked about what they believed Jews to be like. The eight were chosen because they were all unequivocally negative in content and because they satisfied basic statistical criteria for index development.[7] The index summarized the teenagers' responses to these items, with a score of seven signifying strong agreement with each item. Intervening scores of five and six signify that these statements, on the average, were more agreed than disagreed with; scores of two and three mean the opposite. Those scoring four were as likely to accept the anti-Semitic stereotypes as to reject them. The distribution of teenagers' scores on this index is shown in Table 5-3, separately for the three communities.

TABLE 5-3.   Percentage of Students at Each Level on Anti-Semitism Index in Three Communities.

Position on Index of Anti-Semitic Belief		Commutertown	Oceanville	Central City
High	7	3%	2%	1%
	6	13	10	5
	5	24	19	13
	4	25	23	22
	3	18	25	26
	2	10	15	23
Low	1	6	7	10
Anti-Semitic (Scores 4–7)		66%	53%	41%
Extremely anti-Semitic (Scores 6 and 7)		16%	12%	6%
Total cases		(755)	(612)	(1,331)

SOURCE: Reproduced from Glock *et al.*, *Adolescent Prejudice*, p. 32.

A judgment about how much anti-Semitism exists in the three communities depends on what criterion is used to define anti-Semitism. If it is decided that anti-Semitism is indicated only if a student has strongly agreed with all or almost all of the eight items—a score of six or seven on the index—then 16 percent score as anti-Semitic in Commutertown, 12 percent in Oceanville, and 6 percent in Central City. If the criterion is adopted that anti-Semitism is indicated when more negative beliefs are accepted than rejected—scores of five, six, and seven on the index—then 40 percent of teenagers in Commutertown are anti-Semitic, 31 percent in Oceanville, and 19 percent in Central City. Finally, if an even harder criterion is adopted, namely, to score as not being anti-Semitic requires that negative beliefs are more often rejected than accepted, then 66 percent, 54 percent, and 41 percent respectively in the three communities would be judged anti-Semitic. Whichever procedure is adopted, the anti-Semitism is greater the larger the Jewish presence in the community.

This index of anti-Semitic belief is strongly related to other measures of prejudice. Teenagers scoring high in anti-Semitic beliefs tended also to object to having personal contacts with Jews, to say that they would react unfavorably to meeting a Jewish stranger, and to have few Jewish friends. The summary measure thus reflects different manifestations of teenage anti-Semitism.

The Social Location of Teenage Anti-Semitism

As in the study of adult prejudice, the next task is to uncover the social location of teenage anti-Semitism. Where in school populations is anti-Semitism most and least likely to be found? Most particularly, is adolescent prejudice more pronounced among the socially deprived or the socially privileged?

Among adults, it will be recalled, anti-Semitism is most common among those of lower SES—among those with blue-collar jobs, low incomes, and less exposure to education. Youths in this study are not divided along the same status lines as the adult population, since they are roughly of the same age and rank in school. However, they do differ in the social and economic privileges available to them and in their academic achievement and success. These differences tend to be cumulative, with some youths being considerably more advantaged than others.

In all three school systems, less privileged youngsters are found to be more prejudiced toward Jews, and more privileged youngsters to be less prejudiced. With respect to social and economic status, this tendency is weak but consistent. Youngsters whose parents are well-to-do and highly educated and who themselves are well off financially are in each instance less prejudiced than their counterparts. This is true in all three communities, and the effects are cumulative. The more socio-economic privileges a teenager enjoys, the less likely he or she is to be prejudiced.

With respect to academic privilege and achievement, the same relationship holds but to a much stronger degree. Whatever measure of academic status is employed—whether grades in school, time spent on homework, feelings of satisfaction with school, being in college rather than a vocational track, wanting and expecting to go to college—the less privileged teenagers are always the more anti-Semitic. Once again, this is true for all three communities, and the effects are cumulative. The greater the number of academic privileges, the less the anti-Semitism.

With teenagers, as with adults, then, anti-Semitic prejudice is located largely among the less privileged. Among teenagers, moreover, it is the educational factor that likewise most distinguishes the prejudiced from the unprejudiced. Having wealthy or better-educated parents is not by itself associated with lower levels of teenage prejudice. It is only when socio-economic privileges are accompanied by academic achievement that anti-Semitism is reduced.

Thus the underlying process at work among teenagers is for socio-economic privileges to facilitate academic privilege and achievement, which in turn leads to a relative absence of prejudice. The opposite process, of course, operates among the more deprived. Being in less privileged socio-economic positions, such youngsters are less active and successful in school and are less oriented toward college. Their lower levels of academic achievement, in turn, result in higher levels of anti-Semitism.

Thus the social location of prejudice is roughly the same for teenagers and for adults. In both instances, anti-Semitism is most common among those with lower social, economic, and educational status. That these patterns occur among eighth-, tenth-, and twelfth-graders is a significant finding. It shows how early status- and education-linked factors affect prejudice.

Causes of Teenage Anti-Semitism

The next question addressed was "Why should this be?" Why should less privileged, particularly academically less privileged, youngsters be considerably more prejudiced than their more privileged counterparts? Moreover, since not all students who were at the top of their class are unprejudiced, why are some of them prejudiced and others not? In turn, what accounts for some disprivileged youngsters ending up not scoring as anti-Semitic?

The search for answers to these questions involved tests of four theories of prejudice, each of which purports to explain why anti-Semitism is most often found among the socially deprived. One of these theories involves the emotive explanation discussed in Chapter 3. Emotive theory, it will be recalled, holds that hostility toward minority groups results from anxiety produced by frustration.[8] According to this view, repeated failures to get what one wants—whether it be economic rewards, social status, academic success, or other desires—result in anxiety, guilt feelings, and repressed wishes that build up like steam in a boiler until they must find some outlet. Hostility toward others results when more direct means of resolving such tension break down. Frustrations and guilt feelings in this case are not confronted directly but are projected onto others. Since minority groups are easily identified and frequently without power to defend themselves, they often become targets or scapegoats for such aggression. This theory suggests that, among teenagers, those failing to compete successfully for grades, friends, admission to college, and other rewards may find themselves beset by anxiety and self-blame to the point where they seek excuses for their failures. Groups other than themselves, such as Jews, provide easy excuses and thus become likely candidates for jealousy and hatred.

A second theory about why anti-Semitism is more prevalent among the socially deprived holds that prejudice is produced and maintained primarily through interaction with other prejudiced persons.[9] Contrary to the frustration/aggression argument, this theory points out that people acquire most of their attitudes simply because they are exposed to them, not because they need these particular attitudes to cope with psychic problems. Thus persons with prejudiced attitudes hold such notions simply because they learned them from their associates. Once acquired, prejudicial attitudes, to be sure, may function to relieve anxieties and tensions. But to concentrate only on psychological needs and their resolution, the proponents of the interactionist view contend, misses the social and cultural setting in which prejudice is learned. When applied to teenagers, this theory suggests that the reason the academically deprived are more prejudiced may lie simply in the fact that they associate with peers who are more prejudiced, thereby reinforcing one another's views.

The third theory has to do with enlightened values.[10] A widespread assumption, and one that governs many schools' approach to the problem of prejudice, is that the absorption of enlightened values of brotherhood, equality, civil liberties, and respect for the rights of others will affect the reduction of prejudice. This theory, discussed in Chapter 3, would account for the greater prejudice of academically less privileged teenagers as resulting from their failure to have learned the enlightened values that mitigate prejudice.

The fourth theory argues that the academically deprived are more susceptible and the academically privileged less prone to prejudice because of differences in their levels of cognitive sophistication.[11] Underlying this theory, it will be recalled from Chapter 3, is the idea that prejudice is an inherently complex phenomenon. Highly developed powers of reasoning are required to recognize it, to judge it for what it is, and to reject it. Awareness of stereotyping and sensitivity to its dangers is called for. Recognition of the sometimes subtle distinction between relative and absolute differences is required, as in an avoidance of the pitfall of automatically assigning to particular members of the group traits or characteristics that characterize the group as a whole only to a degree. An understanding of the cultural, historical, and social forces at work that make for group differences is also demanded, as well as knowledge and sophistication enough to separate true differences from false ones.

Having the cognitive capacity to do all these things does not necessarily guarantee freedom from prejudice. Circumstances can be imagined, for example, where peer group pressure might be a more powerful stimulant to prejudice than reason and restraint against prejudice. Nevertheless, a cognitively sophisticated understanding of prejudice, according to cognitive theory, is a necessary if not a sufficient condition for its prevention. Thus the reason that academically deprived youngsters are more prejudiced is that they lack the cognitive sophistication to combat it.

Earlier it was found that, of the several theories tested, the cognitive and enlightened-values theories contributed most to the understanding of prejudice among adults. What now is their power in comparison to other theories to account for adolescent prejudice?

FRUSTRATION/AGGRESSION

Three separate tests were made of the theory that the anti-Semitism of the socially deprived is a result of frustration over one's status for which release is sought through aggression against members of an outgroup. One of these tests involved the use of a version of the F scale, a measure designed to identify the presence of such characteristics as social rigidity, status anxiety, self-glorification, and a tendency to project guilt and inadequacy onto others.[12] As interpreted by the authors of *The Authoritarian Personality*, high F scorers have become that way largely because of a strict and repressive upbringing. This causes repressed feelings of resentment toward one's parents and insecurities and rigidities as one grows older—feelings that are often "resolved" by venting hostility upon such minority groups as Jews.

The second test of frustration/aggression theory substituted for the F scale a revision of the Gough self-acceptance scale, a measure of low self-confidence and anxiety.[13] A lack of self-confidence about which one experiences anxiety, it was assumed, is a way of expressing frustration. If frustration/aggression theory is correct, a lack of self-confidence should be especially characteristic of the academically deprived and should account for their greater disposition toward prejudice.

The third test, a slight variant of the second, utilized Rosenberg's scale of self-esteem.[14] This scale was developed to measure the degree to which individuals respect themselves and consider themselves worthy persons. This scale was adopted to test frustration/aggression theory on the grounds that one who is low in self-esteem would be frustrated as a result, and if the theory is correct, would be found more anti-Semitic than those with high self-esteem.

The results of the three tests were all negative. It turns out that academically deprived youngsters were no more likely to score high on the F scale than academically privileged youth. It is also the case that scores on the F scale are not related to scores on the anti-Semitism index. There was a slight tendency for the academically deprived to score lower on self-esteem and self-acceptance than the academically privileged. Scores on these scales were totally unrelated to the scores on the anti-Semitism index.

These were the consistent findings in all three communties. Caution must be exercised, of course, in drawing generalizations from a single study. However, these results, coupled with those reported in Chapter 3, indicate that frustration/aggression theories do not explain contemporary forms of anti-Semitic prejudice.

PRIMARY GROUPS

The second theory tested emphasizes the importance of primary groups in influencing individual attitudes. It posits that the relationship between academic deprivation and prejudice may result from the greater likelihood that academically deprived youth will associate with peers who are prejudiced, from whom, then, prejudice is learned, nourished, and reinforced.

That prejudice breeds prejudice, or at least is nourished and sustained by it, receives support from the data. Teenagers whose close friends are anti-Semitic show a tendency, although not an overwhelming one, to be anti-Semitic themselves. This could occur because anti-Semitic youngsters seek each other out. It is more likely to come about because academically deprived youngsters seek out their own kind, and their own kind, like themselves, tend also to be prejudiced.

While the effect of associating with prejudiced others is to exacerbate one's own prejudice, such associations were not found to be the underlying reason why prejudice tends to be located among the less privileged. Among teenagers with no anti-Semitic friends, as well as among those with such friends, low achieving, non-college-oriented youths continue to be more anti-Semitic than their high achieving, college-oriented counterparts. What these results signify is that academic deprivation and anti-Semitic friendships both contribute independently to prejudice. It is not the case, however, that academic deprivation leads to having anti-Semitic friends, which in turn leads one to become anti-Semitic oneself.

ENLIGHTENED VALUES

The theory ascribing the link between academic deprivation and prejudice to the fact that the academically deprived are less likely to have absorbed enlightened democratic values was subjected to three independent tests. In the first, the teenagers were asked the extent to which they supported such "civic values" as being useful citizens, working for civil rights for everyone, and assuring a society in which everyone has a fair share. For enlightened-values theory to be correct, academically privileged adolescents should be more likely to subscribe to these values, and, in turn, subscribers should be less prone to anti-Semitism than nonsubscribers.

The second test substituted "moral" for "civic" values. Students were asked how important it is that people work hard, follow the rules, and be religious, honest, and moral. Reducing life and moral values to such simplistic notions leads, according to enlightened-values theory, to stereotyping minority groups and others different from oneself as immoral, treacherous, lazy, debauched, and irreligious—in general as the antithesis of all good moral virtues. Consequently, confirmation of the theory would be a discovery that teenagers who support such values as important are more likely to be anti-Semitic than those who do not.

The third test focused on interpersonal rather than political and moral values. Here the assumption was that, for enlightened-values theory to be correct, teenagers who have been more privileged in their socialization, both at home and in school, should have received more careful training in the codes of interpersonal contact than those who have been deprived of such advantages. In turn, youngsters who have internalized such codes should prove to be less prejudiced than those who have not. To find out, students were asked a set of questions about the standards of interpersonal behavior to which they subscribe. It was then possible to determine whether the subscribers were more likely than the nonsubscribers to be both socially and academically privileged and unprejudiced.

The results of these several tests, unlike for adults, afford no substantial support of enlightened-values theory. The academically privileged were no more likely to subscribe to "civic" or to deny "moral" values than the academically deprived. Moreover, there was no relationship between harboring these values and anti-Semitism. The academically privileged were somewhat more disposed than the academically deprived to subscribe to the interpersonal values. In turn, those subscribing to such values were less often anti-Semitic than the nonsubscribers. The relationships were relatively weak, however, and afford no illumination as to why teenage anti-Semitism is especially prevalent among the academically deprived. The deprived remain high in anti-Semitism, irrespective of their interpersonal values.

COGNITIVE SOPHISTICATION

The final proposition tested was that the association between academic deprivation and anti-Semitism occurs because the academically deprived have not developed the cognitive sophistication to recognize prejudice in themselves and others, to judge it for what it is, and to reject it. A test was made using three different approaches for measuring cognitive sophistication.

The first measure sought to assess students' interests in intellectual pursuits through asking them the extent to which they like science and poetry, value the ability to think clearly, read books for pleasure, and perceive teachers as people whose ideas about things matter. The second measure was Gough's Flexibility Scale, which measures one's willingness to entertain new and complicated ideas and to risk uncertainty and ambiguity in the pursuit of such ideas.[16] The third measure was based on students' responses to questions about how they interpret human nature; for example, do they think "most people are honest chiefly through fear of getting caught"? Students who rejected more cynical and simplistic interpretations were judged to be more cognitively sophisticated than students who accepted them.

These measures were conceived as tapping different aspects of cognitive sophistication. In all three communities, and for black and white non-Jewish teenagers examined separately, all three measures proved to be related to students' anti-Semitism. The greater the teenagers' interests in intellectual pursuits, the more their cognitive flexibility; and the less simplistic their thought processes, the less their anti-Semitism. These measures were likewise related to the students' academic status. Academically privileged youngsters were found considerably more likely to exhibit more interest in intellectual pursuits, to have greater cognitive flexibility, and to be less simplistic than the academically deprived. Thus, whereas there was little or no support for the other theories of adolescent prejudice, there was relatively strong support for a cognitive theory of prejudice. From these results it would appear that, as with adults, cognitive sophistication is a primary factor working to reduce the incidence of anti-Semitism among teenage Americans.

The Effects of a Jewish Presence

Further support of the theory that prejudice is a result of cognitive failure came from the investigation of why anti-Semitism was greater the larger the size of a Jewish presence in a community. It will be recalled that in the community with the largest Jewish presence, Commutertown, there was considerably more anti-Semitism than in Oceanville, the town with a smaller proportion of Jewish teenagers, and that the incidence of anti-Semitic stereotyping was lowest in Central City, where there are virtually no Jewish adolescents. Just the opposite result had been anticipated in light of other studies indicating that contact reduces rather than aggravates prejudice.

Contact where it flowers into friendship does reduce prejudice. The white non-Jewish teenagers in Commutertown and Oceanville who had Jewish friends were less prejudiced than those who had no Jewish friends. Not all contact generates friendships, however. As is evidenced by the greater incidence of prejudice in Commutertown and Oceanville than in Central City, contact can be a source of hostility as well as of friendship. But how does the hostility come about? One source of it in the communities under study was the relative success of Jewish youngsters; another was their relatively greater disposition to clannishness.

Jewish youngsters were on the average far more successful in academic life than their non-Jewish counterparts. This was true in both Commutertown and Oceanville; it was also true of the thirteen Jewish students in the

Central City sample. Jewish teenagers got better grades, spent more time working on studies, and were more active in school affairs. They were also more often enrolled in college programs and more likely by far to plan to go to college. Moreover, the parents of Jewish teenagers were on the average more affluent, better educated, and, judging from their greater concern to have their children go to college, more solicitous for their children's success.

Many people in the Jewish community, as well as outside of it, have been sensitive to the possibility that Jewish success may be a cause of anti-Semitism. The common view, however, has been that if success has this effect, it is because of jealousy and envy on the part of non-Jews, an essentially psychological explanation of prejudice along the lines discussed earlier. Successful Jews in one's environment afford a ready scapegoat for those frustrated and struggling to contend with their own failures. The evidence from the present study of adolescent prejudice does not sustain such an interpretation; none of the psychological theories subjected to test were supported.

The explanation that gained the most support from the analysis is that Jewish success is a source of anti-Semitism because of cognitive failure on the part of non-Jewish teenagers. Reflecting on what it means to be successful in school, it soon becomes evident that attributes accrue to successful youngsters that tend to be negatively evaluated by the less successful. For example, young people can be conceited without having any grounds except their own ego needs to be so, and certainly there are other sources of conceit than academic success. In school settings, however, where academic achievement is so highly valued, the probabilities are that the conceited will be found especially among the academically successful. Similarly, someone without leadership qualities may try to throw his weight around and thereby earn for himself the epithet "bossy." Generally speaking, however, being or appearing to be bossy is more often a characteristic of leaders in a social group than of followers. And, of course, leadership and being successful academically also tend to go together. The image of "buttering up" teachers also seems likely to be associated with the successful more than with the unsuccessful. The less successful in school probably have the greater need to "butter up" teachers, but the more successful are likely to be the ones to give the impression of doing so, simply because they are more likely to seek teachers out. Power, too, goes with success, and, for those without either, thinking that the successful are "too" powerful has a basis in fact.

In sum, there are reasons for nonsuccessful youngsters to dislike successful ones on grounds that accrue from success itself. The process through which success breeds anti-Semitism is this: When successful teenagers are Jewish, traits that derive from their being successful are falsely ascribed to their being Jewish. The insidiousness of prejudice and the importance of well-developed reasoning powers to overcome it are revealed in this act of false reasoning. In a school setting where the more successful students tend to be Presbyterian or Episcopalian (as the more academically successful youngsters in Central City tend to be, incidentally), it would never occur to anyone to attribute tendencies toward conceit, vanity, or slyness on such students' part to their religion. There simply is not the kind of anti-Episcopalianism or anti-Presbyterianism in the culture to cause an observer to falsely identify these traits as having their roots in religion.

Where a successful Jewish youngster exhibits these traits, however, even the unprejudiced observer must contend with the ready explanation afforded by the prevailing cultural anti-Semitism. It requires extraordinary sophistication not to fall victim to its appeal. One must possess a profound understanding of the nature of prejudice to be able to recognize the true source of the disliked traits and to be knowledgeable about the historical and social forces making for group differences. For those without such sophistication, the barriers to falling prey to prejudice and feeling quite vindicated in doing so are simply not there.

In analogous fashion, anti-Semitism appears to be nourished by the tendencies of Jews to want to associate with other Jews and of Jewish parents to want their children to date and marry Jews. Such tendencies toward clannishness are not unique to Jews. In Commutertown and Oceanville, however, both in their behavior and by their own admission Jewish youngsters are more likely to be clannish than non-Jewish teenagers.

How Jewish clannishness is responded to by non-Jews, the results suggest, depends on how they understand the clannishness to have come about. If the explanation is racist—"Jews stick together too much because of a flaw in Jewish character"—the result is hostility. If, however, a non-Jewish youngster is knowledgeable about the persecution of Jews throughout history and sophisticated enough to recognize a natural tendency for the victims of persecution to band together in order to survive, then the response to Jewish teenagers' clannishness is one of understanding and sympathy rather than hostility and prejudice.

Summary

Anti-Semitism remains a significant feature of adolescent life in America and resembles in character the anti-Semitism exhibited by adults. As with adults, a substantial minority of adolescents are highly prejudiced in their attitudes toward Jews. Like adults, teenagers also are less anti-Semitic in their feelings about interacting with Jews than in attributing negative traits to them. Moreover, both adolescents and adults are much more anti-Semitic when they come from economically and academically deprived backgrounds.

The most important conclusion to emerge from the inquiry is that this latter tendency is apparently not a result of psychological processes, as has been widely thought. Rather, it appears to be principally a result of cognitive failure. Prejudice is nurtured especially among youths who have not developed the cognitive skills and sophistication to combat it.

This result for adolescents is highly concordant with findings reported earlier for adults. Within both age groups, the cognitive factor proves more central to explaining the presence or absence of prejudice than the emotive one.

The adolescent study afforded an opportunity to investigate the effects of the size of a Jewish presence on anti-Semitism. Unexpectedly, it was found that anti-Semitic beliefs are more prevalent when Jews are present in a school population than when they are not. This result was accounted for as another example of how cognitive failure can lead to prejudice. Lacking the knowledge and cognitive skills to recognize the true source of group differences, many youths are disposed to explain them in racist terms. Thus, in Commutertown and Oceanville certain negatively evaluated traits exhibited by Jewish youngsters are interpreted falsely as deriving from their Jewishness rather than, in this instance, their success.

These last findings are especially indicative of the invidiousness and subtlety of prejudice. Anti-Semitic stereotypes are often based on half-truths, partial distortions, and erroneous interpretations. In such circumstances, it requires a high degree of sophistication not to be prejudiced.

The possibility of a pedagogical approach to prejudice reduction based on trying to raise levels of cognitive sophistication is suggested by the findings of the adolescent study. This possibility, among others, will be addressed in the concluding chapter on the implications of the findings of all of these studies.

CHAPTER 6

Christian Sources of Anti-Semitism

FOR CENTURIES, CHRISTIANITY WAS a principal force behind the segregation and persecution of Jews. It was the official religion of much of the Western world, and its followers displayed little tolerance or mercy toward those not accepting Christian teachings. To many Christians, furthermore, Jews were not just religious heretics, but Christ-killers. They were held personally responsible for the Crucifixion of Jesus and believed to have brought down upon themselves the wrath and vengeance of God. In murdering the Redeemer, they had supposedly sealed their fate and that of their children for eternity. This charge of deicide served as the inspiration for the medieval segregation of Jews and for the bloody pogroms—officially sanctioned massacres—that have recurred throughout Western history.

The Christian roots of anti-Semitism are thus strong; Jews have been stigmatized as religious heretics, defilers, and murderers. Indeed, such images have been so powerful that they have often been invoked even when religious issues have not been directly at issue. Adolph Hitler—who otherwise had little to say about religion—found it convenient to evoke Christian symbols in justifying the confinement and execution of more than six million Jews.

While all this is true of the past, what is its relevance in America today? Heretics are not being burned at the stake, and no respected Christian leader refers to the Jews as "accursed." It is an age of *rapprochement* between Jews and Christians, a time of mutual acceptance and even of cooperation. American history is not without examples of religiously inspired prejudice and bigotry, of course, but over time the nation has learned to live with its religious differences reasonably well. The differences have made necessary a quest for ways to minimize disagreement and to emphasize the values of religious tolerance and pluralism.

94

Americans are thus understandably puzzled when it is suggested that they are religiously prejudiced. Religious intolerance is admitted to exist in the backwoods—or perhaps within certain untutored sections of the country—but not among the majority of Christians.

It is certainly true that Americans do not actively persecute one another on religious grounds and that Christian and Jewish religious bodies now work with one another openly and positively in a variety of ways. Yet there remain reasons to doubt that Christians are entirely free from anti-Semitic prejudice. Once a social pattern becomes deeply entrenched within a culture, it does not easily die out. In the past, Christianity was a prominent source of anti-Semitism, and it seems unlikely that there are no remaining vestiges of this legacy. Further, while the official position of Christian churches is one of tolerance, this does not mean that such a norm will necessarily be observed by all church members or, indeed, by all church leaders. Numerous examples can be cited of discrepancies between an institution's formal norms and the informal practices of its members.

Because such doubts were entertained, it was decided to make religion a subject of special investigation in the series of studies on anti-Semitism in America. If anti-Semitism is nourished by certain interpretations of Christian faith or by some forms of Christian worship, this fact ought to be known so that remedial steps might be taken. By the same token, if modern Christianity proves to be a positive force helping people to transcend their old prejudices, this too should be understood so that it can be made even more effective.

As reported earlier, three studies were undertaken to explore the interconnections between religion and anti-Semitism. One study involved the participation of a sample of 3,000 church members residing in the San Francisco Bay Area. A second study, designed to assess whether the findings from the Bay Area study would hold true for the adult population of the country as a whole, involved 2,000 interviews with a sample of that population.[1] A third study focused on clergy rather than laity and was based on 1,580 questionnaires completed by a sample of Protestant pastors serving parishes in the state of California.[2] The results of the two studies of laity were highly concordant. Consequently, this report on the findings is restricted to the more comprehensive of the two lay studies—the one based on Northern California churchgoers—and the study of clergy.

Christian Beliefs and Anti-Semitism: A Model

The basic propositions tested in these three studies can be stated rather simply (see Figure 6-1). They are that certain interpretations of Christian faith are conducive to producing religiously based hostility toward Jews, and that this religious hostility makes those who harbor it especially prone to secular anti-Semitism.

FIGURE 6-1.   Causal Sequence: Orthodoxy to Anti-Semitism

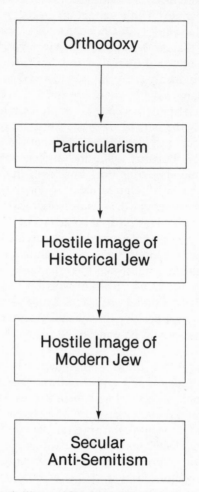

SOURCE: Rodney Stark *et al., Wayward Shepherds* (New York: Harper & Row, 1971), p. 12.

The beginning of this postulated causal chain is orthodox Christian belief, a commitment to those doctrines which historically have been central to
the Christian religion. These include beliefs in an omnipotent, all-knowing
God who imposes certain requirements on man; in Jesus Christ as the Son
of God, sent to earth so that men could be forgiven for their sins and receive
the blessing of eternal life; and in the existence of Hell, to which those who
turn their backs upon such Christian beliefs will be sent.

As will be seen, not all church people today—clergy or laity—accept
these doctrines in such literal terms. Those who do, it was predicted, would

be especially likely to be caught up in the second link in the chain leading to anti-Semitism, a disposition to see Christian truth as the only religious truth and to view all other faiths as fallacious and misguided.

The importance of such a particularistic religious orientation is that it may lead to hostile feelings toward those not accepting traditional Christian doctrines. If only right-thinking, orthodox Christians are saved, non-Christians are by definition damned. This imputation can extend to Buddhists, Hindus, Satanists, or other religious outsiders. Historically, however, Jews have been a special object of Christian invectives, and in this country Jews are by far the largest and most conspicuous non-Christian group. For these reasons, if hostile feelings flow from particularistic religious conceptions, it is likely that they will most often be directed against Jews. This can take the form of *hostility toward historical Jews*—the renegades from the Christian faith and the crucifiers and revilers of the Son of God. It can also take the form of a *hostility toward the modern Jew*—the heretic and the nonbeliever in essential Christian truths. That *particularistic* Christian belief does lead to religious hostility toward both historical and modern Jews is the next link in the postulated causal chain.

The final link in the causal model is the crucial one—the linkage between religious hostility toward Jews and *secular anti-Semitism*. The idea here is rather simple and straightforward, namely, that ideas have consequences. It is proposed that people who maintain hostile attitudes toward Jews on religious grounds will be especially vulnerable to hostile secular stereotypes of Jews. In effect, if it is believed that Jews are heretics or out of favor with God, it is a small step to also believing that they are wicked or evil in other ways as well.

Christianity and Religious Hostility Toward Jews

This causal sequence provided the theoretical framework used to investigate and explain the existence of anti-Semitism among American Christians. In order to determine its accuracy, it was necessary to devise ways to measure the various critical components of the theory—orthodoxy, particularism, religious hostility toward Jews, and secular anti-Semitism.

ORTHODOX CHRISTIANITY

The measurement of commitment to orthodox Christian belief was approached through asking respondents to express their degree of acceptance of such traditional articles of Christian faith as belief in God, the divinity of Jesus, the devil, life after death, and the Biblical accounts of Jesus' miracles. It was discovered that there are considerable differences in what church people believe about these central tenets of Christianity. The differences are illustrated in Table 6-1, which shows the proportion of Protestant and Roman Catholic laypersons and Protestant clergy who responded in an orthodox way to a sample of the questions asked. The range is from 86 percent of Roman Catholics who expressed unequivocal belief in the divinity of Christ to 38 percent of Protestant laypersons who acknowledge without qualification the existence of the devil. On most questions the majority give orthodox responses, but the majority is rarely overwhelming, and it is clear that there are many Christian church members and clergy who do not subscribe to traditional tenets of faith.

TABLE 6-1.   Christian Laypersons' and Protestant Ministers' Acceptance of Orthodox Religious Beliefs.

	Laypersons		Protestant Ministers
	Protestants	Catholics	
"I believe in God and I have no doubts about it." (percentage agreeing)	71%	81%	67%
"Jesus is the Divine Son of God and I have no doubts about it." (percentage agreeing)	69	86	61
"There is life after death." (percentage accepting as completely true)	65	75	79
"The Devil actually exists." (percentage accepting as completely true)	38	66	41
100% (N) =	(2,326)	(545)	(1,580)

SOURCE: Adapted from Charles Y. Glock and Rodney Stark, *Christian Beliefs and Anti-Semitism* (New York: Harper & Row, 1966), pp. 5, 7, 12; and Rodney Stark, Bruce D. Foster, Charles Y. Glock, and Harold E. Quinley, *Wayward Shepherds: Prejudice and the Protestant Clergy* (New York: Harper & Row, 1971), pp. 17, 19, 23.

That there is variation made it plausible to develop a summary measure of it. To this end, an index of orthodoxy was constructed based on lay answers to the questions asking them about the existence of a personal God, the divinity of Christ, the authenticity of Biblical miracles, and the existence of the devil. In the construction of the index, a respondent received a score of 1 for each of these belief questions on which he or she expressed certainty about the truth of the Christian position. Respondents received a score of 0 for each item on which they acknowledged doubt or disbelief about the orthodox response. Thus a person could score as high as 4 by being certain in his faith on all four items, or as low as 0 by reporting doubt or disbelief on all four. Following the same procedure, an index of orthodoxy was also constructed for Protestant clergy.

Table 6-2 reports the proportion of laypersons and clergy who scored 4 on the orthodoxy index; that is, respondents who gave an orthodox response to each of the four items included in the index, and therefore can be considered highly orthodox. In this table results are presented not only for Protestants taken as a whole but also broken down to show the figures for members of different faiths. Overall, Roman Catholic laymen are much more likely to score high on orthodoxy than Protestants. The figure for total Protestants, however, masks great variations by denomination. At the one extreme are the members of the United Church of Christ, where only 4 percent score as highly orthodox. At the other extreme are the Southern Baptists and sect members, where respectively 88 percent and 86 percent score as highly orthodox. This variation by denomination also holds true, as can be seen, for Protestant clergy. (Catholic priests, it will be recalled, were not surveyed in these studies; thus there is no figure for the degree of their orthodoxy.)

TABLE 6-2. Orthodox Religious Beliefs of Laypersons and Protestant Ministers.

| | Percentage Scoring High in Religious Orthodoxy | |
	Laypersons	Protestant Ministers
United Church of Christ	4% (141)	7% (137)
Methodist	10 (381)	6 (350)
Episcopal	14 (373)	19 (204)
Disciple of Christ	18 (44)	[a]
Presbyterian	27 (457)	24 (225)
Lutheran Church in America	43[b] (195)	39 (86)
American Lutheran Church		59 (115)
American Baptist	43 (76)	65 (144)
Missouri Synod—Lutheran Church	66 (111)	89 (131)
Southern Baptist	88 (76)	95 (167)
Sects	86 (247)	—[a]
Catholic	62 (500)	—

[a]None included in this study.   [b]Figure is for L.C.A. and A.L.C. combined.
SOURCE: Adapted from Glock and Stark, *Christian Beliefs and Anti-Semitism*, p. 13; and Stark *et al.*, *Wayward Shepherds*, p. 33.

PARTICULARISM

The main interest in these inquiries lay not with religious orthodoxy *per se*, of course, but with the consequences it has for other beliefs in the causal chain leading to secular anti-Semitism. The first of these, it will be recalled, was religious particularism—the belief that one's own religion is the only true one and that all others are false and even pernicious. Particularism can be viewed as a kind of religious chauvinism. It is a dismissal of all religious perspectives different from one's own.

Within Christianity, particularistic attitudes have historically centered on the question of salvation: Who will and who will not receive God's grace and be rewarded with eternal life. One traditional answer has been that one must accept Jesus Christ as savior in order to be so saved. In recent years, this definition has been liberalized in many denominations so that salvation is a possibility for Jews, Moslems, and other non-Christians.

However, as has been observed already in the discussion of orthodoxy, the gap between official pronouncements and individual attitudes—whether among the clergy or the laity—is often a large one. So it is with religious particularism. Two-thirds of the Protestant laypersons and half of the Catholics agreed that a belief in Jesus Christ as savior was "absolutely necessary" for salvation. Among Protestant clergy, this figure reached 69 percent. The majority of Christians clearly continue to hold beliefs that would condemn non-Christians to damnation (as well as those Christians not accepting Jesus as the Son of God).

As above, this "total" statistic is something of a fiction, varying greatly from denomination to denomination. Among Protestant laity, the percentage holding to such a belief ranges from a low of 38 percent among United Church of Christ to a high of 97 percent among Missouri Synod Lutherans and Southern Baptists. Among clergymen, the figures similarly vary from 29 percent of the United Church of Christ ministers to 97 percent among Missouri Synod Lutherans and 99 percent among Southern Baptists. The belief that non-Christians are damned is thus virtually unanimous in some churches, while a minority viewpoint in others.

Since these denominational distributions correspond to those found above for orthodoxy, it seems likely that orthodoxy and particularism are closely linked (as the model suggested they would be). In fact, they are. Among clergy and laity alike, an orthodox theological world view leads to the belief that those rejecting Jesus Christ as the savior of mankind are personally doomed.

The potential importance of such particularistic attitudes for anti-Semitism lies in what they may imply for how persons of the Jewish faith are responded to. In the past, particularist beliefs have led to a missionary zeal to convert those not believing in orthodox Christian truths and, on frequent occasions, to the persecution of those rejecting such conversion. Christianity today has lost much of its previous fervency but perhaps not all of its righteousness. Orthodox, particularistic Christians may continue to have feelings of hostility toward nonbelievers and, because of their visability, especially toward Jews.

IMAGES OF THE HISTORICAL JEW

Undoubtedly the most pernicious and sinister of all Christian images is that of Jews as Christ-killers—the murderers of Jesus Christ, the Christian Redeemer. The principal source of this epithet is a passage in the Book of Matthew describing the trial of Jesus before the Roman Procurator of Judea, Pontius Pilate. According to Matthew's account, Pilate thought Jesus to be innocent of any wrongdoing and sought to avoid his execution. A long-standing Jewish custom allowed a condemned prisoner to be pardoned at feast time, and Pilate gave the Jewish multitude the choice of releasing Jesus or another prisoner, Barabbas, who had been found guilty of murder and sedition. Instead of Jesus, however, the crowd was persuaded by their priests and elders to pardon Barabbas. When Pilate protested Jesus' innocence, the Jewish multitude cried out, "His blood be on us, and on our children."

The charge that Jews are collectively responsible for the execution of Jesus has been repeated through the centuries and has been used to justify continued Jewish persecution. In a 1939 pastoral letter, for example, Konrad Grober, the Roman Catholic Archbishop of Freising, Germany, wrote that the Jews were entirely responsible for the Crucifixion of Christ and that "their murderous hatred of Him has continued in later centuries."[3] Bishop Hilfrich of Limburg echoed this viewpoint, adding that for their murder of God the Jews have been under a curse since the original Good Friday.[4] Such religious attitudes were fairly typical of the German Roman Catholic hierarchy—and to a lesser extent of Protestant church leaders—at the time. In this country much the same charges were being made by Father Charles E. Coughlin and revivalist preachers such as Gerald B. Winrod and Gerald L. K. Smith.

Following the destruction of European Jewry, the Roman Catholic Church and most of the major Protestant churches recanted their previous positions on this issue. They denounced the doctrine of Jewish guilt for the Crucifixion and taught that all mankind is responsible for the death of Jesus. Today only a few denominations—most notably the Missouri Synod Lutherans and Southern Baptists—have failed to condemn the age-old charge of deicide.

Official church actions, however, can hardly be expected to change people's minds overnight. Indeed, research has shown that most Protestants remain completely unaware of their denominations' official pronouncements and that in many issue areas Catholics openly rejected their church's stands (such as in relation to birth control).[5] Thus it was felt that some church members might continue to hold Jews responsible for the Crucifixion, even though their church's official teachings were otherwise.

The presence among contemporary Christians of a belief that Jews were responsible for the Crucifixion was explored somewhat differently in the lay and clergy studies, although both studies confirm that such a belief continues to be widely held. In the lay study, which dealt with the subject more comprehensively, an effort was made to assess not only Matthew's account of Jewish responsibility for the Crucifixion but also the themes that Pilate tried to prevent the execution and that the Jewish multitudes, stirred up by their priests and elders, forced the Crucifixion to be carried out.

Seventy-nine percent of the laity (Catholics and Protestants alike) agreed that Pilate "wanted to spare Jesus from the cross." Forty-seven percent of the Protestants and 46 percent of the Catholics acknowledged that "a group of powerful Jews wanted Jesus dead." When given a choice of choosing the Romans, the Greeks, the Jews, the Christians, or none of these as the group most responsible for crucifying Christ, 58 percent of the Protestants and 61 percent of the Catholics chose the Jews.

At least as an historical interpretation, it is evident from these figures that many Christians continue to hold Jews responsible for the Crucifixion. Further, many of them assign questionable or evil motives to the Jewish rejection of Jesus. When asked why the Jews rejected Christ as the Messiah, 44 percent of the Protestants and 39 percent of the Catholic supported the assertion that the Jews "couldn't accept a Messiah who came from humble beginnings," 21 percent of Protestants and 16 percent of Catholics charged that "the Jews were sinful and had turned against God."

Protestant clergy were asked only the question about which group was most responsible for crucifying Christ, but the option "all mankind" was added to those made available to the laypersons. Given that option, the majority of clergy—54 percent—chose it, but 32 percent still chose the Jews. Thus, even among clergy there is a substantial minority who blame the Jews for Christ's death.

HOSTILE RELIGIOUS CONCEPTIONS OF THE CONTEMPORARY JEW

The persistence of specifically religious, as distinct from secular, hostility toward Jews was also investigated with respect to the modern Jew. Is it believed that Jews today continue to bear the stigma of their rejection of Jesus? To measure this dimension of belief two propositions were put to the lay and clerical respondents. The first suggested that Jews are still to be blamed for the Crucifixion: "The Jews can never be forgiven for what they did to Jesus until they accept him as the true savior." In the lay study, 33 percent of the Protestants and 14 percent of the Catholics agreed with this statement, while another 27 percent and 32 percent, respectively, were uncertain in their beliefs. All together, then, 60 percent of the Protestants and 46 percent of the Catholics at least acknowledge the possibility that Jews are unforgiven for their treatment of Jesus. Clearly, for many Christians the Crucifixion remains a salient point of reference in their judgment about Jews.

The second statement was even more strongly worded. It asked, in effect, whether the contemporary Jew is "cursed by God": "The reason the Jews have so much trouble is because God is punishing them for rejecting Jesus." To agree with this statement is tantamount to viewing the mistreatment of Jews today as divinely ordained. It was accepted by 13 percent of the Protestants and 11 percent of the Catholics in the lay study. If we add to these figures those who were uncertain in their views, 39 percent of the Protestants and 41 percent of the Catholics allowed the possibility that Jews were under God's curse.

Many rank-and-file church members thus hold hostile religious images of Jews. Considerably fewer clergy subscribe to such images, although the number, particularly with respect to the view that "the Jews can never be forgiven for what they did to Jesus until they accept Him as the true savior," is not insubstantial. Nineteen percent of the clerical respondents agreed with this statement, while another 6 percent were uncertain of their position. On the more strongly worded statement—that Jews are being punished for rejecting Jesus—8 percent agreed, with another 4 percent uncertain.

Feelings of religious hostility toward Jews thus also exist among the clergy, albeit at a lower level than among the laity. The anomalous nature of these attitudes can be better appreciated if they are compared with the way in which Americans characteristically think about other ethnic or population groups. With very few exceptions, judgments are made about them in contemporary terms and not from the perspective of past history. For example, the atrocities of the Romans is virtually never considered in present-day conceptions of modern-day Italians, or the vicious raids of the Vikings in thinking about Scandinavians. Those are simply past events holding little relevance to contemporary values or beliefs. Even an occurrence as recent and as murderous as World War II is today of small consequence to the images held of our former adversaries. The Germans and the Japanese of contemporary times are seldom equated with the hated enemies of forty years ago.

To make such judgments of Jews is thus a rare and peculiar practice. Even if Jewish leaders were active agents in the execution of Jesus some 2,000 years ago, it is odd that Americans would consider this fact to have any bearing on their evaluations of Jews today.

ORTHODOXY, PARTICULARISM, AND RELIGIOUS HOSTILITY

But are these tendencies among Christians attributable to their religious beliefs? More specifically, is religious hostility toward the contemporary

Jew a product of an orthodox and a particularist vision of Christian faith? The answer is yes, but not absolutely. Not all Christians whose faith is highly orthodox and particularistic exhibit religious hostility. In turn, not all Christians whose faith is other than orthodox and particularist are entirely free of such hostility. There exists, however, rather strong tendencies for the beliefs and hostilities to go together.

Among Protestant laity, 86 percent of those who are highly orthodox and highly particularist, and who attributed Christ's death to the Jews, feel that Jews still cannot be forgiven for rejecting Jesus. In contrast, only 1 percent feel this way among those low on both orthodoxy and particularism and who did not blame the Crucifixion on the Jews. Fewer Catholics than Protestants harbored a negative religious image of the modern Jew in the first place, and thus the actual percentage differences for them are smaller. However, a majority of Catholics holding the negative image scored high on particularism and orthodoxy and also blamed the Jews for the Crucifixion.

The same pattern of relation holds for Protestant clergy. Among clergy who are highly orthodox and highly particularist, and who attribute the Crucifixion to the Jews, 89 percent agreed either that the Jews can never be forgiven until they accept Christ or that the Jews are being punished by God or both. In comparison, such agreement is only 18 percent among nonorthodox, nonparticularist clergy who reject an image of the Jews as responsible for Christ's death.

As a consequence of these patterns, anti-Jewish feelings are found largely within those denominations where religious views of an orthodox and particularist nature are most commonly taught. In the clergy study, 69 percent of the Southern Baptists and 53 percent of the Missouri Lutherans agreed that Jews would remain unforgiven until they accept Christ as savior, as contrasted with only 3 to 4 percent of the United Church of Christ, Methodist, and Episcopalian clergy. A similar range of opinions was found among laypersons. Eighty percent of the Southern Baptists and 70 percent of the Missouri Synod Lutherans agreed that the Jews remain unforgiven. Among members of the United Church of Christ, Methodists, and Episcopalians, the figures were respectively 10, 12, and 11 percent.

In summarizing these findings, it must be pointed out exactly what is involved in the holding of such beliefs. To consider Jews to be unforgiven and an object of God's punishment is an unmistakably hostile attitude. It represents a highly damaging conclusion—one that is almost certain to affect the holder's general feelings toward Jews. To entertain such notions is thus a form of religious bigotry and prejudice.

From the perspective of traditional Christianity, this judgment may seem unfair or overly harsh. For conservative Christians it is often an article of faith that Jews—a group not accepting Jesus as the Son of God—remain unforgiven and unsaved; it may not seem that such a position involves any hostility or prejudice. This argument, for example, was made by the Reverend Wayne Dehoney, then president of the Southern Baptist Convention, in criticizing the results just reported. He was quoted in *Newsweek* magazine:

> Christians do believe that all Jews who reject Christ as the Messiah are therefore lost from God's redeeming love—as are all men of all races who have not personally responded to God's grace through faith in Jesus Christ. This is not racism; this is the Christian doctrine of personal salvation.[6]

A similar position was taken by a Missouri Synod Lutheran minister respondent in the clerical study:

> I feel sorry for all Jews who have rejected Jesus and thus have no God. There is only one God (Father–Son–Holy Ghost). "He that knoweth not the Son honoreth not the Father," said Jesus. The unrepentant Jew is unsaved. God loves the Jews and chose them, and my Savior is a Jew. But they have chosen to reject Him. What more could they have wanted from the Messiah?

While such statements might seem perfectly reasonable from an orthodox point of view, they amount to a demand that Jews renounce their own religious convictions and heritage and accept Christianity; if they do not, they will be punished for eternity.

Christian Beliefs and Anti-Semitism

The first four stages of the model have thus been substantiated. A commitment to an orthodox and particularistic version of Christian faith does indeed lead to the holding of hostile religious feelings toward modern-day Jews. It does so through a cognitively related chain of beliefs; once certain basic assumptions are made about religious reality, it follows logically that Jews will be viewed as religious outsiders or heretics.

It is time now to present evidence on the final and most controversial step in this model. The central purpose of these investigations was to determine whether religious convictions play any part in contemporary anti-Semitism. It was thought that people who held hostile religious conceptions of Jews might tend also to develop anti-Jewish feelings of a more general or secular nature—simply put, that people who disliked Jews on religious grounds would easily fall prey to disliking them in more secular ways as well.

ANTI-SEMITISM AMONG CHURCH MEMBERS

A long battery of questions was included in the study of laity for the express purpose of measuring various forms of secular anti-Semitism. These items included most of the same belief statements considered in earlier chapters, as well as questions designed to measure the respondents' feelings toward interacting with Jews and their potential reaction to Jews under certain hypothetical conditions. Since little difference was found among these various indicators of anti-Semitism, attention here will be limited to anti-Semitic beliefs.

First, how anti-Semitic in their beliefs are churchgoers? Are the values of Christian brotherhood reflected in a greater acceptance of Jewish people? Or do the religious feelings outlined above produce greater hostilities toward Jews? Speaking generally, the level of anti-Semitism found among church members is about the same as that found among the general public. The proportion of respondents in this study accepting negative stereotypes of Jews was almost identical to that in the national study cited in Chapter 1. For example, 33 percent of the Protestants and 29 percent of the Catholics agreed that it was true or somewhat true that "Jews are more likely than Christians to cheat in business." Thirty-one percent and 26 percent, respectively, felt that "Jews, in general, are inclined to be more loyal to Israel than to America." And 57 percent and 55 percent agreed that "Jews want to remain different from other people, and yet they are touchy if people notice these differences."

Such figures indicate that church members are not much different from anyone else when it comes to anti-Semitic prejudice. In the national study it was estimated that a third of the American people were highly prone to hold anti-Semitic beliefs; in the present study the figure was set at 33 percent for Protestants and 29 percent for Catholics.[7] Again, it should be pointed out that such percentages do not refer to the virulent form of anti-Semitism associated with Nazi Germany or with certain hate groups in this country. Anti-Semitic feelings of this type are relatively rare in present-day America. These figures do, however, refer to individuals who are highly disposed to stereotype Jews in negative ways, including stereotypes of an overtly belligerent and hostile nature.

Anti-Semitism can thus be found within the churches as well as outside of them. This in itself is hardly a surprising finding; there are few knowledgeable observers who believe that organized religion is entirely free from prejudice. To what extent, however, are such anti-Semitic beliefs a product of distinctly religious convictions rather than of something else?

Previously, four distinct sets of Christian beliefs were identified, and their causal connections demonstrated. Orthodoxy was seen to produce a particularistic world view in which only right-thinking Christians were subject to salvation; theological beliefs of this nature, in turn, were associated with hostile religious images of both the historical and modern Jew. Upon examination, *all four of these religious beliefs were found to be strongly associated with secular anti-Semitism.* Indeed, taken together, they prove a powerful predictor of secular anti-Semitism. This is indicated in Table 6-3, which combines these four dimensions of Christian belief into a single composite index of "religious bigotry." As this table indicates, the respondents' anti-Semitism varies in direct relation to their positions on this measure. Among Protestants, the proportion of anti-Semites ranged from 10 percent among those low in religious bigotry to 78 percent among those high on this dimension; among Catholics, the range was from a low of 6 percent to a high of 83 percent. These variations are among the greatest of any encountered in the studies in this series. Moreover, these variations are sustained when such controls as age, education, and socio-economic background are taken into account. That is to say, whether persons are young or old, educated or uneducated, rich or poor, the more the religious beliefs are subscribed to, the greater the anti-Semitism.

TABLE 6-3. Percentage of Christian Laypersons Scoring High in Anti-Semitic Belief at Each Level of Religious Bigotry Index.

Percentage scoring high and medium high on index of anti-Semitic belief	Index of Religious Bigotry						
	Low 0	1	2	3	4	5	High 6
Protestants	10% (216)	15% (233)	28% (206)	37% (146)	46% (159)	57% (124)	78% (97)
Catholics	6% (31)	17% (54)	19% (78)	39% (59)	40% (33)	58% (21)	83% (6)

Source: Adapted from Glock and Stark, *Christian Beliefs and Anti-Semitism*, p. 136.

It is important to recognize, however, that the process through which this occurs is not directly from orthodox and particularist belief to secular anti-Semitism. Believing that salvation is possible only through Christ, for example, does not lead believers directly to be disposed to accept the additional belief that Jews are more likely than Christians to cheat in business. Rather, what the religious beliefs do is generate hostility to Jews as religious outsiders. For those believing that Jews are damned on religious grounds, it is apparently a small step to believing that Jews are also avaricious, unethical, clannish, and unpatriotic.

The significance of the linkage of Christian orthodoxy and particularism to secular anti-Semitism should not be underestimated. A large proportion of churchgoers in this country are orthodox and particularist in their religious outlooks, and in this respect *most Christians are susceptible to such religious sources of anti-Semitism*. It is not a small or deviant perspective in Christianity that contributes to anti-Semitic sentiments among people; it is the theological convictions of a large part of the religious mainstream of America.

ANTI-SEMITISM AMONG PROTESTANT MINISTERS

Anti-Semitism among Protestant ministers is less prevalent than among Protestant laity. For example, while 53 percent of the Protestant laity agreed that it was at least somewhat true that "Jews were more likely than Christians to cheat in business," only 10 percent of the California ministers answered this way. Similarly, while 31 percent of the laity accepted the possibility that Jews were more loyal to Israel than to America, only 19 percent of the ministers agreed. Overall it was estimated that 17 percent of the Protestant clergy surveyed were anti-Semitic, as against 33 percent of the Protestant laity.[8]

This difference is attributable in part to the fact that clergymen, on the average, are better educated than lay persons. When clergy are compared with laity who have had more than a college education, which most clergy have had, the difference in anti-Semitism rates is considerably less—the clergy's 17 percent is measured against 22 percent for highly educated Protestant laity. However, among lay persons it was found that, to a large extent, the lower anti-Semitism of the more-educated was the result of their being less likely than the less-educated to subscribe to orthodox and particularist beliefs. When the more-educated did subscribe to such beliefs, they were as likely as the uneducated believers and considerably more likely than uneducated nonbelievers to be anti-Semitic.

Besides being less anti-Semitic, clergy also differ from laity in that their religious convictions are less likely to produce anti-Semitism. Among highly educated Protestant laity, for example, 86 percent are anti-Semitic of those who are highly orthodox particularists and feel some religious hostility toward Jews. Only 9 percent are anti-Semitic among those without the religious convictions and the hostility. Among clergy, the range is from 9 percent to 47 percent. Thus among both laity and clergy it is clear that religious convictions are a source of anti-Semitism, but the relation is considerably stronger for laity than for clergy. This is attributable to the clergy's greater ability than laity, while believing in the eternal damnation of the Jews, not to permit this to spill over into secular anti-Semitism.

That the links in the causal chain leading from religious convictions of the kind specified to anti-Semitism are not inexorable affords some promise that the chain can be broken without asking people to abandon their religious convictions. It would appear, however, that the clergy who are able to do this for themselves are not helping their parishioners to follow suit. Such clergy may well proclaim that Christian doctrines of love, brotherhood, compassion, and forgiveness erase any potential for prejudice contained in their Christian convictions. For themselves this may indeed hold true. The evidence suggests, however, that relatively few of the laity whose religious convictions are conservative are receiving the message.

Summary

The model set forth at the beginning of this chapter proved to be accurate. The acceptance of orthodox Christian beliefs leads to a particularistic religious orientation in which only right-thinking Christians are seen as saved and all others are damned. These views, in turn, are associated with hostile feelings toward Jews—which have both a historical dimension (Jews being held responsible for the Crucifixion) and contemporary effects (Jews being condemned for their rejection of Jesus as savior). Such religious beliefs, finally, are associated with secular forms of anti-Semitism. Christian laypersons and ministers holding these religious conceptions are disproportionately prejudiced in their attitudes toward Jews.

The churches today, then, may not openly preach anti-Semitism, and their official position may be one of reconciliation and rapprochement. In reality, however, orthodox Christianity continues to serve as an agent of anti-Semitic prejudice in America. It does so by introducing a set of cognitive assumptions that provide people with reasons to dislike Jews. Not everyone who accepts these assumptions draws from them the same hostile conclusions about Jews, but the majority of theologically conservative churchpeople do make such connections. Thus, despite the liberalization of American religion, Christianity continues to have a strong impact upon what people think about Jews. Indeed, of the various factors examined in the entire series of studies, religious beliefs were second only to a lack of education as a primary source of anti-Semitic prejudice among Americans.

CHAPTER 7

Anti-Semitism in the News

THE RESEARCH PROGRAM ON ANTI-SEMITISM was addressed primarily to measuring the incidence and to investigating the causes of this form of prejudice, rather than to mounting or evaluating efforts to reduce and combat it. It was intended, of course, that consideration be given to the implications of the findings for such ameliorative efforts (a task taken up in the final chapter of the book). The original research plan did not, however, call for any effort to assess the efficacy of then ongoing efforts by Jewish defense agencies and others to contain and reduce prejudice. In part, this decision was made because no existing effort was substantial or extensive enough to warrant such an effort. Primarily, however, evaluation was not conceived to be a task appropriate to a program whose purpose was basic research.

A change in plans came about because an international event occurred that serendipitously produced a situation in which the population of the world was exposed, over an extended period of time, to news stories depicting in vivid detail the extraordinary evil to which anti-Semitism can lead. It was decided that it would be an opportunity lost if some effort were not made to assess the impact of these news stories in informing the public about the nature of anti-Semitism and in changing public attitudes toward Jews.

The event, of course, was the Eichmann trial. The events of Eichmann's capture in Argentina and the circumstances of his trial were reported, analyzed, and debated before the American public for well over a year. In the process, the barbaric murders engineered by Eichmann and his associates were vividly recalled and the demonic nature of Nazism and of political anti-Semitism was again revealed. If anything might serve to inform public opinion about the evils of anti-Semitism, the Eichmann trial seemed to be an ideal medium for that purpose. But was anybody listening, and if so, to what effect?

The study undertaken to find out was conducted at that time during the trial when the proceedings had ended and the court recessed for three months to give the judges time to reach a verdict.[1] Thus the subjects of the study were asked about their knowledge and opinions of the trial after more than a year of its having been reported on almost daily in the mass media. The timing of the interviews also meant that respondents could be asked their views of Eichmann's guilt before the judges' verdict was announced. Thus the respondents were placed in the position effectively of being jurors themselves.

The details of the Eichmann trial will probably have been forgotten by now. Before reporting on the study's results, consequently, it is appropriate to review briefly how the trial unfolded.

The Course of the Trial: A Reminder

The Eichmann case first came to the world's attention on the morning of May 24, 1960. On that day Israeli Premier David Ben-Gurion announced that Adolf Eichmann had been found, was being held in Israel, and would be tried for his crimes by an Israeli court. The initial announcement did not provide details about the manner or the location of the capture. However, within a week the Israeli government confirmed that Eichmann had been taken by its agents from a suburb of Buenos Aires, Argentina, and brought to Israel on Foreign Minister Abba Eban's El Al airliner. Few news analysts took seriously Israel's *pro forma* statement that Eichmann had not been kidnapped, but had submitted willingly; most accepted the unofficial explanation that Israel had kidnapped Eichmann because of Argentina's past refusals to extradite ex-Nazis discovered within its territory.

The alleged kidnapping, which was in violation of an extradition treaty signed only two days earlier, was officially protested by Argentina. The issue was subsequently taken to the United Nations Security Council, where Israel was chided for the capture but not directed to return Eichmann to Argentina.

After the Security Council resolution in June 1960, Israel began to make preparations for the trial. The charges against Eichmann were drawn up. Arrangements for press and television coverage of the trial were made. Through a series of public statements, Israel outlined its purposes in conducting the trial.

In February 1961 fifteen charges againt Eichmann were disclosed. The first eight pertained to Eichmann's crimes against Jews and against humanity. The next four accused Eichmann of crimes against non-Jewish groups, specifically Poles, Slavs, and gypsies. The last three charges accused him of membership in organizations branded as illegal by the Nuremberg trial.

At the end of February the composition of the court was announced. The three members were Benjamin Halevi, a judge in the Jerusalem District Court; Itzhak Reveh, a judge in the Tel Aviv District Court; and Moseh Landau, a justice of Israel's Supreme Court, who was named chairman. Earlier, the Knesset (Israel's parliament) had voted to pay a German lawyer, Robert Servatius, to defend Eichmann. Attorney General Gideon Hausner accepted responsibility for the prosecution.

The trial opened on April 10, 1961, with the reading of the indictment against Eichmann. Servatius immediately challenged Israel's illegal abduction of Eichmann and its right to try, and charged that the court was prejudiced against Eichmann. Hausner replied that no court in the world could fail to be biased against Eichmann, but that prejudice would not be permitted to enter the proceedings. The court denied Servatius's objections and held that Israel did have jurisdiction. Eichmann pleaded not guilty to all fifteen counts of the indictment, partly on the ground that he had been a mere subordinate carrying out official orders.

Hausner devoted part of his opening statement to a summary of the evidence showing that Eichmann did more than follow orders. He described Eichmann's role in the deportation of German and Austrian Jews in 1938, and his statement summarized the Nazi mass executions and tortures, including the death march of Hungarian Jews organized by Eichmann in 1944.

From the middle of April to the middle of June, Hausner introduced evidence of Nazi crimes and Eichmann's complicity in them. Survivors of the pogroms, the shootings, the labor camps, and the death camps told of their experiences. They told not only of the organized slayings but of gratuitous and sadistic torture. Some of the evidence did not mention Eichmann by name, but the court held such information to be relevant because it sought to show not only that crimes had been committed but that they had been of a particularly heinous nature. Much of the testimony dealt with Eichmann directly.

In late June and July Eichmann himself testified. Servatius's examination tried to establish that Eichmann had been no more than a bureaucrat following orders and that he had actually shown kindness to Jews when he could. Hausner's cross-examination persistently sought to destroy this image. Eichmann was continually confronted with documents describing his activities, some of which contained his own signature. At the beginning of the cross-examination Eichmann admitted his "moral guilt" in the slaying of European Jewry, but only by way of arguing that he was an accessory, not a perpetrator. Before his testimony ended, he admitted that the slaughter of Jews was a "hideous crime," but he continued to maintain that he was merely following orders and that it was his duty to do so.

Eichmann's testimony ended with an examination by the judges on July 25, 1961. The early weeks in August were taken up with the summations of prosecution and defense. The court then recessed until December. On December 10, Eichmann was convicted on all fifteen counts. On December 14, he was sentenced to hang but was granted the right to appeal to the Israeli Supreme Court. His appeal was unanimously rejected by that five-man tribunal on May 28, 1962. Eichmann's appeal to President Itzhak Ben-Zvi was also rejected. He was hanged on May 30, 1962, and his ashes, in an act that symbolized the dissolution of Nazi racism, were scattered over the Mediterranean.

Exposure to the Trial

The Eichmann trial placed the atrocities of Nazi Germany in the news. It reminded the public what had happened to the Jews in Germany and what could result when anti-Semitic prejudice went unchecked. Given the nature of these events, it might be expected that the publicity given to the Eichmann trial might serve to educate the public on the dangers of prejudice and to produce greater sympathy toward the Jews. At least this was the hope of Israeli officials in carrying out the trial. A principal objective was to remind the world about what had happened in Nazi Germany so as to provide firmer resistance to anti-Semitism and to the reenactment of such atrocities. How well these objectives were achieved can first be gauged by looking at the public's awareness and knowledge of the trial.

AWARENESS OF THE TRIAL

The citizens surveyed in this study had ample opportunity to become exposed to and informed about the Eichmann trial. The trial and events leading up to it received prominent attention in newspapers and on local radio stations. It was the subject of several national television programs. It was featured in stories in mass circulation magazines—*Life, Time, Look, Reader's Digest*—and in more sophisticated journals of opinion—*Harper's, Atlantic Monthly, The Reporter, Saturday Review*. In addition there were opportunities to hear about it through neighbors, friends, and co-workers.

Not all of these sources of information were available to everyone, but all persons in the study were in touch with at least one source of information. Eighty-six percent reported that they regularly read a daily newspaper. Fifty-seven percent were regular readers of magazines that carried some kind of report on the trial and on Israel's capture of Eichmann. Eighty-nine percent owned at least one television set, and 91 percent owned at least one radio.

For the events of the Eichmann trial to have an impact on public opin-ion, the first requisite was that the public be aware of the trial. When asked, 84 percent said they had heard of the trial; 16 percent had not.[2] It may be wondered how it was possible for one out of six members of the public to have managed to escape exposure to an event that had been in the news for more than a year. Others, familiar with past data on levels of public knowl-edge, may find it surprising that as many as 84 percent had heard about the trial. In order to set the figure of 84 percent in proper perspective, the amount of attention given to the trial may be compared with that given to other news events of the day. Compared to other events, the Eichmann trial did not get unusual attention. More people, for example, knew that the movie actor Gary Cooper had just died than knew about the trial. At the same time, as many people knew about the trial as were aware of other seri-ous news stories of the day. It received about the same attention as did other serious news events of the time.

Generally speaking, those who paid attention to the trial were more news-oriented than those who were unaware of it. The two groups differed especially with respect to giving attention to serious news events. Thus the 16 percent who had not heard about the Eichmann trial paid little attention to serious news generally.

KNOWLEDGE OF THE TRIAL

Awareness is only a minimum indicator of exposure to an event. It says nothing about the extent of people's knowledge and understanding of the trial. Two questions pertained to the capture: "Do you happen to remember in what country Eichmann was arrested?" "What country arrested him?" One question dealt with Eichmann's identity: "Do you know whether Eich-mann was a Communist, a Nazi, or a Jew?" A final question tapped knowl-edge of the Nazi persecution: "An official estimate has been made of the number of Jews killed before and during World War II. Would you please look at this card and tell me which number comes closest to this official esti-mate?" These questions were asked, of course, only of the 84 percent who said they had heard of the trial.

Judging from the responses to these questions, a considerably larger proportion of the public was aware of the trial than possessed minimum knowledge about it. Of those aware, only about a third replied correctly that Eichmann had been captured in Argentina, 50 percent knew that he had been arrested by Israel, 59 percent correctly identified him as a Nazi (9 percent thought he was a Jew!), and 33 percent correctly identified the of-fical estimate of the number of Jews killed by the Nazis as six million. The impression conveyed by these figures is that the trial did not penetrate very broadly or deeply into the minds of the public. This impression is reinforced when the answers are considered in combination. Only 13 percent of the awares answered all four questions correctly. Twenty percent had three correct answers, 20 percent two, 23 percent one, and 24 percent none.

These figures do not take into account those who had not even heard of the trial. When that group is included, it turns out that 36 percent were not reached by the trial at all, being either unaware of it or unable to answer any of the four simple questions asked about it. This is more than three times the number who knew the answers to all four questions.

These results may be distressing, but they are hardly surprising. It has been documented over and over again that the details of even the most publicized national and international events elude the majority of the public. Only when an event has deep personal meaning for a population is lack of interest and concern overcome. The Eichmann trial held such meaning for the Jewish population. All of the Jewish respondents in the survey were highly informed about the trial. However, if extent of factual information is any test, then it must be concluded that the majority of the non-Jewish population did not perceive the trial as personally relevant or interesting. This does not mean necessarily that those with little knowledge of the trial's details were uninfluenced by its message. The trial's impact on attitudes is a matter still to be addressed. Nevertheless, it is evident that only a minority of the public was enough caught up in the drama of the trial and in the lessons to be learned from it to pay close attention to the proceedings.

Who was it among the general public that paid close attention to the trial? Alternatively, who was unaware and unknowledgeable of the proceedings? The results of other studies reported earlier suggest that better-educated, more privileged Americans are likely to have paid more attention to the Eichmann trial, as they do news events generally. Such was the case. Among respondents with eighth-grade educations or less, only 21 percent were aware of the trial and answered two or more of the above questions correctly. Among those with some high school, the figure reached 31 percent, while among high school graduates it was 49 percent. Among respondents who had attended college, it was 68 percent, and among college graduates it was 81 percent.

The significance of these patterns should be apparent from findings reported in earlier chapters. Less-educated Americans tend disproportionately to be anti-Semitic in their beliefs. Thus those who were least aware and knowledgeable of the trial were those whom it was intended to affect most—those most prejudiced toward Jews. Table 7-1 presents the relevant figures. On both measures of anti-Semitism developed in this study, the more prejudiced respondents were the least likely to be knowledgeable about the trial and the events it sought to publicize.[3] Moreover, prejudice itself was found to be an independent factor in producing such low levels of knowledgeability. The anti-Semitic were less knowledgeable of the trial than their lack of education and social privileges alone would predict.

TABLE 7-1. Knowledge About the Eichmann Trial, by Anti-Semitic Belief and Acceptance of Discrimination.

| | General Anti-Semitism Index | | | |
	None 0	Low 1	Medium 2	High 3
Percent knowledgeable[a]	57%	40%	40%	15%
(Number)	(213)	(92)	(50)	(27)

| | Discrimination Index | | |
	Reject Discrimination	Mixed	Accept Discrimination
Percent knowledgeable[a]	55%	36%	28%
(Number)	(232)	(126)	(100)

[a]Answered two or more of the four knowledge questions correctly.
SOURCE: Adapted from Charles Y. Glock, Gertrude J. Selznick, and Joe L. Spaeth, *The Apathetic Majority: A Study Based on Public Responses to the Eichmann Trial* (New York: Harper & Row, 1966), p. 43.

It is not surprising that the more prejudiced Americans would be found least aware and knowledgeable of the Eichmann trial. Prejudice often leads people to avoid issues and situations that threaten their own viewpoints. Nevertheless, it is evident that those individuals toward whom the educational aspects of the trial were most directed were least attentive to it.

The Public's Response to the Issues of the Trial

On this first dimension, then, it is evident that Israel was not altogether successful in its attempt to arouse public concern regarding anti-Semitism through the trial of Adolf Eichmann. The trial did not receive any more attention than is generally accorded serious news stories, and it was the most anti-Semitic who were least attentive to the trial and the details it sought to make public.

As already suggested, however, knowledge and attitudes do not always depend on one another; it is possible for people to be persuaded by the case made against Eichmann without knowing all the details of the trial. Thus it seemed appropriate to inquire into the public's response to the issues raised in the trial. First, to what extent was the public persuaded of Eichmann's complicity and guilt as portrayed by the prosecution? Second, how many viewed the trial as legal and how many as illegal? Third, how many approved of the death penalty for Eichmann and how many did not?

EICHMANN'S COMPLICITY AND GUILT

The evidence presented at the trial and the way it was reported and interpreted in the responsible mass media offered three images of Eichmann's complicity. One image was that he was a monster—a sadist, a moral degenerate who had personally committed murder. A second image was that he was a zealot, probably not personally engaging in murder, but carrying out his assignment with enthusiasm and zeal. A third image was that he was a bureaucrat, an acquiescent cog in the Nazi machine acting primarily out of obedience and performing his tasks with impersonal efficiency.

The main burden of the prosecution's case was to present Eichmann in the second of these three images. Eichmann was portrayed as performing his tasks with an efficiency and initiative that could have been inspired only by zeal and enthusiasm for Nazi policy. There was ample evidence indicating that he had in fact actively participated in making decisions and formulating policy. The allegation that Eichmann had personally murdered (the first image) was not pursued actively except at one point in the proceedings when it was charged that Eichmann had killed a Jewish boy in his Budapest garden. The image of Eichmann as a monster was thus not the dominant one presented by the prosecution. The third image, that of Eichmann as a bureaucrat, was rejected by the prosecution, which also argued that, even if it were accepted, no ground for acquittal existed. Subordinates are responsible for crimes against humanity even when ordered to commit them by their superiors.

The defense made no attempt to deny that Eichmann had helped to administer and facilitate the mass murder of European Jews during World War II. It did, however, seek to minimize Eichmann's role, arguing that he had merely been following orders he was morally and legally bound to obey. The defense did deny that Eichmann had participated in decision making and that he had personally engaged in murder. The defense case was legal rather than factual. Its argument was that, while Eichmann had perhaps participated in a moral crime, it was out of an excess of loyalty and subservience. He had not, strictly speaking, committed a legal crime and was thus innocent.

The part of the public that was aware of the trial sided in substantial proportion with the case presented by the prosecution. Seventy percent judged Eichmann to be guilty, 6 percent not guilty, and 22 percent said they didn't know. Omitting the don't knows, the proportion judging Eichmann guilty was an overwhelming 92 percent. Most respondents also agreed with the prosecution's portrayals of Eichmann's complicity. Twenty-one percent of those aware of the trial subscribed to the image of Eichmann as a monster who had personally engaged in the murder of Jews. Another 24 percent rejected the charge that Eichmann had personally murdered but accepted the prosecution's principal position that Eichmann was a zealot who pursued his assignments even beyond what his superiors had ordered. The defense's portrayal of Eichmann as no more than a bureaucrat was accepted by 23 percent of the public. However, the majority of this group—61 percent—judged Eichmann guilty nonetheless, whereas only 11 percent supported a verdict of not guilty. The balance of those holding the bureaucratic image had no opinion as to Eichmann's guilt. Twenty-two percent of the respondents, finally, held no opinion about what Eichmann had done, while 2 percent adopted a view presented by neither the defense nor the prosecution, namely that Eichmann was being used as a scapegoat by Israel to further its own interests and that the charges against him were false.

In sum, then, the prosecution's case was supported in some part by 70 percent of the public. Only 8 percent sided totally with the portrait of Eichmann as a guiltless bureaucrat. The remaining 22 percent had no opinion.

This information regarding images of Eichmann and attitudes about his guilt should be evaluated against the background of what has been learned about the public's knowledge of the trial. Only 33 percent of those aware of the trial could correctly answer at least three of the four basic questions regarding the trial and pretrial events. Yet 78 percent formed an image of Eichmann's role in the Nazi crimes and 76 percent reached a verdict concerning his guilt or innocence.

Knowledgeability was found to be most closely associated with the bureaucratic image of Eichmann.[4] This means that, while most respondents agreed with the prosecution in depicting Eichmann as a monster or zealot, the greatest dissent came from those who knew most about the trial. Why this was so can be explained in terms of the cognitive factors discussed in previous chapters. The image of Eichmann as a bureaucrat required a more sophisticated understanding of fascism as a political phenomenon. A movement such as German Nazism, in fact, comprised many little people blindly following whatever they were told—precisely the position taken by Eichmann's defense attorney. Those who understood what facism is like, then, could view Eichmann as a bureaucrat and still condemn him. The prosecution's portrayal of Eichmann as a zealot (and possibly a monster) was an image that could more easily be grasped by an undiscerning or inattentive public. And it was this more simplistic image of evil that less knowledgeable members of the public most often formed to make sense out of the trial.

This tendency explains what would otherwise seem to be a paradox of orientations. Overall, respondents who held images similar to that advanced by the prosecution (Eichmann as a zealot or monster) were the most anti-Semitic in their own personal beliefs. Respondents who viewed Eichmann as a bureaucrat (the defense position) were the least anti-Semitic. The explanation has to do with the low level of information of the anti-Semitic. Among the uninformed, nearly half of those who viewed Eichmann as a monster were themselves anti-Semitic.

THE LEGALITY OF THE TRIAL

Several questions were raised about the trial's legality by the media and legal scholars, as well as by the defense. First, Eichmann's capture by Israeli agents in Argentina and his delivery to Israel in an El Al plane were said to be contrary to international law. This was probably the most frequently raised issue in the media and news commentary in this country. Second, it was argued that Israel had no jurisdiction in the case since it was not a state during World War II when Eichmann helped to perpetrate the atrocities of the Nazi regime. According to this viewpoint, Israel's laws must be considered *ex post facto* and inapplicable to Eichmann. Third, the applicability of Israeli laws to a citizen of Germany was questioned. In international law generally, the laws of a nation are not applicable outside of its own boundaries. Finally, one student of constitutional law, Yosal Rogat, criticized Israel's apprehension of Eichmann on the grounds that, besides being ambiguous under present international law, it did not serve to advance international law to a higher level.[5]

Besides replying to critics on each of these legal points, Israel argued its case on the principle of a "higher morality." The Israeli premier, David Ben-Gurion, stated it as follows: "Those whose brothers and sisters were murdered by Eichmann and who undertook to search him out were right morally, although perhaps not formally. I know they committed a breach of law, but sometimes there are moral obligations higher than formal law." Ben-Gurion also argued, "It is historic justice that [Eichmann] be tried by a Jewish state. Only a Jewish state can try him from a moral point of view."[6]

The trial itself did not and could not settle the legal issues it raised, but the fact that they were raised caused the Israelis concern that they might prevent the trial's broader educational purposes from being served. If it came to be widely believed that the trial constituted an illegal proceeding, this might redound to the disadvantage of Israel and world Jewry, however much the public might be in sympathy with the case against Eichmann.

Eighty-two percent of the public who knew about the trial expressed an opinion about its legality. Of these, 50 percent believed without qualification that the trial was legal, while an additional 22 percent thought it was legal but qualified their answers in some way. The remaining 28 percent thought the trial was illegal, 11 percent adopting this position with qualifications. All together, then, nearly three-quarters of the respondents with an opinion thought that the trial was legal.

The grounds for giving a qualified answer tended to be the same whether the person believed the trial to be illegal or legal. Almost all of the qualifiers—eight out of every ten—mentioned Eichmann's capture in Argentina by Israeli agents as the source of their equivocation. Some, while critical of Israel in this respect, adopted the view of many observers that the capture did not impugn the trial itself:

> It may not have been legal to go to another country and arrest him, but from a subjective point of view everyone should be brought to trial for his crimes.

> Actually, they kidnapped him, which was illegal, but they certainly were justified in bringing him to trial. He certainly needs to be punished.

For others, however, the alleged kidnapping was enough to lead them to judge the entire proceedings as illegal:

> No, I don't think they had any right going into another country and kidnapping him. [There are] channels you should go through to extradite him.

> I don't think it was legal the way they did it, by kidnapping him. They should have served papers and done it legally.

> No, I don't. They had no right to arrest a man in another country and kidnap him out. According to international law, they didn't have the right. Definitiely, it's illegal.

The only other qualification raised with any frequency bore on the question of Israel's right to jurisdiction in light of its not being in existence during World War II, when the crimes were committed. Again, some people were willing to overlook their reservations on the grounds that a "higher justice" was being served, but others were not.

> Yes, it was legal. Even though Israel was formed after the crimes were committed, many people or relatives in Israel suffered the crimes. So [I] feel it's legal for them to try Eichmann.

> From a technical point of view it wasn't, since the crimes were committed before there was an Israel and the crimes were not committed on Israeli soil.

> No, since Israel wasn't a state at the time of the crime.

Only one respondent raised any question about Israel's ability to conduct a fair trial. All in all, the alleged kidnapping was conceived as the main point at issue. That few respondents explicitly rejected Israel's right to try Eichmann is one thing, however; whether people thought it desirable that Israel should try him is another. After the question on legality had been asked, respondents were presented with four possible actions Israel might have taken with regard to Eichmann and asked to choose the one which, in their opinion, would have been the right course for the Israeli government to follow: (1) try him as they were doing before an Israeli court, (2) hand him over to Germany for trial, (3) hand him over to an international court for trial, (4) let him go free. The idea of trying Eichmann in an international court might not have occurred to many people had the questions not brought it to their attention. Nevertheless, 51 percent of those who knew about the trial would have preferred having it conducted by an international court. Thirty-six percent favored the status quo, that is, having Israel try Eichmann. There was little sympathy for having Eichmann tried by Germany (4 percent) and even less for letting him go free (3 percent). Very few respondents (6 percent) had no opinion on this question.

Israel thus succeeded in winning the public to its view regarding the trial's legality to almost the same degree as it succeeded in gaining acceptance of the prosecution's image of Eichmann's complicity and guilt. The support, however, was frequently accompanied by the opinion that it would have been preferable, all things considered, had Eichmann been tried by an international court. As above, it was the least educated and least knowledgeable respondents who most fully accepted the trial's legality. Those who knew more about the trial and the events leading up to it were less willing to support the legality of the trial, whatever image they had of Eichmann's complicity in the murder of Jews. Thus the ironic pattern emerges again of the more anti-Semitic segments of the population giving the most unqualified support to Israel's conduct in the trial.

EICHMANN'S PUNISHMENT

The study of the Eichmann trial, it will be recalled, was conducted while the jury was out, so to speak. The interviews were collected during the three-month period when the trial was in recess to allow the judges time to consider their verdict. Thus the respondents were asked to state their opinions about Eichmann's guilt and punishment without knowing the official verdict. The overwhelming verdict of respondents with an opinion was that Eichmann was guilty, as has already been reported. Among those who personally found Eichmann guilty, there was general agreement that the court would also find him guilty. There was no such agreement, however, about how Eichmann would or ought to be punished.

Respondents who gave and expected a verdict of guilty were asked two questions about his punishment: "What sentence do you think the court will impose?" "What sentence would you personally give him, were the matter up to you?" A bare majority (55 percent) said they expected the court to impose the death sentence. Twenty-six percent expected a sentence of life imprisonment, a handful (3 percent) expected some other sentence such as limited imprisonment, and 16 percent declined to offer a prediction. Were the matter up to them, only 37 percent of the respondents would personally impose the death sentence, almost half (43 percent) favored a sentence of life imprisonment. Of the balance, 11 percent favored a different sentence (two respondents favored letting Eichmann go free), and 9 percent said they did not know what sentence to impose.

The attitudes expressed by the public toward Eichmann's punishment thus did not correspond very closely with the verdict eventually handed down. Whereas Eichmann was sentenced to death by the Israeli court, only 37 percent of the respondents personally favored the death penalty. Those who did not, as might be expected, tended to be more knowledgeable about the trial and to have more reservations as to its legality. They also tended to score low in anti-Semitism.

Summarizing what has been learned thus far, Israel was most successful in winning the public to its view of Eichmann's complicity and guilt, somewhat less successful in persuading the public that it was proper for Israel to have conducted the trial, and least successful in getting the public's support for the death penalty. In all of these respects, the least educated and knowledgeable (and most anti-Semitic) segments of the population most heavily sided with the Israeli position. The central research question, however, was what effect the trial would have on public opinion. Given the educational objectives in conducting the trial, what information was it able to convey about the Nazi attitudes, and what effect did it have in influencing public attitudes toward Jews?

Impact of the Trial

The manifest purpose of the Eichmann trial was to bring a criminal to justice, but the trial was also conceived as a means of combating anti-Semitism. However painful to the survivors, a recapitulation of the unspeakable horrors suffered by the Jews would be a reminder to non-Jews everywhere of the continuing need to struggle against all manifestations of anti-Semitism, whether passive, polite, or rabid. Not only would the facts of Jewish suffering serve to justify Israel's capture of Eichmann, they would create a reservoir of sympathy for the Jewish people as a whole.

The mass media, even when they had reservations about Israel's handling of the trial, had no such qualms about the validity of the educational aims. Much of the trial was given over to documenting the facts of the "final solution," and the mass media reported sympathetically and in detail the many eyewitness accounts of Nazi depravity introduced into evidence. Editorial opinion, too, was sympathetic, and during the course of the trial almost all of the mass media, local as well as national, took occasion to underline their concern that the trial accomplish its long-run educational purposes.

It is open to question, however, whether Israel, the mass media, and responsible citizens everywhere were not guilty of wishful thinking in harboring the hope that the trial could accomplish its educational goals. The Nazi horrors when they occurred had failed to stir the conscience of a passive and indifferent world. The chance that a recapitulation of the horrors would succeed where the horrors themselves had failed seemed remote indeed. Yet the very viability of the trial as an educational instrument rested on this premise. To what extent was it warranted?

Not only past experience, but the data of the present study indicate that the educational message of the trial could not have, in any case, reached all of the public. At the time of the interviews, 16 percent were not even aware that the trial was taking place. Moreover, analysis revealed that the Eichmann trial was largely ignored by that section of the American public which does not generally follow serious news. This tends to be the less-educated and less privileged members of the public—precisely those who are most anti-Semitic and who would presumably benefit most from the educational message. Those who were well informed of the trial consisted of that handful of people who ordinarily and routinely attend to serious events, whatever their nature. If paying close attention to the trial was a necessary condition for grasping and internalizing its message, there is good reason to doubt that the educational aims of the trial could be accomplished.

While the grounds for pessimism seem overwhelming, it is also true that critics of the trial were in a minority. Most people were favorably disposed to the prosecution's case against Eichmann and to the legality of the trial. The relative absence of criticism in the general public may, of course, merely reflect an apathy with which the trial was viewed. One cannot be sure, however, and the possibility remains that people's hearts were touched by the messages of the trial, even though its factual details were not impressed on their minds. It is also possible that criticisms of the trial did not blind people to its message.

In order to test these possibilities, three questions were explored. First, to what extent did the public view the trial as in the end a good thing? Second, how much understanding of the scope and extent of the Nazi atrocities did the trial convey? Third, to what extent did the public feel greater sympathy for the Jewish people as a consequence of the trial?

GENERAL ACCEPTANCE OF THE TRIAL

After being queried on the details of the trial, respondents were asked, "Do you think it's a good thing that Eichmann was brought to trial or not so good?" The danger that the trial would have a boomerang effect was always present, and the answers to this question provide a clue as to the extent, if any, to which it occurred. Judging from the results, the effect, while present, was minor. Most respondents were disposed to feel that it was a good thing that Eichmann had been brought to trial. Seventy-seven percent of the respondents who were aware of the trial gave this response. Of the remainder, 15 percent replied negatively, and 8 percent said they did not know.

Anti-Semitism does not seem to have been a significant factor in influencing the public's response to the wisdom of holding the trial. As might be expected, however, those who disapproved of the trial were more critical of Israel's handling of it than those who approved. For example, 43 percent of the disapprovers viewed the trial as definitely illegal, as compared to only 11 percent of the approvers. Among disapprovers, only 52 percent judged Eichmann to be guilty, as against 97 percent of the approvers. Among disapprovers, finally, the dominant image of Eichmann was that of an acquiescent bureaucrat, while most approvers viewed Eichmann as a monster or zealot. Thus degree of acceptance of the trial was influenced by the public's response to the way it was conducted, and to a large extent the high degree of acceptance of the trial is a result of the public's belief that it was conducted properly.

There remains a question about the significance of these findings. Did most people view the trial favorably because they were deeply moved by the trial's message? Or was the response an essentially superficial one reflecting lack of attention to the trial and automatic acceptance of the position of a sympathetic press? Clearly, to allow a conclusion, more evidence is required than that the majority judged the trial a "good thing."

RESPONSE TO THE NAZI ATROCITIES

It remains today a disquieting fact that world opinion was not uniformly outraged by the Nazi crimes against the Jews. Examination of opinion polls conducted in the United States during that time convey the impression that, by and large, Americans were not deeply touched by the news from Nazi Germany. To some extent, people simply were unable to believe that such horrors were in fact taking place. Present too was sheer indifference to what was going on in Europe as none of America's business.

Since the end of World War II there have been several occasions for presenting to the world incontrovertible evidence of the extent and horror of the Nazi atrocities. Any lingering doubts that the Nazi persecution of the Jews was exaggerated were quickly dissipated with the end of the war as the evidence became directly accessible to investigation. At that time the results of the investigation were widely reported in the world press and in films of the concentration camps, the gas chambers, the mass burial grounds, and the pitiful condition of the few survivors.

The Nuremburg trials of 1945–49 served once more to remind the world of what had occurred and to do so with all the authority that an international tribunal commands. The facts were again given wide publicity, and the estimate of six million Jews killed was given official status on the basis of Nazi records. Until the Eichmann trial, no other occasion presented itself to communicate on a worldwide scale what the Nazis had done. The task was, in effect, turned over to the world's classrooms.

By the time of the Eichmann trial, the generation that had lived through World War II was middle-aged and older. A large proportion of the world's population was represented by those who were children or as yet unborn during the Nazi era. The trial shared in part the audience that had been exposed to the war and to the Nuremburg trials, but it was also a vehicle for reaching those who were at the time too young to have been informed by those earlier events. Thus the trial provided a unique opportunity to reeducate an older generation and to educate a newer one in the cruelties of which man is capable. How well did it succeed? It is impossible to say how many of the public were led to a better comprehension of the Nazi atrocities because of the Eichmann trial. However, it is possible to say that by the time the trial proceedings were over there was still a substantial segment of the public who thought that the Nazi persecutions were partly or mostly the Jews' own fault and who contended that the official estimate of the number of Jews killed was inflated.

The question asked in the interview concerning the degree to which the Jews were responsible for their fate was similar to one used in previous surveys. It read: "Thinking back to the treatment of the Jews by Nazi Germany before and during World War II, do you think the persecution of the Jews was mostly their own fault, partly their own fault, or not at all their own fault?" Once again, only respondents aware of the trial were asked the question. Of these, 53 percent said that the Nazi persecution was not at all the Jews' fault, but 30 percent said it was partly the Jews' fault, and 2 percent said it was mostly the Jews' fault. The remainder—15 percent—did not know. Thus after the trial 47 percent of the public either had no opinion or still believed the Jews to be partly or mostly to blame for the unmitigated horrors that befell them during the Nazi period.

Additional evidence to the effect that the trial failed to overcome the abiding propensity of many people not to face up to the reality of the Nazi horrors and, indeed, to exhibit some wish to explain them away, is provided by the responses to two questions concerning the official estimate of six million Jews killed by the Nazis. Throughout the entire trial proceedings, probably the single piece of information about the Nazi period most often repeated in the mass media was the fact that six million Jews had been annihilated. At a bare minimum, it would seem that the trial, if it was to succeed at all, had to communicate this simple fact. Yet, as has already been reported, by the time the trial proceedings had ended, only 33 percent of the public aware of the trial were able to say that the official estimate was six million. This ignorance looms larger when it is remembered that information about the official estimate had been certain for a long time before the trial began.

Communicating the official estimate is one thing, of course; persuading people to accept it is another. Respondents, after being asked what they believed the official estimate to be, were told that it was six million. They were then asked whether they thought this was too high, about right, or too low. Of the respondents who were aware of the trial, only 40 percent were willing to accept the official estimate of six million as correct. Twenty-four percent claimed that the figure was less than this, and 5 percent that it was more. Thirty-one percent said they really didn't know.

As might be expected, respondents who were more knowledgeable about the trial were also more knowledgeable about the number of Jews killed by Nazi Germany and more likely to accept the official estimate as accurate. Conversely, the less-educated and less knowledgeable members of the public were more likely to reject the six million figure. Being anti-Semitic, moreover, was found to play some part in how the figure was perceived and responded to. Anti-Semitic respondents were less likely to know the official estimate and to reject its accuracy after being informed about it.

Thus, on the important issue of communicating to the public the extent of the Nazi atrocities, the trial can only be judged as relatively unsuccessful. Most members of the public remained unaware of the official estimate of six million Jews annihilated by Nazi Germany, and most rejected the official estimate even when told about it. Less knowledgeable and more anti-Semitic respondents, in particular, exhibited these tendencies.

SYMPATHY FOR THE JEWS AND FOR ISRAEL

The final criterion on which the net impact of the trial was judged was its success in winning increased sympathy for the Jewish people and for Israel. Two questions were asked to this end: "Has the Eichmann trial made you feel more sympathetic or less sympathetic toward the Jews?" and "Has the Eichmann trial made you feel more sympathetic or less sympathetic toward Israel?"

A much larger proportion of respondents—37 percent as against 2 percent—said that the trial made them feel more rather than less sympathetic toward Jews. The ratio of favorable responses was about the same for Israel—34 percent as against 7 percent. While the alternative answer "about the same" was not included in the question, 57 percent volunteered this response with respect to Jews, 55 percent with respect to Israel. As the figures suggest, responses to the questions were highly correlated.

On the positive side, these results indicate that the trial did not produce a significant boomerang or negative effect. Moreover, in view of the perennial difficulty of engaging the public in issues they do not perceive as of direct personal concern, the fact that more than one-third of the public was moved to express greater sympathy appeared to constitute a relative success. On the negative side is the fact that a majority of the public said that the trial had no effect on their feelings either way. This result reinforces the tenor of earlier findings that by and large the public was only passively involved in the trial and what it was seeking to accomplish.

Before such a conclusion can be firmly stated, it is necessary to explore what it meant to say that one's sympathy toward the Jews "stayed the same" despite the trial. It may have meant that one was already so favorably disposed that nothing, not even the trial, could make one's attitude more positive, or it may have meant that, while there was room for improvement, the trial did not make a contribution in this direction. To separate the two clearly, it would have been necessary to have a measurement of sympathy both before and after the trial proceedings. In the absence of such comparative data, results must be interpreted with caution, yet further analysis of the data suggests that the reason the majority of people reported no improvement was not because no room for improvement existed.

Summary and Conclusions

The first step in any effort to reduce prejudice, if the Eichmann trial can be viewed as an effort to this end, is to win the attention of one's intended audience. This is easiest when the audience is a captive one and cannot escape exposure. Even here, of course, the audience has the option of closing its ears and eyes or of misinterpreting what is going on before it. The Eichmann trial had no captive audience except for those in the courtroom. If it was to reach the general public, the only channels available to it were the mass media. A spectacular achievement of the trial was the amount and quality of attention it received from the mass media over its entire course. The trial was reported in great detail, for the most part in highly sympathetic terms. If the coverage given to the trial by the mass media is any criterion, the public had more than ample opportunity to become exposed to the trial and its message.

For all the opportunity, few people availed themselves of it. The trial was not able to transcend the general tendency of people to ignore the serious news event. To be sure, only 16 percent of the public missed it entirely. At the same time only 13 percent paid enough attention to it to be able to answer correctly four elementary questions on the details of the trial and its background. Even those people did not single out the trial for special attention; they were highly educated members of the public who customarily paid attention to all serious news events.

Involving people in the trial could not have guaranteed the achievement of its educational objective. Involvement in an issue may produce a boomerang effect instead of the intended one. Nevertheless, a prerequisite for conveying the message of the trial was that the public be persuaded to pay attention to it. Judged on this criterion alone, the trial failed in large measure to achieve its purpose. Not only was the general level of attention low, but the least attentive were those most in need of hearing the trial's message—the less-educated and more anti-Semitic members of the community.

The question may be raised as to whether the apathy exhibited by the public was inevitable. Greater involvement would have been achieved had it been possible to make the trial personally more relevant to more people. It is difficult, however, to imagine anything that Israel could have done to imbue the trial with this kind of salience. Much of the public was apathetic when the Nazi persecutions were taking place. To overcome this apathy some twenty years later by reminding people of what they had allowed to happen was a remote possibility indeed.

The failure of the trial to overcome public complacency, while virtually assuring the failure of its ultimate educational objectives, did not eliminate all possibility of a positive effect. There was nothing to be hoped for, of course, from the minority who were not even aware that the trial was going on. The prospect remained, however, that in spite of their relative apathy, the majority who paid only scant attention to the trial would end up feeling more positive toward Israel and more sympathetic to the Jewish people. Moreover, there was a larger prospect that the small but elite group who did pay attention would be deeply moved and persuaded of the need to eradicate anti-Semitism.

To a surprising extent, the trial did win the sympathy of the apathetic majority. Most of them felt that the trial was a good thing, and many were moved to feel greater sympathy for Israel and for the Jewish people. Moreover, they were relatively uncritical of Israel's conduct of the trial—more so than those members of the public who were knowledgeable about the events of the trial.

Is this generally uncritical and sympathetic response to be taken seriously, or does it merely mean that the apathetic majority tends to adopt the prevailing attitude of the mass media? These people were not really involved in the drama of the trial. They were likely not to know who Eichmann was and not to have grasped the enormity of the Nazi atrocities. Their favorable response appears largely to have been a reflection of their desire to conform to the favorable attitudes they discerned in the mass media. Had the mass media adopted a negative stance, the apathetic majority might well have responded in kind. They might have acted upon their own greater anti-Semitic feelings toward Jews.

That the mass media were the instrument through which this generally positive response was elicited is thus of importance. It suggests that the mass media may have a powerful cumulative effect on issues that remain of low salience for extended periods of time. On such issues, the majority do not take the trouble to become even minimally informed so that they can arrive at an independent judgment. Rather, when it becomes appropriate for them to have an opinion, they search for clues as to what the proper opinion is. A natural source is the impression they have been absorbing almost subliminally from habitual if superficial attention to the mass media. This would appear to be the process through which the apathetic majority formed their generally favorable opinion about the trial. They were primed to form this opinion, not only by what they discerned to be the proper attitude from their limited exposure to the trial via the mass media, but by prior exposure to what may be described as a long-term propensity on the part of the mass media to present stories about Jews in a sympathetic light.

If it is generally true that the mass media have a large role in determining the climate of mass opinion on issues of low salience, then over the long run they must help to establish the perspective from which issues are evaluated when they do in fact become salient. By itself, a stimulus such as the Eichmann trial is not likely to have much effect. However, seen as one of a series of stimuli directed to establishing a sympathetic image of the Jewish people, it is of some importance that the trial did make a positive impression on most people, even though the impression lacked depth because at the time the underlying issue of anti-Semitism lacked salience.

There is always the danger that the mass media may not be persuaded to present an issue from a particular point of view. Here Israel took a calculated risk, and its success in winning the mass media to its side paid off in the positive response it obtained from the majority of the public.

CHAPTER 8

Anti-Semitism and Racial Prejudice

ALL OF THE STUDIES WHOSE RESULTS have been reported upon thus far were addressed principally to investigating anti-Semitism in America. Curiosity about whether or not what was being learned about anti-Semitism also applied to other forms of prejudice led, in a number of the studies, to parallel investigation of racial prejudice. This chapter presents the results of these studies, making comparisons, where appropriate, with the results for anti-Semitism.

As in the studies of anti-Semitism, the questions addressed in the investigations of racial prejudice bore on how much of it exists in America, where it is located in the social structure, and how it is to be accounted for. This chapter begins by presenting information on the first of these three questions. To trace the changes that have occurred in racial prejudice over time, the data from the study series on anti-Semitism have been supplemented with the results of national polls conducted by the National Opinion Research Center (NORC), the Center for Political Studies (CPS), the Gallup Organization, and Louis Harris and Associates. The next section examines the social location of racial prejudice as compared to anti-Semitism. It shows whether the same class, educational, age, and regional patterns found for anti-Semitism also exist with respect to racial prejudice.

Finally, racial prejudice and anti-Semitism are compared within two of the special populations examined in the study series—Christian laypersons and teenagers. The objective in the first instance is to determine whether the same religious factors found to be a source of anti-Semitism also contribute to racial prejudice. (They should not if the theory concerning religion and prejudice presented in Chapter 6 is correct.) The objective in the latter case

130

is to compare the nature, prevalence, and causes of the two kinds of prejudice among adolescents.

The Extent of Racial Prejudice

Racial prejudice, as anti-Semitism, was measured in the studies to be reported on in terms both of the acceptance of negative stereotypes and of tolerance for different forms of discrimination. It is also possible to make comparisons of the amount of sympathy that non-Jewish white Americans feel toward the two minorities.

ACCEPTANCE OF NEGATIVE STEREOTYPES

Blacks, like Jews, are frequent victims of negative stereotyping. The ideology of racial prejudice, however, differs substantially in its "racist" components from the ideology of anti-Semitism. Blacks are viewed as being inferior, unintelligent, unambitious, immoral, gaudy, trouble-prone, and sloppy. Such images reflect the generally poorer, lower-class existence of blacks in America. They provide a highly disparaging and contemptuous view of what blacks are like, essentially blaming deficiencies in the black character for their relative state of poverty.

Information on white acceptance of anti-black stereotypes is somewhat limited, especially for earlier periods. Existing studies show, however, that many whites believe these negative characterizations to be true. They also suggest that acceptance of these stereotypes declined between the 1940s and early 1960s but has dropped at a slower rate, if at all, since then. These trends are comparable to those found for anti-Semitism.

Earlier trends in the acceptance of antiblack beliefs are demonstrated by the responses to the following questions about black intelligence, asked of national samples of the white population on six separate occasions between 1942 and 1964: "In general, do you think blacks are as intelligent as white people? That is, can they learn just as well if they are given the same education and training?"[1]

In 1942 only 42 percent of white respondents replied that blacks are as intelligent as whites. Forty-eight percent thought blacks to be less intelligent, with the rest undecided. On a regional basis, 50 percent of non-Southern whites but only 21 percent of Southern whites said blacks were of equal intelligence.[2] The percentage of whites rejecting this stereotype rose in subsequent askings of the question. In 1964, 85 percent of non-Southern whites and 58 percent of Southern whites said blacks were of equal intelligence.

Nineteen percent said blacks were less intelligent—12 percent outside the South and 37 percent in the South.[3]

Comparable questions were not asked about other antiblack stereotypes during this period. However, national samples of whites were asked in Harris polls conducted in 1963 and again in 1971 whether or not they agreed with various negative statements about blacks. These results—shown in Table 8-1—provide an excellent summary of white attitudes during this tumultuous period in racial history. In 1963, as seen, two-thirds of all whites agreed that blacks "have less ambition," a majority thought blacks "have lower morals than whites," and close to a majority said blacks "keep untidy homes," "want to live off the handout," and "have less native intelligence." Some decline in stereotyping occurred between 1963 and 1971, but in 1971 these stereotypes were still held by substantial proportions of white Americans. A majority of whites still saw blacks as less ambitious, a central image in racist ideology. On another key stereotype, the number of whites viewing blacks as less intelligent dropped only from 39 percent to 37 percent. A large minority of whites also accepted stereotypes of blacks as immoral, living off the handout, violent, and sloppy.[4]

TABLE 8-1.   White Americans' Acceptance of Stereotypic Images of Blacks, 1963 and 1971.

Statement	1963	1971
Blacks have less ambition.	66%[a]	52%
Blacks have lower morals than whites.	55	40
Blacks want to live off the handout.	41	39
Blacks have less native intelligence.	39	37
Blacks are more violent than whites.	—[b]	36
Blacks keep untidy homes.	46	35
Blacks breed crime.	35	27
Blacks care less for the family than whites.	31	26
Blacks are inferior to white people.	31	22

[a]Percentages indicate the degree of acceptance by whites of each of the statements.
[b]Not asked in 1963.
SOURCE: National polls conducted by Louis Harris & Associates.

More recent surveys examining the acceptance of these stereotypes worded questions differently, so strict comparisons are impossible. However, whenever questions have been asked about black intelligence and ambition, a substantial minority and sometimes a majority of whites reply that blacks are unintelligent and unambitious. In a national survey conducted in 1977, for instance, white respondents were told that "on the average, blacks have worse jobs, income, and housing than white people." They were then asked which of several explanations accounted for these differences. Forty-nine percent said "because most blacks just don't have the motivation or will power to pull themselves out of poverty"; 25 percent said "because most blacks have less inborn ability to learn." By way of contrast, only 39 percent said that these differences were "mainly due to discrimination."[5]

In sum, these findings show that the acceptance of antiblack images, like anti-Semitic stereotyping, has declined since the 1940s, but that today's acceptance rate is still far from the vanishing point. As with anti-Semitism, most of this decrease seems to have taken place between the 1940s and 1960s. Strict comparisons of the prevalance of these two kinds of prejudice cannot be made since they involve different imagery and characterizations. Judging from the relative acceptance of more negative stereotypes, however, racial stereotyping appears to be more prevalent than anti-Semitic stereotyping, at least since the 1940s. More adequate comparison of the incidence of the two forms of prejudice is possible when attention is turned to the second dimension of prejudice—support for discrimination.

TOLERANCE OF DISCRIMINATION

The extent to which whites are willing to support racial discrimination has been examined on numerous occasions over the years. Since the early 1940s whites have periodically been asked their opinions about discrimination in such areas as schooling, housing, and employment. The results, when compared with similar information about discrimination against Jews, show that support for discrimination against both groups has declined sharply since the 1940s, suggesting a general decline in discriminatory attitudes over this period. However, support for discrimination against blacks was and is far more prevalent than support for discrimination against Jews. This holds true for all kinds of discrimination on which comparable evidence exists.

Trends in white attitudes toward public forms of antiblack discrimination are presented in Table 8-2. These responses show that a dramatic turnaround in white opinion has occurred since the 1940s, from a stance largely supportive of racial discrimination to one largely opposed. As will be seen, however, white Americans are more often opposed to racial discrimination in principle than in practice.

Education. Discrimination in schooling has probably been the most controversial racial issue of the recent past. Prior to 1954 it was legally permissible for school districts to maintain separate schools for whites and for blacks, and most Southern school districts (and some in the North) did so. This practice was ruled unconstitutional in 1954 in *Brown* v. *Board of Education*, ushering in a series of controversial government actions designed to enforce the principle of school integration. These efforts included the use of federal troops and federal marshals, the withholding and threatened withholding of federal funds from segregated school districts, and the busing of schoolchildren from one area to another to create more racially balanced

TABLE 8-2.   Whites' Acceptance of Racial Integration in Public Areas, 1942 to 1970s.

School Integration

"Do you think that white students and black students should go to the same or different schools?"	1942	1956	1963	1970	1977
Percent saying "the same"	30%	49%	62%	74%	85%

Percent who would object to sending their children to a school where:	Southern White Parents		
	1963	1970	1975
A few are blacks.	61%	19%	15%
Half are blacks.	78	43	38
More than half are blacks.	86	69	61
	Non-Southern White Parents		
A few are blacks.	10%	6%	3%
Half are blacks	33	24	24
More than half are blacks.	53	51	47

Housing Integration

"If a black with the same income and education as you have moved into your block would it make any difference to you?"	1942	1956	1963	1972
Percent saying "no difference"	35%	51%	61%	84%

"Blacks have a right to live wherever they can afford to."	1964	1976
Percent agreeing	57%	85%

White people have a right to keep blacks out of their neighborhoods, and blacks should respect that right."	1963	1970	1977
Percent disagreeing	44%	50%	56%

Employment

"Do you think blacks should have as good a chance as white people to get any kind of job?"	1944	1963	1972
Percent saying "yes"	42%	82%	96%

Public Transportation

"Do you think there should be separate sections for blacks in street cars and buses?"	1942	1956	1963	1970
Percent saying "no"	44%	60%	77%	88%

Public Facilities

"Do you think that blacks should have the right to use the same parks, restaurants, and hotels as white people?"	1963	1970
Percent saying "yes"	71%	85%

SOURCES: See notes pertaining to the discussion of this table.

schools. For many years, these federal actions were directed primarily at the South and were generally favored by whites outside the South and opposed by most Southern whites. Beginning in the late 1960s governmental actions increasingly were directed toward Northern schools, with a corresponding hardening of attitudes among Northern whites.

The first question in Table 8-2 is one of several asked by NORC of a national sample of the population at repeated intervals over the years. In 1942 and several times thereafter, white respondents were asked whether they thought that "white students and black students should go to the same or different schools." In 1942 two out of three whites said they should go to different schools. The percentage saying "the same," however, has risen steadily over the years, from 30 percent in 1942, to 62 percent in 1963, to 85 percent in 1977.[6] Very few whites today support the principle of racially segregated schools.

The responses to the second question provide some indication of how whites feel about actually sending their children to school with blacks. It asked white parents whether they would object to sending their children to a school where "a few are blacks," where "half are blacks," and where "more than half are blacks." Consistent with the above patterns, by the mid-1970s few whites said they would object to sending their children to schools where there are "a few" blacks. This represents a major change in attitudes among Southern whites since 1963, when 61 percent said they would object. About one in four white parents, however, object to sending their children to schools where half of the other students are blacks, while half object when the majority are black.[7] Non-Southern whites are only slightly more supportive of school integration under these circumstances than are Southern whites. About half would object to sending their children to schools where they would constitute a minority—a situation found in many cities outside of the South.

It is not necessarily inconsistent, of course, for white parents to be against segregated schools and yet be reluctant to send their children to schools where the number of black students is large. Such reluctance, however, shows that there are limits to white acceptance of the implications of integrated schooling.

Since the late 1960s school busing has been a primary means of achieving more racially balanced schools. Polls show that this policy has been consistently and overwhelmingly opposed by whites. Depending upon the wording of the question, between 75 and 90 percent of whites have regularly taken an antibusing position in opinion surveys.[8] Since school busing is an important instrument of school integration, such opposition might be taken as a sign of antiblack prejudice. That there can be other reasons to be against school busing, however, is suggested by the fact that a majority of blacks also oppose it. They do so by lesser margins than whites and support many of the objectives associated with busing; nevertheless, blacks also are largely opponents of school busing.[9]

Housing. White attitudes toward discrimination in housing follow similar patterns. In the 1940s whites widely accepted the idea that blacks should live in separate sections of the community and should be kept out of white neighborhoods.[10] As the next three items in Table 8-2 show, the distribution of white attitudes has virtually reversed since then. In 1942 almost two in three whites said they would object if a black person, even of the same income and education, were to move into their block. The percentage saying it would make no difference, however, rose from 35 percent in 1942 to 84 percent in 1972.[11] By the mid-1970s most whites had come to accept the principle that "blacks have a right to live wherever they can afford to."[12]

White opposition grows, however, when the principle of housing integration is to be put into practice. White respondents have on several occasions been asked whether they agree or disagree that "white people have a right to keep blacks out of their neighborhoods, and blacks should respect that right." As Table 8-2 shows, opinions shifted only slightly in a pro-integrationist direction on this question between 1963 and 1977. In the former year, a slight majority agreed with this position; in the latter year, a slight majority disagreed.[13] Whites are largely opposed, as other polls show, to laws that would make it illegal to discriminate against blacks in the selling of private homes.[14] They are even more firmly opposed to programs designed to encourage blacks to buy homes in white suburbs, whether these programs are government-sponsored or private and voluntary in nature.[15]

As with schooling, then, there has been a dramatic turnaround in white attitudes toward housing discrimination from a pro-segregation to a pro-integration position. At the same time, many whites remain reluctant to give up what they conceive to be their right to keep blacks out of their neighborhoods, and most whites oppose laws that would promote residential desegregation.

Employment. Much the same patterns are found in the next item in Table 8-2, discrimination in employment. In the 1940s a majority of whites rejected the principle that blacks should have an equal chance in getting any kind of job and opposed government actions to require nondiscrimination in hiring.[16] By the early 1960s, however, white opinion again had reversed itself. More than four in five whites agreed that blacks should have as good a chance to get any kind of job, and a slightly larger proportion favored laws requiring employers to hire people without regard to color or race.[17] By the early 1970s nearly all white Americans accepted the principle of nondiscrimination in employment.

Discrimination in employment was thus rejected at a somewhat earlier date than discrimination in schooling or housing. As in the previous two instances, however, white support decreases when it comes to government actions to provide employment opportunities for blacks. Most whites oppose affirmative action policies in employment which give blacks "special preference" or "extra consideration."[18] They are also against the idea that, because blacks were discriminated against in the past, they deserve special treatment in job placement or in school admittance today.[19]

Public Transportation and Facilities. Other realms in which black Americans have been discriminated against in the past are in their use of public transportation and such public facilities as parks, restaurants, and hotels. The civil rights movement began in the early 1960s largely as an effort to desegregate restaurants and public transportation. As seen in Table 8-2, white Americans held discriminatory attitudes in these areas as in others under examination, but by the mid-to-late 1960s the vast majority had come to accept the principle of integration here as well. These issues largely affected the South, and it is among Southern whites that attitudes have correspondingly changed the most.[20]

Taken together, the information in Table 8-2 shows that a remarkable turnaround in white attitudes toward public forms of discrimination has occurred since the 1940s. In early polls a majority of whites were opposed to racial integration in all five of these areas. By the 1960s whites had largely come to accept the norm of nondiscrimination in employment, public transportation, and public facilities; by the 1970s they had largely accepted this norm in schooling and housing. Very few whites today say that blacks should be openly discriminated against in any of these public areas.

These trends in opinion parallel, in a general way, those found for anti-Jewish discrimination. Support for discrimination against Jews was also relatively high in the 1940s and dropped progressively thereafter. It is apparent, however, that fewer Americans hold discriminatory attitudes toward Jews than toward blacks, at least over the period for which information exists. By the mid-1960s, as seen in Chaper 1, barely any support existed for anti-Jewish discrimination in any of these areas. In housing, for example, only 3 percent of non-Jews in the early 1960s said it would make a difference to them to have a Jewish neighbor, while on another question 7 percent stated that they would prefer not to have Jewish neighbors. In contrast, 33 percent of whites at the time said they would object to having a black person move onto the same block.[21]

White Americans, while mostly agreeing today that blacks should not be discriminated against, are largely opposed to many specific policies or actions that might put the principle of nondiscrimination into effect. By lopsided margins, they are against school busing, fair housing legislation, and affirmative action policies in hiring and school admissions.

These findings suggest a reluctance on the part of whites to engage in more personal or intimate forms of contact with blacks—a subject to which attention is now turned.

Intermarriage. White attitudes toward racial intermarriage have undergone changes similar to those noted above but remain, on the whole, decidedly negative. Where change has most occurred is with respect to laws (now unconstitutional) making it illegal for a black person to marry a white person. While most whites once favored such miscegenation laws, a majority now oppose them. Opposition rose from 36 percent in 1963, to 49 percent in 1970, to 71 percent in 1977.[22]

White Americans thus largely oppose overt or legal discrimination against blacks in this area as in others. Relatively few whites, however, express approval or support for racial intermarriage. In 1972 only 29 percent of a national sample of whites said they approved of intermarriage—up from 2 percent in 1958 and 20 percent in 1968.[23] In a national survey conducted in 1977 more than three-quarters of the white respondents said it would make them feel "very" or "somewhat" uneasy if a close relative were planning to marry a black person, while nine in ten agreed that "you can expect *special* problems with marriages between blacks and whites."[24]

It was pointed out in the discussion of intermarriage between Jews and non-Jews that one could oppose intermarriage without being prejudiced—that other values often affected opinions on this issue as well. The same is true in this instance, with many blacks also opposing or seeing special problems in intermarriage. Nevertheless, disapproval of intermarriage between blacks and whites is much higher than disapproval of intermarriage between Jews and non-Jews.

Social Club Discrimination. White attitudes toward social club discrimination follow the same patterns. In a recent national survey, white respondents were asked: "If you and your friends belonged to a social club that would not let blacks join, would you try to change the rules so that blacks could join?" Thirty-nine percent said yes, 54 percent no; the rest were undecided. Those who said they would try to get the rules changed were then asked if they would resign if they were unsuccessful "even if their friends didn't." Forty-two percent of this group said they would—only 16 percent of all whites in the survey.[25]

Again, such attitudes are not necessarily indicative of antiblack prejudice; other values might also affect one's views on the subject. Opposition to social club discrimination, however, is much higher when it is directed against Jews than against blacks.[26]

A Black as a Dinner Guest. White feelings toward having personal relations with blacks can be gauged on one additional measure—having a black person home to dinner. White respondents have on several occasions been asked the following question: "How strongly would you object if a member of your family wanted to bring a black friend home to dinner? Would you object strongly, mildly, or not at all?" The proportion of whites saying they would "not object at all" rose from 49 percent in 1963 to 71 percent in 1977. In this last poll, 11 percent said they would object "strongly," 16 percent "mildly."[27]

While fewer whites today object to having a black as a dinner guest, one in four still think that way. It is difficult to interpret this response as other than prejudice.

Political Discrimination. The final dimension of prejudice to be considered is represented by a willingness to engage in political discrimination—to favor disqualification of blacks from holding public office. This dimension has traditionally been measured by asking respondents whether they would vote for a qualified black for President. In 1958 only 38 percent of whites said they would vote for a black presidential candidate. Subsequently, this figure rose to 50 percent in 1961, 70 percent in 1973, and 75 percent in 1977.[28]

Support for political discrimination against blacks has thus likewise decreased and at a rapid rate. In comparison with Jews, however, black Americans are again the more frequent target of discriminatory attitudes. As seen in Chapter 1, the percentage of non-Jews saying they would vote for a qualified Jew for President was 62 percent in 1958, 80 percent in 1965, and 86 percent in 1969.

SYMPATHY WITH THE BLACK PLIGHT

A somewhat different perspective on these two forms of prejudice is provided when comparisons are drawn between the sympathy expressed for difficulties experienced by the two minorities. As was pointed out previously, one common problem in the elimination of prejudice is that the majority often has little sympathy for the victims of prejudice. Imbued with the stereotypes of prejudice, they often feel that the victimized minority is undeserving of help or has brought the problem upon itself. Those in the majority, moreover, may have little association with minority group members and thus not be personally aware of the debilitating effects of prejudice. They may feel that the minority group is not being treated so badly and reject claims that the situation needs improving.

Various questions about Jews show that sympathy for the Jewish plight is not as strong as one might suppose. On balance, however, there is no doubt that non-Jewish Americans think about Jews in generally sympathetic and positive ways. They are sympathetic toward Jews because of the historical suffering of Jews; they see Jews as an especially warm and friendly, industrious, and intelligent people; and, in situations such as the Eichmann trial, they show a proclivity to take the side of Jews, even when not well informed.

In contrast, white responses to any number of questions reveal a lack of sympathy toward blacks and toward black demands for racial progress. This has been a consistent finding throughout the period in which polls have been conducted, showing little change over time.

This lack of sympathy can best be illustrated through a series of questions asking whites how blacks are being treated in America. Whites consistently reject the notion that blacks are being treated poorly. NORC, for example, has asked a national sample of white Americans whether they thought "most blacks in the United States are being treated fairly or unfairly" on at least three separate occasions. In each instance, a large majority of whites replied that blacks were being treated "fairly": 66 percent in 1944, 66 percent again in 1946, and 69 percent in 1956.[29] Two later NORC polls asked whites how well they thought blacks were being treated in the country—whether "the same as whites are," "not very well," or "badly." In 1967, 72 percent of whites said "the same"; in 1968, 70 percent gave this response.[30]

White attitudes in more recent years are illustrated by responses to relevant questions asked in several national Harris polls dealing with discrimination. It might be thought that white Americans would readily acknowledge the existence of racial discrimination in America, so thoroughly has it been documented and reported upon. Most whites do not, however, at least in specific instances. Harris asked national samples in 1969, 1972, and 1977 whether they thought blacks were discriminated against in such things as "decent housing," "full equality," "white-collar office jobs," "fair wages," and "quality education in the schools." The predominant response in all three years was that blacks were not being discriminated against. (Needless to say, this was not the perception of black respondents asked these same questions.) The percentage of whites acknowledging discrimination in these areas, moreover, declined noticeably in 1977.[31]

Still other questions indicate that white Americans have mixed feelings about racial integration and respond negatively to black demands for better treatment. Whites, for example, have regularly been asked whether they favor integration, segregation, or some in-between policy. The main tendency both in Harris and CPS surveys is to choose the middle category. In 1976, for example, Harris found that 28 percent of whites favored "full racial integration," 12 percent "separation of the races," and 48 percent "integration in some areas of life."[32] Roughly the same responses have been given in CPS surveys using slightly different wording.[33]

Whites have also been asked their opinions about the pace of racial change in the country and have consistently replied that it is moving "too fast." Harris asked respondents whether they felt "that blacks in this country have tried to move too fast, too slow, or at about the right pace." The proportion of whites saying "too fast" was 63 percent in 1972 and 55 percent in 1977.[34] The CPS asked respondents whether "the civil rights people" have been moving too fast, too slowly, or about right. Sixty-eight percent said "too fast" in 1964 and again in 1968, when the civil rights movement was most active. Thereafter the percentage dropped, reaching 43 percent in 1976.[35]

NORC, finally, has regularly asked respondents whether they agree or disagree with the statement, "Blacks shouldn't push themselves where they're not wanted." In every instance, a large majority of whites has agreed. The percentage taking a pro-integrationist position by disagreeing, moreover, has remained relatively constant over the years: 25 percent in 1963, 16 percent in 1970, 23 percent in 1972, and 26 percent in 1977.[36] These findings again suggest a more negative reaction during times of civil rights advocacy.[37]

In sum, while white Americans have come to accept the principle of non-discrimination, they have not become much more sympathetic toward the plight of blacks. During all the years in which surveys on the topic have been taken, the predominant response has been unsympathetic. Most whites deny that blacks are being treated unfairly, reject the notion that blacks are discriminated against, favor only partial integration, think that blacks have tried to move too fast, and feel that blacks should stay out of places where they're not wanted. Such beliefs appear to have changed little over the years surveyed. Whites were somewhat more likely to acknowledge the existence of discrimination during the period of civil rights militancy, but they were also more likely to respond negatively to the civil rights movement itself.

All of this evidence shows that racial prejudice is more prevalent than anti-Semitism in America. This is not to underplay the amount of anti-Semitism that exists. As has been demonstrated throughout this book, a substantial minority of Americans are prejudiced against Jews. Relatively, however, over the entire period covered by opinion polls—from the early 1940s until the present—and on all existing measures, more racial prejudice is revealed than anti-Semitism. Why racial prejudice should be so pervasive in America is a subject beyond the scope of this book. Historically, however, racism has deep roots in the attitudes of early settlers, the institution of slavery, and efforts to keep freed blacks in subordinate roles. It has been intimately connected with and reinforced by economic, social, cultural, and educational practices in this country. Anti-Semitic prejudice, in contrast, developed much later in American history and was largely transported from Europe. While taken up with vigor in this country, especially in the 1920s and 1930s, it has not been as fully absorbed into the institutional mainstream of American life.

In a more contemporary sense, it is apparent that class prejudice contributes substantially to the greater incidence of racial prejudice among Americans. Blacks are relatively poor in this country, while Jews are relatively well-to-do. Other factors aside, Americans are usually more willing to interact with those of the same or higher social status than themselves and less willing to have social relations with those of lower class standing. Such class feelings undoubtedly lie behind the reluctance of whites to have more intimate contacts with blacks and to have blacks move into their neighborhoods or go to school with their children.

This class factor is reflected in the imagery of anti-Jewish and antiblack beliefs. The ideology of anti-Semitism recognizes the accomplishments and power of Jews but explains this success in negative terms, as somehow deviously gained. As a result, non-Jews often have mixed or contradictory attitudes toward Jews. They admire Jews for their achievements but view these attainments as tainted or ill-gotten. With blacks, no such equivocation exists. Racist imagery portrays black Americans as possessing lower-class traits and blames deficiences in the black character for this condition. Blacks are poor because they are unintelligent, lazy, unambitious, disrespectful of property, and wasteful in their consumption. If such behavioral patterns are accepted as factual, it follows that blacks themselves are responsible for deprived conditions, not whites or American society generally. Blacks are thus to be given little sympathy for their plight as an underprivileged minority. If they would take advantage of the opportunities available to them—work harder and follow the Protestant ethic—they could lift themselves out of poverty and share in the affluence of American life.

Racist ideology is thus reinforced and strengthened by class ideology. As a result, prejudice toward blacks remains deep, pervasive, and stubbornly resistant to change. White Americans today largely reject overt discrimination against blacks but oppose actions that might produce greater racial equality or integration.

The Social Location of Racial Prejudice

Further insight into these two kinds of prejudice is obtained by comparing their locations in the social structure. How is racial prejudice distributed along the social dimensions examined for anti-Semitism in Chapter 2—education, age, religion, region, and so forth? Do the same kinds of people who are prejudiced toward Jews tend also to be prejudiced toward blacks?

SOCIAL CLASS AND EDUCATION

Americans of lower SES hold the most prejudiced attitudes toward blacks, as is true for Jews. It is a lack of education, moreover, that is again primarily responsible for these class patterns of prejudice. As with anti-Semitism, the statistical associations of income and occupation to antiblack prejudice are largely explained by education.[38]

This tendency for less-educated Americans to be racially prejudiced can be demonstrated by figures from the national study. Outside the South, 58 percent of grade-school-educated whites scored high in racial prejudice, as compared with 41 percent of the high-school-educated, 25 percent of those with some college, and 16 percent of the college-educated. In the South, the comparable figures at each educational level were, respectively, 87, 77, 50, and 43 percent. Similar results have been obtained in other surveys of racial prejudice conducted both before and after this one.[39]

A lack of education is thus a prime factor in racial prejudice, as it is in anti-Semitic prejudice. The main difference is that racism is more prevalent at all educational levels, as it is in the population at large. Education apparently provides people with the cognitive skills and information to reject prejudice in general. It makes them more aware of minority group differences, of the socio-economic history that produced them, and of the dangers of prejudiced thinking. Conversely, those with little schooling are likely to lack such knowledge and skills. They will be more likely to accept prejudiced beliefs when exposed to them and to accept them as true.

The effect of education in discouraging prejudice in general helps to explain the decline in antiblack and anti-Jewish beliefs over the last several decades. Americans have, as a whole, become much more educated during this period. In the 1940s the average American had between eight and nine years of education; by the late 1970s the average American had between twelve and thirteen years.[40] American schools have also given greater attention to minority group issues in recent years and have rejected such formerly taught theories as that blacks are biologically inferior. In a broad sense, it can be said that antiprejudice, antidiscriminatory norms have become a part of the official or ideal norms of the country over this period. And the schools are their main purveyors as such.

Education, of course, is not the only element involved in prejudice. Other factors have contributed both to the decline of the two kinds of prejudice and to their maintenance. Furthermore, it is not necessarily true that education always produces enlightened minds or that the schools could not do better in reducing the vestiges of prejudice. How the schools might improve their efforts is discussed in the concluding chapter.

AGE

Given these common links to education, it is not surprising to find that racial prejudice and anti-Semitism are distributed similarly along other social dimensions as well. One of these is age. Opinion polls have consistently found that younger Americans are less racially prejudiced than their elders, as was the case with anti-Semitism.[41] In the national study, for example, strong generational patterns in racial prejudice were found among both non-Southern and Southern whites. Outside of the South, 29 percent of those under the age of thirty-five scored high in racial prejudice, as compared with 37 percent of those between thirty-five and fifty-four, and 55 percent of those fifty-five or older. In the South, the comparable figures were, respectively, 63, 71, and 81 percent.

As with anti-Semitism, education explains much of this age variation in racism.[42] Younger Americans are less racially prejudiced than their elders primarily because they are better-educated. They have spent more years in school and, in general, have been exposed to more racially enlightened values during those years.

RELIGION

It was reported in Chapter 2 that Catholics are somewhat less prejudiced than Protestants, as a whole, toward Jews. The same tendency exists for racial prejudice.[43] Less racially prejudiced yet, however, are Jews—a finding consistent with the images of black respondents reported in Chapter 4.[44] It would appear that being objects of discrimination themselves makes the members of the two ethnic minorities more aware of and sensitive toward prejudice. As reported earlier, Jews in particular have traditionally been strong supporters of civil rights.

One way in which religion affects anti-Semitism is through the configuration of theological beliefs examined in Chapter 6. Whether or not these same religious orientations produce racial prejudice is examined later in this chapter.

REGION

It is with respect to region, as would be expected, that anti-Semitism and racial prejudice differ most strongly in social location. Racism developed out of the institution of slavery in the South and from white efforts to keep freed blacks in subordinate positions. Until recently, most civil rights efforts were aimed at alleviating discriminatory practices in the South—outlawing segregated schools, integrating public transportation facilities and restaurants and motels, and assisting blacks to register and vote.

The regional differences in racial prejudice have been demonstrated in figures reported throughout this chapter. These differences are considerable, as indicated both on the individual questions examined above and on various more refined measures of racial prejudice. In the national study, for example, 72 percent of Southern whites scored high on an index of racial prejudice as compared to 40 percent of whites living outside the South. On a measure of pro-integration attitudes developed at NORC, the index scores of Southern white respondents to a national survey are about half those of non-Southern whites.[45]

Polls show that these regional differences in racial prejudice have narrowed somewhat over the years. In large part, this is because there was much more room for improvement in the South than outside it. In 1942, for example, only 2 percent of Southern whites approved of school integration, while only 4 percent supported integration in public transportation. Most non-Southern whites also held discriminatory attitudes on these issues but not nearly to the same degree.[46] More recently, white attitudes outside the South appear to have stiffened as the center of the civil rights controversy has shifted to that region of the country. As non-Southern whites have faced black demands for greater integration in housing, education, and employment, they have taken positions on racial issues more closely resembling those of Southern whites.

Still, racial prejudice in the South remains considerably higher even today than racial prejudice elsewhere. This remains true on all or almost all measures of racial belief. It will be recalled that anti-Semitism was also found to be more prevalent in the South than outside of it. Relatively, however, region is a considerably more important factor in racial prejudice than it is in anti-Semitism.

URBAN–RURAL RESIDENCE

Urban–rural differences in racism followed the same patterns existing for anti-Semitism. Prejudice toward blacks is, as a whole, more common in rural areas of the country than in urban areas.[47] It is especially in the rural South, moreover, that prejudice toward blacks is prevalent. As with anti-Semitism, the relatively low levels of education among rural Southern whites account for some, although not all, of these differences in racial prejudice.

ETHNICITY

Ethnicity is difficult to measure in national surveys, because only a few members of each ethnic group are likely to be included in the typical national sample. What evidence exists, however, suggests that racial prejudice and anti-Semitism are distributed about the same among different ethnic groups. Some ethnic groups, however, appear to score relatively higher on both forms of prejudice than others, but, given the size of the samples on which the comparisons are made, no firm conclusions on the importance of the ethnic factor are warranted at present.

SEX

Sexual differences in racial prejudice, finally, are slight, as they are in anti-Semitism. No significant differences exist in the extent of racial prejudice or anti-Semitism between men and women.

For all their differences, then—in history, in content, and in degree— anti-Jewish and antiblack prejudice are very much alike in social location. Both kinds of prejudice are found disproportionately at lower socio-economic levels, among the less-educated, and in older age groups. They also tend to be more prevalent among Protestants than Catholics, in the South than the North, and in rural as opposed to urban areas.

Such findings suggest that a considerable overlap is likely to exist between the holding of anti-Semitic and antiblack beliefs. The same people who are prejudiced toward Jews are apt to be prejudiced toward blacks as well.

Table 8-3 shows the overlap between anti-Semitic and antiblack prejudice found in the national study. Respondents scoring high on one measure of prejudice, it is seen, are likely to score high on the other. Among anti-Semites, roughly three in four are also racially prejudiced. Among those scoring high in racism, about four in seven also score high in anti-Semitic prejudice. In total, 26 percent of Americans held prejudiced beliefs toward both minorities, 45 percent toward neither. These figures are to some degree arbitrary, since they are based upon estimates of prejudice. Nevertheless, they leave no doubt that Americans who are prejudiced toward one minority tend to be prejudiced toward the other as well. Alternatively, Americans free of one kind of prejudice are usually free of the other.

TABLE 8-3.   Relationship of Antiblack and Anti-Semitic Prejudice, Non-Southern and Southern.

	Outside the South	South	Total
Neither antiblack nor anti-Semitic	48%[a]	25%	45%
Antiblack only	18	35	20
Anti-Semitic only	12	3	9
Both antiblack and anti-Semitic	22	37	26
(N) =	(1,173)	(444)	(1,617)

[a]Percentages indicate the proportion of whites scoring high on the index of antiblack beliefs and the index of anti-Semitic belief.
SOURCE: Reproduced from Gertrude J. Selznick and Stephen Steinberg, *The Tenacity of Prejudice* (New York: Harper & Row, 1969), p. 182.

To a considerable extent, it is lack of education that is responsible for these common tendencies. The less-educated have a weak resistance to racial prejudice as well as to anti-Semitism; they possess fewer cognitive skills with which to detect prejudice and to reject it. This is not to suggest, however, that anti-Semitism and racism are entirely interchangeable phenomena or are identically caused. They grew out of unique historical circumstances, are expressed in different ideological languages, and have some independent sources. One source of anti-Semitism, presumed in this series of studies not to be a factor in racial prejudice, is Christianity. A report on a test made of that assumption is presented next.

Christian Beliefs and Racial Prejudice

The racial attitudes of white Americans were examined in the study of Christian laypersons, whose findings on the subject of anti-Semitism have already been presented in Chapter 6, for two reasons.[49] One objective was simply to learn how extensive racial prejudice is among contemporary churchgoers living in a cosmopolitan urban setting (recall that this study was conducted among churchgoers living in the San Francisco metropolitan area). A second objective was to test further the thesis that belief in an orthodox-particularistic version of Christian faith is a still operating source of contemporary anti-Semitism. If that theory is correct, the same religious factors should *not* produce racial prejudice. The religious hostility directed against Jews for rejecting Jesus as savior should not be directed against black Americans, since they are predominantly Christian. If this "null" hypothesis is true, it would increase confidence in the findings concerning Christian beliefs and anti-Semitism.

Table 8-4 shows how these Christian laypersons responded to several questions asked about race. These churchgoers, it is seen, overwhelmingly accept what might be called the "moral clichés" of Christian brotherhood. They agreed that " 'love thy neighbor' means that we should treat all races the same," and that "blacks ought to have the same rights and opportunities as others." When it came to putting these general principles into practice, however, the situation was different. Significant numbers of these laypersons perceived blacks in stereotypic terms as sloppy, unintelligent, and immoral and were reluctant to have blacks as neighbors and, to a lesser degree, in their churches and schools. These expressions of antiblack sentiment are similar to those of nonchurchgoers studied at the same time. Being a Christian is no more a guarantee against racial prejudice than against anti-Semitism.

But do Christian beliefs actively promote racial prejudice? More specifically, does that configuration of orthodox-particularistic beliefs examined in Chapter 6 produce racial prejudice, as it does anti-Semitism? The answer to these questions is no. Racial prejudice was distributed relatively uniformly across the church groups studied—unlike anti-Semitic prejudice, which was most prevalent in the more conservative denominations and in the sects.[50] Likewise, no relation was found between the index of religious bigotry, which so powerfully predicted anti-Semitism, and racial prejudice. Religous orthodoxy, particularism, and hostility do not generate racism as they do anti-Semitism.

TABLE 8-4.   Christian Laypersons' Acceptance of Clichés About Brotherhood and Their Application to Issues of Consequence.

	Protestants	Catholics
Moral Clichés		
" 'Love thy neighbor' means that we should treat all races the same."	91%[a]	91%
"Blacks ought to have the same rights and opportunities as others."	91	88
Issues of Consequence		
Antiblack imagery		
"Most black neighborhoods are rundown because blacks simply don't take care of property."	50	53
"It's too bad, but in general, blacks have inferior intelligence to whites."	30	29
"It's a shame that blacks are so immoral."	26	28
Antiblack discrimination		
"Suppose you owned your own home and several black families moved into your block. Would you be apt to move elsewhere provided you could get a fair price for your home?" (percent who would probably move)	42	40
"It would probably be better for blacks and whites to attend separate churches."	29	15
"It would probably be better all around if blacks went to separate schools."	22	18

[a]Except where indicated, percentages refer to the proportion of Christian laypersons agreeing with these statements.

SOURCE: Adapted from Charles Y. Glock and Rodney Stark, *Christian Beliefs and Anti-Semitism* (New York: Harper & Row, 1966), p. 168.

That such doctrinal beliefs are unrelated to racial prejudice confirms their unique link to anti-Semitism. Jews as non-Christians and disbelievers in Jesus as savior are special objects of religious enmity. The same hostile feelings do not attach themselves to blacks, who are largely Christians themselves.

Racial Prejudice Among the Young

Antiblack and anti-Semitic prejudice can be compared in one final way—in the eyes of the young. The teenagers whose anti-Semitic beliefs were reported upon in Chapter 5 were also studied for their antiblack beliefs. All of the questions asked about their attitudes toward Jews were also asked about blacks. The results afford a unique opportunity to compare the prevalence and content of the two kinds of prejudice as they exist among teenagers, as well as to examine their respective social locations and causes.

The study of adolescent prejudice, it will be recalled, was conducted within three communities in the Northeast, each with student populations from 14 to 16 percent black. Included in the study were all youth in the eighth, tenth, and twelfth grades.[51]

ANTIBLACK IMAGES

The first method used to measure prejudice was to ask these teenage respondents whether they agreed with various stereotypic statements about blacks and about Jews. Both positive and negative statements were included, as were traditionally antiblack and traditionally anti-Semitic imagery.[52]

Table 8-5 reports the average proportion of white, non-Jewish teenagers in the three communities accepting stereotypes as true of blacks as compared to the proportion accepting them as true of Jews. The results reveal a great deal about the prejudiced beliefs of American youth. On the positive items, these young respondents clearly held more favorable images of Jews than of blacks. Most notably, a large majority of these teenagers agreed that Jewish students are intelligent (78 percent) and concerned about getting good grades (73 percent), while relatively few described their black classmates in these terms. The only positive stereotype disproportionately associated with being black is having a lot of athletic ability.

TABLE 8-5.   Teenagers' Images of Jews and Blacks.

	Average Rate of Acceptance[a]		Average Rate of Overacceptance[b]	
	Blacks	Jews	Blacks	Jews
Positive Stereotypes				
Athletic (have a lot of athletic ability)	91%	40%	51%	
School spirit (have a lot of school spirit; know what's going on around school and take part in activities)	49	74		25%
Intelligent (are quite intelligent and well informed; think clearly about things)	31	78		47
Ambitious (are very concerned with getting good grades; are always working for A's)	20	73		53

TABLE 8-5.   Continued.

	Average Rate of Acceptance[a]		Average Rate of Overacceptance[b]	
	Blacks	Jews	Blacks	Jews
Negative stereotypes				
Troublemakers (frequently in trouble with school authorities and the police; often break rules and laws)	81	20	61	
Gaudy (often dress in a loud and flashy way)	75	38	37	
Vain (are loud and show-offy; will do almost anything to gain recognition and draw attention to themselves)	68	52	16	
Sloppy (do not keep their property and possessions in good condition)	62	18	44	
Untrustworthy (are likely to be untrustworthy; lie and cheat more than others)	57	22	35	
Bossy (force their wishes and beliefs on others; are bossy)	57	45	12	
Quitters (give up on hard problems easily; never seem to try very hard in school)	56	18	38	
Pushy (try to push into groups where they are not really wanted)	56	39	17	
Selfish (are likely to be selfish; concerned only for themselves or their own group)	52	49	3	
Conceited (think they are better than other students; easily develop a superiority complex)	50	55		5
Unfriendly (are unfriendly; do not mix with others; go around with their own group)	46	38	8	
Powerful (have too much to say about what goes on in school; run pretty much everything)	22	53		31
Sly (often try to "get ahead" by "buttering up" the teachers)	22	50		28

[a]Average rate of acceptance is the percentage of white non-Jewish students in the three communities agreeing with these statements.

[b]Average rate of overacceptance is the difference between the average acceptance of these statements as they apply to blacks and to Jews.

SOURCE: Based upon Tables 2 and 74 in Charles Y. Glock, Robert Wuthnow, Jane Allyn Piliavin, and Metta Spencer, *Adolescent Prejudice* (New York: Harper & Row, 1975), pp. 7, 134.

On the negative items, a parallel pattern prevailed. A majority of the teenagers agreed that ten of these thirteen stereotypes were applicable to black students. They perceived blacks as being troublemakers, gaudy, vain, sloppy, untrustworthy, bossy, quitters, pushy, selfish, and conceited. Anti-black attitudes, moreover, were considerably more common than anti-Jewish attitudes. In comparison with Jewish students, black youth were especially viewed as being troublemakers—as "frequently in trouble with school authorities and the police" and often breaking "rules and laws." Eighty-one percent of these teenagers described their black peers in these terms, while only 20 percent associated such characteristics with Jews. Blacks were also disproportionately seen as not keeping "their property and possessions in good condition"; as giving up on "hard problems" easily and never seeming to "try very hard in school"; as dressing in "loud and flashy" ways; and as "likely to be untrustworthy" and lying and cheating more than others.

The teenagers polled are thus considerably more prejudiced in their attitudes toward blacks than toward Jews. The average rate of acceptance for all thirteen negative statements was 54 percent for blacks and 38 percent for Jews. Similarly, a greater percentage of the teenagers scored as prejudiced on the index of antiblack beliefs than on the index of anti-Semitic beliefs (both of which were based upon the same eight items). Taking as prejudiced those with scores of 4 through 7, 82 percent of the students in Commutertown were judged to be racially prejudiced, as were 73 percent of those in Oceanville and 84 percent in Central City. On equivalent criteria, the number of anti-Semites was set at 66 percent in Commutertown, 53 percent in Oceanville, and 41 percent in Central City. In all three communities studied, then, racial prejudice is more prevalent than anti-Semitism.

These teenage patterns of prejudice thus correspond fairly closely with those found among adults. As with adults, negative stereotyping is more prevalent in relation to blacks, while favorable images are more often held of Jews. Also as with adults, it is traditional imagery that is most often accepted. Blacks are seen as less intelligent and less ambitious and as trouble-prone, gaudy, sloppy, and untrustworthy. Jews are seen as disproportionately powerful, sly, and conceited, and also as being vain, selfish, bossy, and pushy.

SOCIAL DISTANCE

White non-Jewish teenagers' feelings about interacting with black students were measured in the same way as their feelings about interacting with Jewish students—by means of a social distance scale. This scale, it will be remembered from Chapter 5, was created by asking respondents whether they would be willing to interact with a student, in this case a black student, in situations of varying degrees of intimacy. As before, these scale questions were repeated for "a student in the college preparatory program who is black and is getting B's" and "a student in the vocational program who is black and is getting failing grades."

When the hypothetical student is successful, these teenaged respondents were generally willing to have social relations with a black classmate. The most disapproved activity was having a black student date one's sibling—rejected by just over half of the white non-Jewish youth. Roughly a third also expressed unwillingness to have a successful black student home to dinner, as a close friend, as a member of the same club, or as a member of the same committee. These rates of social rejection were not nearly as high as the rate of antiblack stereotyping. Indeed, they were only slightly higher than when the successful student named was Jewish.

When the hypothetical student was unsuccessful—in the vocational program and getting failing grades—the rate of social rejection was much greater. Nearly all of the students (96 percent) were unwilling to have a low-status black student date their brother or sister. More than three-quarters were likewise unwilling to have such a student as a close friend or home to dinner, while a majority were against engaging in four of the six other items in the social distance scale. In this instance, the rate of social rejection was much higher than when the unsuccessful student was Jewish.

Status considerations thus greatly affect how these youngsters feel about interacting with minority students. They greatly prefer having social relations with a higher-status student, whether the student is black or Jewish. This tendency is illustrated by comparing the teenagers' attitudes toward interacting with a higher-status black pupil on the one hand and a lower-status Jewish youth on the other. On all nine items in the social distance scale, they were least willing to have social contacts with the lower-status Jewish student.

In reality, of course, Jewish youngsters are likely to come from relatively high-status families, while black students are apt to have relatively poor parents. This was true in all three communities studied and is the pattern in most communities in America. The teenage study thus provides clear evidence of what was discussed for adult prejudice. The desire to associate with one's social equals or betters—and to avoid having contacts with social inferiors—has opposite effects upon racial prejudice and anti-Semitism. It reinforces the tendency not to associate with blacks, while leading to less discriminatory feelings toward Jews. Blacks, in other words, would be better received by nonblacks if they were not so disproportionately poor and underprivileged. Jews, in contrast, would likely be the targets of greater discrimination if they were not, as a group, relatively successful and well-off.

INTERRACIAL FRIENDSHIPS

Social distance was also measured in two additional ways—by asking the teenagers how they would feel about meeting someone who is black and by determining how many of their friends were in fact black. Both measures were also used in studying anti-Semitic prejudice as reported in Chapter 5.

The first question elicited little outright hostility when it was asked about Jews and it elicited little more when asked about blacks. The majority of teenagers in all three communities said they would feel "friendly" or "quite friendly" if they met someone about whom the only thing they knew was that he was black. The proportion saying they would feel unfriendly was 11 percent in Commutertown, 12 percent in Oceanville, and 22 percent in Central City. The equivalent figures for Jews were, respectively, 16 percent, 10 percent, and 9 percent. These teenagers were thus only slightly less friendly overall toward blacks as toward Jews on this second measure of social distance.

These verbal expressions of friendliness, however, were not carried over into behavior. It will be recalled from Chapter 5 that these teenagers were also asked to name their five closest friends of the same sex. Heterophily scores were then created from these responses, ranging from + 1 for maximum acceptance of an outgroup to − 1 for maximum rejection. The heterophily scores of white non-Jewish teenagers with respect to blacks was strongly negative in all three communities: − .85 in Commutertown, − .92 in Oceanville, and − .89 in Central City. White non-Jewish students thus report having relatively few close friendships with black students in all three of these community settings. These negative scores, moreover, were much higher than the − .41 recorded in the two communities with Jewish students. Far fewer friendships thus exist between non-Jewish whites and blacks than between non-Jewish whites and Jews.

In sum, these findings show that teenage racial prejudice and teenage anti-Semitism are similarly patterned. In both instances, the non-Jewish white youth more often held negative images of minority group members than refused to associate with them. In both instances, they were less willing to have social contacts with a minority student in more intimate situations or when the minority group member was of lower social status. In both instances, finally, most of the teenagers said they would have friendly feelings upon meeting a minority group member but in fact had relatively few close friends who were black or Jewish.

As with adults, the chief difference is in the frequency with which prejudice is expressed. These teenagers, like their elders, more often hold prejudiced beliefs toward blacks than toward Jews. This was true on all the measures of prejudice developed in this study. In addition, class considerations appear to have a greater bearing upon teenage racial prejudice than anti-Semitism. The fact that black students are poorer and less successful academically contributes to their becoming victims of prejudice.

Given the sample of subjects used in this study, these results cannot be considered applicable to young Americans in the country as a whole. However, the teenagers in this study all lived in the Northeast, an area where adult prejudice is especially low. Thus it can be presumed that teenage racial prejudice would, if anything, be higher on a national scale. Certainly this would be true if teenagers in the South had been included in the study.

THE SOURCES OF TEENAGE RACIAL PREJUDICE

These similarities in the holding of prejudice suggest that teenage anti-Semitism and racism may have common origins, as is largely true for adults. To test this possibility, the teenagers' racial prejudice was subjected to the same analysis as their anti-Semitic prejudice. Whether or not racial prejudice is located among the same social groups was first determined. The four theories of prejudice outlined in Chapter 5 were then tested as possible explanations of racial hostility.

With some exceptions, racial prejudice and anti-Semitism were found to be similarly located and caused. As with anti-Semitism, prejudice toward blacks is most commonly found among the less privileged teenagers economically and especially among the less privileged academically. The most racially prejudiced teenagers were those who studied least, had the worst grades, and were least oriented toward college. It was among teenagers from less wealthy families that these academic deficiencies most often occurred. The relationship between deprivation and racial prejudice, however, was not as strong as that with anti-Semitism. Relatively more adolescents from wealthy families or with good grades held prejudiced attitudes toward blacks than toward Jews.

The very prevalence of racial prejudice among these respondents is partly responsible for the weaker nature of this relationship. At this age, negative stereotyping of blacks is common, occurring at high levels among youth from different backgrounds and with different future aspirations. In addition, it appears that class attitudes generate more prejudice toward black students than toward Jewish students. This factor appears to increase the likelihood of racial prejudice while counteracting anti-Jewish feelings.

As will be recalled, the four theories of prejudice tested in the teenage study were that it is a result of: (a) anxiety produced by frustration, (b) identification with prejudiced primary groups, (c) socialization to unenlightened rather than enlightened values, and (d) a lack of cognitive sophistication. Of these four theories, only the last was confirmed as a principal explanation of teenage anti-Semitism.

Fairly similar results are found when the teenagers' racial prejudice is tested. As with anti-Semitism, no support is found for the theory that prejudice is produced by psychological tensions and frustrations. No support is found either for the notion that interacting with other prejudiced teenagers produces antiblack beliefs. (Some evidence of this effect was found for teenage anti-Semitism.) Both holding unenlightened values and having a relative lack of cognitive sophistication, however, are positively related to teenage racial prejudice. Cognitive theory thus again receives empirical support, as it has in the other studies reported upon.

The main difference between teenage anti-Semitism and teenage racial prejudice involves the support found for enlightened-value theory in the latter case but not the former. The confirmation of the theory is found with respect to teenagers' degree of agreement that "People should support movements or groups that are working for equal rights for everyone" and "People should let everyone have their fair share in running business and politics in this country." Teenagers who subscribe to these values are less racially prejudiced than those who deny them, even among those who are cognitively unsophisticated. The discriminating power of these items evidently derives from their reference to the theme of equality, absent in other measures of enlightened value. Internalizing norms of equality thus contributes to a lessening of racial prejudice among these youth and presumably among youth elsewhere.

As in teenage anti-Semitism, however, the main source of antiblack prejudice among these youngsters was a lack of cognitive sophistication. Teenagers scoring low in cognitive sophistication were the most racially prejudiced in their beliefs; those scoring high, the least. Of course, the high frequency of antiblack beliefs meant that racist attitudes were often found even among the most sophisticated youngsters. While cognitive sophistication serves to reduce the incidence of teenage racism, then, it does so only in a relative sense. These youth apparently need further exposure to the educational process to develop a stronger cognitive resistance to prejudice. This is true of both anti-Jewish and antiblack youth but especially of the latter.

Summary

The purpose of this chapter was to compare the racial prejudice and anti-Semitic prejudice of Americans. Attention was given to the content, prevalence, distribution, and causes of these two kinds of prejudice, with information drawn from several studies in this research series as well as from other opinion polls and investigations.

Important similarities and differences were discovered between the holding of antiblack and anti-Jewish attitudes. Significantly, prejudiced beliefs toward both groups have declined sharply since the 1940s, when first examined in opinion surveys. This changeover in attitudes has been especially dramatic with respect to blacks. While few white Americans accepted the principle of nondiscrimination in the 1940s, most do so today. By the 1970s relatively few Americans—Southerners or Northerners—thought that blacks should go to separate schools, be prevented from living in white sections of town, or be discriminated against in employment, public transportation, or public facilities. The acceptance of antiblack imagery also declined over this period, although not to the same degree.

Prejudiced attitudes in general have thus decreased in America over the past four decades. In particular, the belief that people should not be discriminated against in public areas of life is now widely accepted. This represents an important turnaround in public thinking since the 1940s, affecting Jews, blacks, and presumably other minorities as well.

Despite these changes, however, prejudiced feelings toward blacks remain widespread in America. Many whites continue to think about blacks in stereotypic terms as lazy, unambitious, unintelligent, immoral, sloppy, and violence-prone. Many object to sending their children to schools where blacks make up half or more of the student body. Many feel they have a right to keep blacks out of their neighborhoods if they so choose. And many support antiblack discrimination in such private areas of conduct as intermarriage, social club admittance, and having a black person home to dinner. A large majority of whites, moreover, oppose governmental programs which promote greater integration or racial equality. They disapprove of school busing, fair housing laws, and efforts to assist blacks to move into white suburbs. They likewise reject the notion that blacks should receive extra assistance because of past discrimination and oppose affirmative action programs in employment and school admissions.

Moreover, consistently since the 1940s whites have expressed little sympathy for the position of blacks or for black efforts to improve their situation. Most whites deny that blacks are being treated unfairly in this country, reject the notion that blacks are victims of discrimination, and feel that blacks themselves, not whites, are to be blamed for the inequalities existing between the races. Most whites likewise feel that blacks have tried to move "too fast" and overwhelmingly agree that "blacks shouldn't push themselves where they're not wanted." When asked to choose among integration, segregation, and something in between, finally, the majority tendency among whites has been to choose the middle course.

Without question, then, antiblack feelings are far more prevalent in contemporary America than anti-Jewish feelings. One source of this difference is the relative poverty and lower-class status of blacks in America. In general, people wish to avoid having contacts and personal relations with those of lower social standing than themselves. If blacks were as well-to-do as Jews, they would undoubtedly be more accepted than they are at present.

Where racial prejudice and anti-Semitism are more alike is in their distribution and causes. As with anti-Semitism, prejudice toward blacks is most prevalent at lower socio-economic levels, among the young, among Protestants more than Catholics, in rural areas, and in the South. The main dissimilarity is in the greater degree of racial prejudice in the South than outside it—a gap that has been narrowing, however.

Most important, it is again education that is found to be the main correlate of prejudice. Racial prejudice increases as exposure to schooling becomes less—a relation that largely accounts for the greater racism of working-class and older Americans. A lack of cognitive sophistication thus appears to be a leading source of racial prejudice as well as of anti-Semitism. Those intellectual deficiencies which contribute to the holding of anti-Semitic beliefs also contribute to the holding of antiblack beliefs.

These findings do not mean, of course, that racial prejudice and anti-Semitic prejudice are the same. Each have different historical origins, unique imagery, and independent as well as common causes. One of the separate causes of racial prejudice, as discussed, is the lower SES of black Americans and the desire of many Americans to avoid associating with those below them in social standing. A unique source of anti-Semitism is the harboring of a particular form of Christian theology.

The final section of this chapter drew from the adolescent study to compare anti-Semitism and racial prejudice among the young. As with adults, the main difference was the greater prevalence of prejudice toward blacks than toward Jews. While these youngsters held highly negative images of Jews, they were even more prejudiced in their beliefs about what blacks are like. One in two scores as anti-Semitic in their acceptance of negative stereotypes about Jews, but four in five were prejudiced in their beliefs about blacks.

In most other ways, teenage racism and teenage anti-Semitism are similarly patterned. As with anti-Semitism, racial prejudice is most common among less privileged teenagers economically and academically. As with anti-Semitism, the main source of adolescent racism is a lack of cognitive sophistication. Everything considered, teenagers appear to be highly susceptible to prejudice. Lacking the resistance to prejudiced thinking that comes with more educational experience, they easily pick up the negative imagery of adults.

In broad terms, then, this review of research findings shows that (a) racial prejudice is more prevalent than anti-Semitism on all dimensions for which measures exist, (b) those kinds of Americans who are most prejudiced toward Jews are also most prejudiced toward blacks, (c) racial prejudice has unique class origins while anti-Semitism has unique religious origins, and (d) a lack of cognitive sophistication is a primary cause of both racial prejudice and anti-Semitism among adults as well as among teenagers.

CHAPTER 9

Politics and Prejudice

IT IS WHEN THE DISLIKES and hatreds of people are carried over into politics that prejudice poses its greatest threat to democratic society. At a minimum, the "politicization" of prejudice is likely to harden and inflame existing societal tensions. It will lead people to define their interests along religious, ethnic, and racial lines and to treat those different from themselves as political enemies. In extreme form, the politicization of prejudice can result in the use of the power of the state to repress or even eliminate unpopular minorities. Of all the political excesses of humankind, probably none have been as vicious as those motivated by personal hate and bigotry.

It hardly need be said that Jews have been one of the chief victims of such political discrimination and repression. The specter of the Nazi holocaust continues to haunt any inquiry into anti-Semitism, so appalling was its reality. An examination of politics and prejudice would thus seem to be an essential part of any general inquiry into anti-Semitism in America. Of critical concern are the nature, extent, and causes of political movements that appeal to public prejudices.

These issues were addressed in a final study in this research series, which is reported upon in this chapter.[1] This project, unlike the previous ones, was somewhat historical in approach. It examined all important instances in American history when prejudice and bigotry entered politics. By studying the dynamics of these situations, it sought to arrive at a general understanding of the causes and consequences of the politicization of prejudice in America. Additionally, the study examined the susceptibility of Americans today to political campaigns of hate and prejudice. To what extent can the elements leading to a politics of prejudice in the past be found among Americans in the present?

In both undertakings, the investigation gave attention not only to the entry of anti-Semitism into politics but to the politicization of other forms of prejudice as well. It sought to describe the general conditions under which

158

minority groups are made the targets of political derision and attack. As will be seen, the politicization of prejudice has been more prevalent in America than is commonly assumed. The Irish, Catholics, Jews, blacks, intellectuals, communists, and several other unpopular and vulnerable minority groups have all been subjected to malicious and defamatory political attacks. Such hate-inducing groups have gained strength on the average of once a generation. They have often attracted millions of followers, elected scores of candidates to office, and succeeded in having their prejudices written into the law.

The factors giving rise to the politicization of prejudice are presented in the first part of this chapter. A short history of these movements comes next, followed by a review of contemporary sources of prejudice and politics. The chapter concludes by examining existing and potential future sources of political prejudice against Jews.

Prejudice and Extremist Politics

Prejudice seldom enters into the political process as an isolated phenomenon. Americans who support a politics of prejudice generally hold other intolerant and unenlightened beliefs as well. They are distrustful of foreigners, have little patience for dissent or deviance, are extreme patriots, and see their political opponents as sinister and evil men. Where political prejudice is found, so too is evidence of cognitive unenlightenment generally.

The existence of prejudicial politics, then, is to be explained in terms of more general patterns of intolerance found in political extremism. To understand the politics of prejudice, therefore, requires a prior accounting of the conditions making for extremist politics.

Political extremism is defined as the tendency to violate the norms and procedures of democracy. It includes the suppression of dissent and the assertion that there is only one "truth" to be known and acted upon. Political extremism thus stands in opposition to such ideals as that Americans must learn to live with their differences, to nurture and protect diversity among themselves, and to maintain a society that is open and accessible to all. Such values are "pluralistic" in nature; the values of political extremism are "antipluralistic" or, to use the more appropriate dictionary term, "monistic." Monism is that impulse which is inimical to the pluralist ideal. It includes the tendency to view the ambivalences of life and the differences among people as illegitimate, and to support extremist parties and movements that assert that theirs is the "right" way and that all other groups are "wrong" and are to be suppressed.

THE ORIGINS OF POLITICAL EXTREMISM

In most general terms, the origins of extremist groups in America can be traced to the existence of certain types of social strain. Periodically, large numbers of Americans find themselves caught in circumstances in which they feel personally threatened but over which they have little control. Frustrated by such conditions, such persons often turn to extremist politics as a way to alleviate their anxieties.

Political extremism thus represents a reaction to the frustrations and ambiguities of life. In a more specific sense, the supporters of extremist movements have typically felt themselves to be deprived—either they have never gained their proper share of status and power in American society, or they feel themselves to be losing it. These groups might be referred to as the "never-hads" and the "once-hads." All such persons are not necessarily extremist in their political beliefs, and indeed most are not. It has been among these two groups, however, that extremist movements have gained their most numerous and most ardent followers.

The extremism of the never-hads and once-hads generally follow different political patterns. For the never-hads in American society, deprivation is primarily experienced in economic terms—they are poor and in need of a greater share of the nation's wealth. The never-hads have generally looked to the government for help and have tended to vote for liberal or left candidates. To the extent that they have supported extremist movements, they have usually associated themselves with left-wing groups (although important exceptions can be found).

Left-wing extremism has, on the whole, been of minor consequence in this country. Not so, however, with the right-wing extremism of the once-hads. The once-hads feel themselves to be losing out in the transformations taking place in society and wish to restore previously existing social and economic arrangements. They tend to be attracted to an ideology that is "preservationist" in content. The once-hads resist rather than support social change. They would maintain or narrow existing lines of power and privilege and preserve the old values and ways of doing things.

Right-wing extremist movements supported by the once-hads have been common in American history, and it is not difficult to see why. New regions, new industries, new religious values, and new migrant and ethnic groups have repeatedly encroached upon the old. Such changes have threatened the positions of many people and created a large pool of potential extremists. Additionally, the social structure in this country is itself relatively fluid and open. While class differences exist, they have not been as firmly entrenched or as widely accepted as those in most other countries. No group has been able to maintain a long-term position of dominance in a manner similar to the upper classes in Europe.

For these reasons, status insecurity has been an enduring characteristic of American life, leaving large numbers of people both vulnerable to and threatened by the effects of social change. Such threats are experienced not just in political terms but in social norms and practices as well. Structural changes have altered prevailing beliefs on such deeply felt issues as religion, sexual relations, parent–child relations, the consumption of alcohol, the use of drugs, and styles of dress. Such changes in morality can be quite threatening to those adhering to older norms and practices. They often lead such persons to feel disinherited and displaced in their own land.

Political extremism is thus to be understood as a form of political "backlash"—a reaction against changes taking place in society at large. Those attracted to extremist movements are generally Americans who have some stake in the existing or past social order. In some instances, it is a declining elite group; in others, it is working-class Americans threatened by changes over which they have no control. Extremist movements have been the strongest when they have combined elements of these two socio-economic groups.

PREJUDICE AND EXTREMISM

While prejudice is not a basic cause of political extremism, it invariably comes to play a central role in extremist movements. Eventually, nearly all threatened groups react by singling out a specific reason for their problems. Minority groups are an especially convenient scapegoat for those upset by the pace of change. Minorities abide by values and customs different from those of most other Americans and are usually already targets of distrust and derision. It is a small step to associate them with the evils besetting the once-hads and, more generally, the nation itself.

Americans suffering losses in status and power have thus characteristically responded by attacking minority groups. They have blamed minorities at various times for political defeats, changes in moral standards, economic recessions, large-scale unemployment, crime, uncivility, and the spread of irreligion. They have often been encouraged to do so by the immigrant backgrounds of minorities. It has been easy to discredit ethnic minorities as "foreigners" and to call them "un-American" or "un-Protestant" (when only Protestants were viewed as true Americans).

Extremist movements, moreover, have not only picked up existing negative stereotypes but have invented new ones as well. Significant additions to the repertory of prejudiced beliefs have been generated in this way, including negative references to alleged Jewish power. In addition, extremist groups have often gone beyond the normal pale in their attacks upon minorities. They have sought to discredit—and even to destroy—their victims. Such fierce hostilities are produced in large part by the very situation giving rise to extremist movements—the intense frustrations of the once-hads. If minority groups are causes or symbols of one's loss in position, it follows that they must be stopped or at least severely punished for their transgressions.

Such hostile feelings are commonly brought together and expressed in a conspiracy theory. The targeted minority is not just being different or acting in a misguided manner; it is part of a secret scheme designed to subvert the very essence of the American way of life. The minority that would perpetrate this deed, moreover, is itself duped. Extremist theories uniformly place the real power in such plots in the hands of a small core of intellectuals. It is this band which, through deception, manipulates minority group values and the national mind. It is the ultimate villain in the conspiracy.

The use of conspiracy theory has served a number of functions for extremist groups. It has provided a concrete focus for extremist propaganda and a more identifiable target of opposition. It has intensified feelings of moral indignation and personal outrage. Finally, it has frequently served as a political bridge between different social classes. The privileged and the underprivileged may not have the same economic interests, but they can share common hatreds and resentments. It is when such a merger occurs that extremist movements have had their most notable successes.

COGNITIVE ELEMENTS OF EXTREMISM

Cognition involves the intellectual abilities of people—their knowledge about social reality, their ability to think logically, and their handling of abstractions and complexities. Cognitive factors figure prominently in political extremism, as they do in prejudice generally. Running through all the important writings on right-wing extremist ideology are two main cognitive themes—simplism and moralism.

Simplism involves a tendency to reduce complex phenomena to singular causes or explanations. Extremist ideology characteristically exhibits a high degree of simplism. The wisdom of the common folk is routinely praised, while that of the experts is belittled. What is needed, according to right-wing extremists, is more simple common sense—not the multifactoral, multidimensional models of the intellectuals.[2]

Such simplistic conceptions are illustrated in the approach of extremist groups to political problems. On most issues, right-wing extremists hark back to an earlier—and often mythical—period in American history; they ignore social complexities and the effects of change. The problem of civil rights, for example, is reduced to "outside agitation"; racial conflicts are "artificially inspired" and easily resolved through a few simple programs. Problems in foreign policy would be ended if only the nation's leaders were tougher and more resolute.

Such simplistic conceptions are reinforced by the second element in extremist thinking—a deeply felt moralism. Right-wing extremists conceive of history as a constant battle between the forces of good and evil. What matters is that one has good intentions and good character on one's side, and triumph will be inevitable (although perhaps not until some distant date). What is wrong with the country is the "softness of American character" or the "moral deficiencies" of the nation's leaders. What is needed is a return to the true values of Americanism, patriotism, and manliness.

Such moralism is closely associated with religious values, specifically with Christianity. The country is seen as a preeminently Christian nation, founded with God's Providence as a beacon to all mankind. It is the betrayal of this trust and religious heritage that has led the country to adopt wrong-headed policies; it is what lies behind the nation's unsolved problems. Such references to Christianity are seldom expressed in theological or doctrinal terms. Rather, the Christian religion is viewed as the embodiment of good intentions and good character in the world and the opposition as the embodiment of evil.

The religious character of extremist ideology strongly reinforces its absolutist and uncompromising tendencies. The victims of extremist attacks are not merely misguided; they are in league with the devil. Right-thinking Americans are thus justified in using any means available to squash and eradicate the wickedness in their midst. This infusion of Christian symbolism has also directed and affirmed the extremists' choice of scapegoat. It has generally been a non-Protestant group (usually Catholics), a non-Christian group (Jews), or the antireligious ("godless communists").

RIGHT-WING VALUES IN AMERICA

A final element in extremist ideology is a close relation to mainstream American values. Both draw upon much the same discontents and moralistic impulses—a fact that often strengthens the appeals of extremist rhetoric.

The core American values can be summarized as an interrelated web of egalitarianism, anti-elitism, individualism, and moralism. Americans have traditionally stressed the inherent equality of people and been hostile to claims of elite status. Such values are often associated with the country's lack of a feudal past, a class structure of severe inequality in which those at the top claimed special privileges. Associated with such liberal and democratic values are strongly felt individualism and moralism. Great emphasis is placed upon achievement and personal success. Getting ahead is not only a personal goal but proof of individual worth and virtue; poverty, by contrast, is a sign of personal failure and inadequacy. Such beliefs have been bolstered by a Horatio Alger view of social mobility and an infusion of certain Protestant notions concerning salvation. Personal attainment has been taken as evidence of divine grace, and failure as indication of personal sin and immorality.

The individual thus suffers a heavy burden in American society; economic defeat involves not only material discomfort but personal and moral disgrace as well. At least one consequence of these stresses is a culture that is more "ends-oriented" than "means-oriented." In America, it is winning that counts and only secondarily how the game is played. This trait is most common in the market place but appears with some regularity in politics as well. Politicians have frequently used unscrupulous and defamatory tactics to gain votes and have appealed to popular prejudices or aligned themselves with extremist groups.

On at least one level, then, the American ethos supports those who would use extremist tactics. An equally important reinforcement of right-wing values is found in the policy area. For Americans, a belief in the individual has often been translated into an antistatist position—an antagonism toward government involvement in social problems. In extreme form, the state is seen as having no special obligation to help the less fortunate in society; indeed, it would be morally wrong and personally corrupting to do so. Some variation of this theme is generally advanced by right-wing extremist groups seeking to preserve the "old ways."

These convergences between mainstream American values and extremist ideology add to the attractiveness of right-wing ideas. They reinforce the extremists' ends-oriented, breach-of-rules approach to politics and lend themselves to moralistic personifications and conspiracy theories. They also allow right-wing groups to evoke symbols of Americanism and patriotism.

Right-Wing Extremism in America

The above conclusions are derived from an examination of all significant right-wing extremist movements in America between 1790 and 1970. A brief review of this history is instructive, since it demonstrates the strength and recurrent nature of extremism in this country and illuminates the factors giving rise to it.

THE ILLUMINATI AND THE SOCIETY OF UNITED IRISHMEN

Extremist movements developed early in the nation's history. The first groups to suffer a decline in status and authority were the Federalists, Congregationalists, and merchants of New England. Those groups had figured prominently in the country's early settlement and government, but by 1790 their power was in rapid decline. The response of those first displaced elites was to charge that an evil conspiratorial group was behind their change in fortunes.

The original culprit in this plot was an alleged international conspiracy known as the Illuminati. Such a society of intellectuals had existed briefly in Bavaria in the 1780s before being repressed. The Illuminati, however, had been linked by European writers with the French Revolution and similar upheavals, and these allegations were seized upon. The Illuminati were said to be the moving force behind both the Jeffersonian Democrats and the forces of irreligion—the twin antagonists of the discontented elites.

The myth of the Illuminati has proved to be a persistent one in this country, reappearing time and again in extremist ideology. For that first group of once-hads, however, it was of little help in attracting a mass constituency. What was needed was a more concrete target, a group that was readily identifiable and was already the object of widespread dislike. The Federalists soon found such a scapegoat in the Irish, who were then entering the country in large numbers. By the turn of the century, the more flesh-and-blood Society of United Irishmen had replaced the Illuminati in extremist propaganda.

This tactic proved to be somewhat more successful, as anti-Irish sentiments were beginning to spread in the country. As a whole, however, this early use of extremist tactics proved a failure. The Federalist party was defeated so soundly by the Jeffersonian Democrats that it soon ceased to function altogether.

THE ANTI-MASONIC MOVEMENT

The conditions for political extremism were created again in the 1820s and 1830s, when new power relations were being formed and old moral standards cast aside. In the process, large numbers of Americans felt themselves under attack and turned to the simplistic appeals of extremism. In this instance, support for extremist politics came from two different groups in the socio-economic spectrum. The first group consisted of relatively privileged elites who felt threatened by the rise of Jacksonian Democracy; the second comprised less affluent, largely rural Americans upset with the drift away from traditional Protestant values. This was to be the first "marriage of convenience" between different classes of once-hads.

This time the target of attack was the Order of Masons, a group presumably consisting of the "select class" in the community. Like their predecessors in this role, the Illuminati, the Masons were viewed as a conspiratorial order of evil, immoral men who sought to manipulate the lives of others. They were said to be guilty of intimidation, terror, and even murder. They were declared foes of evangelical Protestantism, since they openly admitted non-Christians into their ranks.

Convinced that most public officeholders were Masons, the extremists of the period decided to enter politics as a separate party. The anti-Masons held the country's first national convention in 1830 and achieved considerable success electing candidates at the state level. Support for the party came largely from the rural working class, which acted out of a combination of religious bigotry, anti-urban feelings, economic discontent, and nativist dislike for foreign immigrants. Reinforcing these tendencies were the group's low level of education and attendant susceptibility to simplism, moralism, and prejudice.

Politically, the chief significance of the anti-Masonic movement lay in the alliance formed between these working-class voters and the conservative elites displaced by the Jacksonian Democrats. That alliance ultimately culminated in the formation of the Whigs, a conservative party opposed to the liberal reforms of the period.

ANTI-CATHOLIC EXTREMISM

Religious prejudices played an important but largely secondary role in those early extremist movements. By the 1830s, however, the Catholic Church began to emerge as an independent target of extremist propaganda. A growing hate literature accused the Catholic Church of a long list of sins, including secret sexual activities that allegedly went on in convents and monasteries. Not surprisingly, the most frequent charge levied against Catholicism involved its challenge to traditional Protestant dominance. The Catholic Church was said to be bent on conquering and corrupting American society through the importation of Catholic immigrants.

For the next century such anti-Catholicism became the primary source of prejudice in American politics. It resulted in a succession of major and minor right-wing extremist groups, including the Native American party in the 1840s, the Know Nothing party in the 1850s, and the American Protective Association in the 1880s and 1890s. Anti-Catholic sentiments also strongly influenced the politics of the Republican party during much of the period and were a principal factor in the rise of the Ku Klux Klan in the 1920s.

As with the anti-Masonic movement, these recurrent waves of anti-Catholic extremism drew their strength from both the top and the bottom of the socio-economic ladder. Conservative elites, struggling to recapture or maintain power, found in their anti-Catholic campaigns an effective means to gain working-class votes. Less wealthy Americans proved to be highly susceptible to such appeals, because of both their general lack of education and their own uneasiness with societal changes. As in other instances, it was a conspiracy theory that provided the essential link between the two natural class opponents. The Catholic Church, acting on instructions from Rome, was variously blamed for alleged losses in religious faith, declining morals, slavery, alcoholism, the Civil War, economic depressions, and the collapse of the country's banking system. Catholicism thus served as a convenient scapegoat for those threatened by a variety of societal conditions.

THE BIGOTED TWENTIES

Anti-Catholicism did not die with the advent of the twentieth century. Rather, Catholics were joined by other victims of political bigotry—the chief of which were the Jews. Anti-Semitism had first appeared on the American scene in the late nineteenth century, when large numbers of Jewish immigrants began to arrive in the nation's urban centers. Like Catholics before them, Jews came equipped with an arcane presence that lent itself to conspiracy theory. They had no Pope or Vatican, but Jews had an aura of secrecy and intrigue about them that was deeply embedded in the folklore of Christian civilization. In addition, hostilities toward Jews often developed over economic matters. Jewish immigrants tended disproportionately to be merchants and middlemen—occupations viewed with suspicion and distrust in an era of economic discontent. It was also during this period that Jews first came to be identified with the financial power of Wall Street. Farmers in particular felt themselves mistreated by the country's banking interests and tended to blame Jews for their frustrations. For many monetary reformers of the time, furthermore, a concern with bankers and those who controlled the credit system easily slid over into an image of a Jewish international conspiracy.

While anti-Semitism had its initial stirrings in this country in the late nineteenth century, it was not until the bigoted decade of the 1920s that prejudice toward Jews first entered into politics. The Twenties have been characterized as a period when the country "returned to normalcy." What that meant, in effect, was that a strong backlash occurred in response to the changes of the previous decade—the federal government's attempt to regulate the economy and the country's involvement in World War I. Most dramatically, the 1920s were a period of fundamentalist Protestant backlash against liberal trends within the churches as well as within the greater society. The 1920s are perhaps best remembered as a time of anti-evolution laws, Prohibition, and a religiously inspired defeat of the country's first Catholic presidential candidate, Alfred E. Smith.

The most dramatic extremist movement of that period was the Ku Klux Klan.[3] The Klan was then a nationwide movement—strong in both urban and rural areas in both the North and South. It arose chiefly as a response of Protestant fundamentalists to their loss in status and prerogatives, and for a time it drew support from both upper- and lower-class groups. Increasingly, however, the Klan lost its upper-middle-class members until it largely became a movement of the less-educated and less privileged. It stridently preached anti-Jewish, anti-Catholic, and antiblack propaganda.

The 1920s were also marked by the emergence of Henry Ford as a respected spokesman for right-wing extremism and religious prejudice. Through his violently anti-Semitic newspaper, the *Dearborn Independent*, Ford reached upwards of 700,000 American readers. In it, Ford hammered away at the theme of an international Jewish conspiracy. The scope of his attacks is illustrated by some of the headlines in his newspaper: "Jewish Gamblers Corrupt American Baseball," "Jewish Jazz Becomes Our National Music," "How the Jewish Song Trust Makes You Sing," "Jew Wires Direct Tammany's Gentile Puppets," "The Scope of Jewish Dictatorship in America," "The Jewish Associates of Benedict Arnold." In short, Jews were blamed for everything from Communism to jazz, immorality, and short skirts.

Such attacks not only were popular with many Americans, but they also projected Ford into the political limelight: At the height of his anti-Semitism he was widely supported as a presidential candidate. Such activities dramatized the entry of full-scale anti-Semitism into the American political arena. Jews were eminently vulnerable for this role, since conspiracy theories could be spun from their visibility in both radical and capitalist circles. They were also central figures in conspiracy theories that had been spawned for political purposes in Germany and Czarist Russia.

NEO-FASCISM IN THE 1930s

The decade of the 1930s—beclouded by massive unemployment and economic hardship—also witnessed its share of extremist groups. On the right, these included an almost endless array of neofascist movements: the Silver Shirts of William Pelley, the Midwestern Black Legion, Gerald Winrod's Christian Defenders, the Union for Social Justice of Father Coughlin, and the Committee of One Million of Gerald L. K. Smith, to name a few. No one knows just how many active members these groups were able to attract or how many other Americans agreed with them.

The drawing power of these neofascist groups was somewhat different from earlier extremist movements. Immigration had slowed down considerably in the country, and Protestant nativism no longer was such a cogent political force. Instead, virulent nationalism ("Americanism") and an abstract kind of racism came to serve as the ideological core of right-wing extremism. The conspiratorial charges of the period were thus directed largely against Jews and Communists, although Catholics continued to be an occasional target of attack.

The most important neofascist movement of the 1930s was organized by a Catholic priest, Charles Coughlin. The Coughlinites demonstrated, if nothing else, that Catholics as well as Protestants were susceptible to the politics of prejudice. Father Couglin was an admirer of Adolph Hitler, then gaining power in Germany, and an outspoken anti-Semite. Like Hitler, he placed the blame for the Great Depression upon the manipulations of Jews. At the height of his influence, Father Coughlin had an audience of millions for his weekly radio programs, while his political views were endorsed by more than a quarter of the population.

Father Coughlin's pro-fascist views were supported by a varied assortment of Americans, including conservatives opposed to Roosevelt's New Deal. They received their strongest backing, however, from fellow Catholics and from poorer Americans discontent with their economic lot. Such support largely represented a status backlash by groups wishing to establish themselves as "Americans." In this respect, anti-Semitism was not as central to Coughlin's success as prejudicial appeals had been to most previous extremist movements. Coughlin's followers were found to be only slightly more anti-Semitic than the rest of the public. Their tolerance of Coughlin's virulent anti-Semitism resulted not so much from an active embracing of such views as from their own cognitive unsophistication and weak resistance to them.

Support for Father Coughlin fell sharply when the country entered World War II against Hitler. Father Coughlin himself abandoned his radio crusades under threat of defrocking.

THE COLD WAR AND McCARTHYISM

Following the war, a general shift occurred in the ideology and politics of right-wing extremism, with Jews and Catholics no longer serving as the principal targets of extremist propaganda. Supplanting them as subjects for such propaganda were the increasing tensions produced by anticommunism and the country's worsening racial situation. Most extremist movements since the war have drawn their strength from one or the other of these sources—although political attacks upon Catholics and Jews have not been unknown during this period as well,

The first postwar outbreak of extremism was the anticommunist movement spearheaded by Senator Joseph McCarthy in the early 1950s. McCarthy contended that a secret communist conspiracy was behind alleged failings in American foreign policy. He charged that undetected communist agents had infiltrated both the government and the key opinion-forming and policy-controlling institutions of the country. He also alleged that these infiltrators were largely members of the social elite—graduates of Groton and Harvard, State Department personnel, newspaper editors, college professors, the heads of foundations, and others in positions of leadership.

McCarthy thus appealed strongly to the status strains felt by those in socially and economically inferior positions. His anti-elitist tirades were well received by Americans who had moved up a notch on the socio-economic ladder but who felt insecure about their newly won positions. As with earlier extremist movements, however, most of McCarthy's support came from the less privileged and less-educated sectors of the society—those lacking in cognitive ability and sophistication.

Finally, encouragement by the conservative party played a key role in the rise of McCarthyism, as it had in earlier extremist movements. Republican leaders saw in McCarthyism an opportunity to attract the support of normally Democratic voters—working-class men and particularly Catholics—who were strongly anticommunist. Republicans thus generally supported McCarthy's use of intimidation and his violation of First Amendment guarantees; they withdrew their support only when McCarthy turned against the Republican establishment itself.

THE JOHN BIRCH SOCIETY

After the collapse of the McCarthy movement, a host of smaller rightwing organizations came into existence. These groups had a variety of favorite causes and preferred scapegoats and reflected both new and older sources of political prejudice. In several instances, different strains of conspiracy theories were woven together into a single tapestry of sinister design. Thus the civil rights movement was said by some to be a Jewish–communist conspiracy, a plot to stir up disaffection and rebelliousness among the nation's blacks.

The most publicized extremist organizations of the 1960s was the John Birch Society, a highly conservative or antistatist group. The platform of the John Birch Society was an exceptionally broad patchwork of conspiratorial charges. It identified the economic and social trends that it opposed with the efforts of a "hidden conspiracy of Insiders"—the Illuminati. Indeed, Robert Welch, the head of the Society in the 1960s, linked this group with all that he considered wrong in past history. The Illuminati were held responsible for both world wars, the Russian Revolution, the breakup of the colonial empires, the formation of the United Nations, centralized banking, the personal income tax, the direct election of senators, and "everything in the way of 'security' legislation, from the first Workmen's Compensation Acts under Bismarck to the latest Medicare monstrosity under Lyndon Johnson."[4]

Unlike its predecessors, the John Birch Society generally eschewed direct appeals to racial and religious bigotry. It has been antiblack in its policy pronouncements—and often in the tone of its statements—but hasn't attacked blacks directly. The main support for the John Birch Society has come from relatively well-to-do but insecure Americans. With its strong attack on the welfare state, it has had no appeal to the underprivileged and has remained a relatively small and unpopular group.

THE WALLACE CANDIDACY

The most recent example of a large extremist movement was the presidential candidacy of George C. Wallace in 1964, 1968, 1972, and 1976. Wallace achieved considerable success in his campaigns, most notably in 1968, when he headed his own American Independent Party and received 13 percent of the popular vote and 45 electoral votes. His share of the popular vote was the largest received by a third-party candidate in almost half a century; his electoral votes were the most won by a third-party candidate since the Civil War.

The extremist nature of the Wallace movement is clearly demonstrated in both the candidate's campaign speeches and his popular support. In his speeches Wallace was highly simplistic, strident, and emotional. He defended the country against its detractors and called upon the common sense of the "little people." All that is needed is to be tougher and more resolute, he said. We should jail criminals and teach political dissenters a lesson; we should unleash our military might in Vietnam and not let the "commies" push us around.

Wallace also linked the nation's problems with the black minority and with elite conspiracies. In running for national office, he did not attack blacks directly—as he had done earlier in Alabama—but the antiblack content of his message was unmistakable.[5] It was implied in his continual denunciations of "welfare chiselers," school busing, and the absence of "law and order." Wallace pictured himself as head of a crusade of the "little man" in opposition to those in power and especially the "pseudo-intellectuals." He regularly attacked "pointy-headed" professors, "top politicians," the federal bureaucracy, judges, and editors of leading newspapers and magazines. Such elites were seen to be engaged in a grand conspiracy against the interests of the average citizen. They were variously held responsible for student radicalism, the "breakdown in law and order," black discontent, and the "coddling" of Communists.

Wallace's support came predominantly from less educated and poorer Americans and from those upset by ongoing social changes. Low in cognitive sophistication, such Americans were responsive to both the simplistic theme of Wallace's approach to politics and his thinly veiled references to race. The racial factor played an especially strong part in the candidate's mass support. On a social level, Wallace drew disproportionate backing from Southerners, working-class whites, rural residents, and conservative Protestants. The members of these groups are among those most alienated by the main currents of American society in the 1960s and 1970s. They feel threatened by the rise of blacks in the cities, by changes taking place in the moral order, by new currents in religion, and by the decline of the United States as a world power.

Contemporary Sources of Extremism

Right-wing extremist movements have thus been a common phenomenon in American society. They have regularly attracted large public followings and have often had an impact upon the nation's politics. They have been most influential when they have brought together disaffected segments of the lower and upper economic strata. They have had the greatest effect upon government policy when they have been supported by elements of the more conservative of the established parties.

Political extremism is an endemic problem in American society. The rapidity of change in America, coupled with a relatively fluid social structure, creates continual social strains. It leaves many Americans exposed to conditions that might lead them to support a politics of extremism, including political anti-Semitism. In concluding this chapter, then, it is essential to inquire into the contemporary sources of extremism in America. Which groups today appear to be most susceptible to the appeals of right-wing extremism? What might bring these groups together into a powerful extremist coalition?

The foregoing analysis suggests that four interrelated conditions contribute to a politics of extremism: (1) the existence of large numbers of Americans who feel disaffected and frustrated by societal change; (2) a willingness on the part of such Americans to ignore democratic norms and values and to violate the democratic rights of others; (3) a reservoir of minority group hate and prejudice, which can be mobilized for extremist purposes; and (4) an acceptance of right-wing or "preservationist" political ideology. What follows is a brief review of each of these conditions as they exist in the middle-to-late 1970s.

FEELINGS OF DISAFFECTION

Extremist movements develop out of feelings of disaffection brought about by change. They are supported by Americans who feel they have just been, or are about to be, deprived of something important (the once-hads), or by Americans whose rising aspirations lead them to feel they have always been deprived of something they now want (the never-hads). Such Americans provide the main base of support for extremist movements. They are likely to be attracted to extremist politics if they believe that the traditional parties are not responding to their needs.

Many kinds of Americans can develop such feelings of disaffection and experience political dislocation. Such feelings, for example, may derive from tangible deprivations, such as a loss in income, power, privilege, or position. Or they may be caused by psychic deprivations, as when traditional norms of religion, morality, or family life are eroded. In recent years, three very different groups of Americans have been most disposed to feelings of disaffection and thus most attracted to extremist-style politics. They can be identified as follows:

1. more privileged Americans, such as doctors or heads of family-owned corporations, who feel the weight of growing government controls
2. less wealthy but predominantly middle-class Americans whose identity is closely bound up in traditional religious and secular values that are being supplanted by "modern" values, which they consider to be immoral
3. working-class whites who, after making some gains, feel their positions to be threatened, especially by the demands of poor minorities and by the attention given to those minorities by government and other agencies

The three groups that have exhibited the most concrete manifestations of political extremism are thus responding to different social strains and represent different points along the socio-economic spectrum. The most recent extremist movement, that centered on the candidacy of George Wallace, appealed to the third of these groups and to some degree the second. An extremist movement that could attract support from all three groups would obviously be in a position to wield considerable influence in American politics.

Given the constancy of change in this country, furthermore, it is likely that emerging social strains are at the moment producing still additional sources of extremist support. One obvious source of disaffection, for example, is the changing economy. Continuing inflation, high rates of unemployment, decreasing mobility, growing housing and energy costs, and a slowdown in economic growth generally will affect some Americans more severely than others. Some groups, in other words, will experience personal loss or will feel threatened by the possibility of loss in disproportionate terms. These groups might well provide the mass base for extremist movements in the future. Under the right conditions, they may be attracted to extremist groups that promise them relief from their economic frustrations.

A WEAK COMMITMENT TO DEMOCRATIC PRINCIPLES

A substantial protection against extremist politics, it would seem, is a firm public commitment to the norms and institutions of democracy. Extremist movements are likely to receive little support from those who accept and understand the meaning of democratic principles. Such Americans will be especially sensitive to the antipluralist, or monistic, aspects of extremist ideology. They will recognize extremist groups as a threat to democratic processes and—whatever else their views—will tend to reject them on these grounds.

The evidence shows, however, that the democratic commitment of many Americans is weak. Either they lack an intellectual grasp of democracy or they are ignorant of democratic norms in the first place. Such Americans often profess a general acceptance of democratic principles but deny their application in specific instances or under certain circumstances. They may not, for example, accord full democratic privileges to communists, radicals, racial militants, or spokesmen for unpopular causes generally. They would be unlikely to defend minorities or others against extremist charges of immoral or conspiratorial conduct.

This weak or "common" democratic commitment is found among all kinds of Americans, but it is at the lower socio-economic levels that such beliefs are most prevalent (as shown in Chapers 2 and 3). Less-educated, working-class Americans often lack a cognitive commitment to democratic principles. Their support of democratic institutions is based upon a loyalty to the system, not an intellectual grasp of democratic principles. This loyalty is sufficient during times of normalcy, when there is little challenge to democratic procedures. During times of political dislocation, however, it can be fragile. It can provide only a weak resistance to monistic appeals of extremism and to extremist attacks upon minorities or other unpopular groups.

While such tendencies are most prevalent among less-educated Americans, it should be emphasized again that they are found throughout the population, among elites as well as nonelites. As history shows, the leaders of the established parties have often used prejudiced appeals when they thought that doing so would gain them support. This tendency has been particularly common within the more conservative (at present the Republican) party.

PREJUDICE TOWARD MINORITIES

Much the same assessment can be made of the next source of political extremism—prejudice toward minority groups. That prejudice toward Jews and blacks remains prevalent in America has been demonstrated in previous chapters. That many Americans are intolerant of cultural diversity in general was shown in Chapter 3. Again, while prejudice is found among all kinds of Americans, it is most common at the lower socio-economic levels. Less-educated, working-class Americans have less cognitive resistance to prejudice and intolerance, just as they have less resistance to monistic politics.

The existence of such negative beliefs provides fertile ground for the cultivation of extremist politics. Extremist groups have been most successful when they have displaced their grievances onto an unpopular minority. In so doing, they are able to appeal to popular prejudices and to give concrete form to their followers' discontents. In particular, they are able to enlarge their mass support among the less-educated and intellectually unenlightened segments of the population and to create a "marriage of convenience" between disaffected upper- and lower-status groups.

As demonstrated, however, extremist movements do not just draw upon existing public prejudices; they often invent and popularize negative stereotypes in their quest to find a scapegoat for their grievances. The belief in Jewish power—that Jews control the news media, Wall Street, and the motion picture industry—develops in much this way. Thus the relative absence of negative stereotypes is not in itself a guarantee against a minority's coming under extremist attack. Prevailing cultural imagery can easily be adjusted and enlarged to serve extremist purposes. People might speak of "jewing" one another, for example, without actually having the behavior of Jews in mind. But if an extremist movement gains momentum—especially one based on economic discontents—such an image might become the source of political anti-Semitism.

The continuing existence of minority group prejudice, of course, makes such inventiveness unnecessary. Ample negative imagery can be found in contemporary America to provide targets for extremist propaganda.

PRESERVATIONIST IDEOLOGY

The last element in extremism is its preservationist ideology. Extremist movements have on occasion taken liberal or left positions, but this has been rare. More typically, extremist groups oppose change and call for a return to earlier and simpler days. They seek to restore the power and prestige of a declining elite and/or call for the preservation of traditional norms, values, and ways of life.

The conservative nature of this position corresponds most closely with the economic interests of wealthy Americans. It is among upper socio-economic groups, accordingly, that the right-wing ideology of extremism is most readily accepted. Wealthier Americans are most apt to agree with the antistatist positon of extremist ideology and its uncomplicated view of political problems. They favor limited government, oppose the welfare state, and fear socialism.

Different socio-economic groups are thus susceptible to different aspects of extremist appeals. Upper-income Americans are most attracted to the right-wing ideology of extremism; lower-income Americans are drawn more to the prejudicial appeals of extremism and are least resistant to its antidemocratic tendencies. Historically, extremist movements have been most successful when they have attracted support from both upper and lower economic levels. This has generally occurred when elements of both groups have focused upon some symbolic and affective aspects of the changing time: a disappearing way of life, a vanishing power, a diminishing group prestige, a lost sense of comfort and belongingness. Such status deterioration is viewed in political terms as a general social deterioration. Typically, it is an emerging minority group that is held responsible for the deterioration and becomes the principal target of attack. A politics of hate and prejudice thus provides the bridge between upper- and lower-class extremism. It is a mechanism whereby Americans with different class interests can find a common outlet for their frustrations and grievances.

It is possible now to bring together the sources of contemporary extremism discussed in this section by summarizing characteristics of the three groups currently most susceptible to extremist politics, giving them their common names. The first group, the Old Guard, is most attracted to the economic conservatism and preservationism of extremist ideology. Its members tend to be well-to-do, older, Protestant, and Republican; their response to extremist movements is conditioned by their high positions of status. The second group, the Radical Rightists, is characterized by status preservationism and strong commitments to the past. Americans in this category are typically middle-class, fundamentalist Protestant, Southern, and Republican. They are drawn to extremism through their identification with traditional norms and values, especially those of a religious nature. The third group, the Rednecks, have a weak intellectual commitment to democracy and resistance to prejudice. They are more likely to be working-class, Catholic, Eastern and Midwestern, urban, and Democratic. Their main link to extremism is their low democratic commitment and high level of prejudice.

An extremist movement would gain maximum strength if it could attract support from two or more of these groups. At present, the most likely coalition would seem to be that between the Old Guard and the Right Radicals. Members of both groups are attracted to an ideology of conservatism and preservationism. The former is grounded more in economic considerations, the latter in status deprivations, but both are "conservative" in their opposition to contemporary trends. These groups could then easily coalesce around a generally preservationist position. One of the obstacles to such an extremist coalition is the relatively greater ideological commitment of the Old Guard to democratic principles.

Rednecks share the status concerns of the first two groups but are anchored by their economic positions to a more liberal ideological position. This makes it unlikely that large numbers of Rednecks will be attracted to a preservationist-based extremist movement, at least for long. As history shows, however, working-class Americans have supported status-preservationist movements when such status appeals are salient and when they correspond (or at least don't interfere) with their economic self-interests. In recent years, a number of so-called social issues have fitted this description. They include attitudes toward protests and demonstrations, law and order, the legalization of marijuana, welfare cheats, and abortion. Rednecks generally hold conservative or preservationist beliefs on issues of this kind.

What crystallizes extremist movements—what brings such groups together—is a common displacement of grievances upon a minority. An emerging ethnic or racial group is held accountable for deteriorating status conditions; it becomes a backlash target upon which those suffering loss can fix the blame. A number of minority groups have filled and can fill the role of political scapegoat—communists, radicals, protesters, Jews, blacks, Hispanics, intellectuals, media owners, and federal bureaucrats, to name a few. During the 1960s and early 1970s, black Americans were the prime targets of such backlash attacks. However, given the persistence of negative cultural stereotypes, other groups, including Jews, remain available culprits for extremist causes.

Political Anti-Semitism

What, then, are the chances that Jews might become the target of extremist attack? Could it happen here? These questions, while central to this chapter, can be only partially and incompletely answered. What is apparent is that extremist-producing pressures continue to exist in American society. What is less apparent is whether Jews are likely to become the main victims of backlash politics or how "extreme" such actions might be.

As noted, political anti-Semitism reached its historical peak in the United States in the 1930s and early 1940s. Upwards of a hundred groups were formed for the primary purpose of promulgating political anti-Semitism, while Father Coughlin delivered his anti-Semitic diatribes to an audience in the millions. Opinion polls, just then coming into use, indicated that distrust of Jewish power was widespread. Forty-one percent of the public agreed in 1938 that Jews had too much power in the country—a figure that increased steadily to a high of 58 percent in 1945.

Following the war against Hitler, the incidence of political anti-Semitism fell sharply. On the one hand, it became less respectable to single out Jews for political attack; on the other, new groups assumed the center spotlight of extremist ideology—communists, "fellow travelers," and Negroes. The opinion surveys cited in Chapter 1 underscored this trend. By the 1960s very few Americans seemed to be troubled by Jewish power, few said they would vote against a qualified Jew for the presidency, and hardly any would support an avowedly anti-Semitic candidate. Overt support for political anti-Semitism became so rare that such questions were no longer included in major opinion polls.

Few Americans today, then, believe in or express support for political anti-Semitism in its more extreme forms. The political prejudices of contemporary Americans are not those of a Nazi Germany or a Coughlinite America. They are more subtle and indirect, drawing upon cultural myths and stereotypes rather than deep-seated animosities.

What this suggests is that political prejudice alone is an unlikely source of extremist attacks upon Jews. However, it does not follow that political anti-Semitism is an impossibility in America. As shown above, many Americans are susceptible to the appeals of extremist politics. They feel themselves to be losing out to social forces over which they have no control and are attracted to leaders or movements that offer simplistic solutions to their frustrations. Such Americans thus might give support to anti-Jewish groups or candidates on grounds other than prejudice. They may be attracted to extremist movements for other reasons and simply ignore or go along with the anti-Semitic tendencies of these groups.

Thus, as far as the "vulnerability" of Americans to political anti-Semitism is concerned, it is not the level of anti-Semitic beliefs that is the key factor but the level of resistance to political anti-Semitism. It is not merely whether people like Jews or accept the tenets of traditional anti-Semitic ideology. It is whether they understand the insidious nature of political anti-Semitism and are committed against the violation of Jews' political rights. As indicated above, many Americans fail to meet one or both of these criteria.

A brief example, drawn from a case study in this research series,[6] serves to illustrate this point. In the late 1960s what had been a routine school board election in New Jersey was abruptly interrupted by a personal attack upon the two Jewish candidates. One week before the election an incumbent board member strongly urged community voters not to support the two Jews. In a newspaper interview he gave the following reasons:

> Most Jewish people are liberals, especially when it comes to spending for education. If Kraus and Mandell are elected . . . and Fred Lafer [a Jewish board member not up for election] is in for two more years, that's a three-to-six vote. It would take two more votes for a majority, and Wayne would be in real financial trouble.
>
> Two more votes and we lose what is left of Christ in our Christmas celebrations and in our schools. Think of it.

This statement caused an immediate uproar in the local township and brought forth a chorus of condemnations. It was censured by both the full school board and the township council, dozens of protests were made by clergymen and prominent officials, and the incident received national press and television coverage. Public officials and leaders in the community, Jewish and Christian alike, were confident that this injection of prejudice would be overwhelmingly repudiated at the polls. Yet when the votes were counted, the two Jewish candidates—who had been heavy favorites prior to the attack—were soundly defeated.

What caused this unexpected result was discovered during a subsequent investigation. The fact was that the anti-Semitic nature of these accusations was never fully grasped by the local citizenry. The community members never understood that it was an act of political anti-Semitism to single out the two Jewish candidates for personal attack, to stereotype all Jews as big spenders, or to introduce the extraneous (and false) issue of Christmas celebrations in the schools. Local public leaders, for all their condemning, had failed to point out these connections. They had simply dismissed the remarks as being blatant and outrageous examples of anti-Semitic behavior. To the local townspeople, however, it was difficult to see the charges as anti-Semitic. Their idea of political anti-Semitism was closer to the Hitler model of Nazi Germany. They did not see their own community in these terms and strongly resented those who implied otherwise.

This episode thus demonstrates the subtleties and complexities often associated with contemporary political prejudice. The charges made against the two Jewish candidates were not the hateful, inciteful type of traditional anti-Semitism. Yet they were a definite example of political anti-Semitism: They involved the singling out of the two Jewish candidates for defeat *solely on grounds that they were Jews.* That many people failed to see the election in these terms is testimony to the cognitive barriers often involved in detecting and rejecting prejudice. Most local voters failed to understand the anti-Semitic nature of these charges or of their own votes.

Whether such an episode, or something like it, could occur on a national scale is more problematical. Also more problematical is whether such a political backlash could take more extreme forms in the United States. In the present conditions, neither seems very likely. Yet, as recent developments have shown, social conditions can change abruptly and radically, making possible what was once unimaginable. Few experts foresaw the emergence of the civil rights movement in the early 1960s, the student protests of the late 1960s, or the women's movement of the 1970s. Each, however, has profoundly affected and changed American society.

It would seem prudent, then, to end this chapter by inquiring into the type of future occurrences that might foster greater political anti-Semitism among Americans. Three seem worthy of particular mention—a severe economic depression, a crisis involving Israel's role in the Middle East, and the nomination of a Jew for the presidency.

AN ECONOMIC CRISIS

A severe economic depression is often viewed as a potential source of political anti-Semitism, and the reasons for this concern are not difficult to understand. Economic crises have regularly produced extremist reactions in this country. Those suffering economic losses were among the principal supporters of the extremist movements of the 1830s, 1880s and 1890s, and 1930s. Jews, moreover, have traditionally been viewed with economic suspicion. Among the most enduring anti-Semitic stereotypes today are those which characterize Jewish economic behavior as deceitful and unscrupulous and depict Jews as having too much power in the business world. For centuries, finally, Jews have been blamed for economic misfortunes. In the United States it was during the Great Depression of the 1930s that political anti-Semitism was most prevalent and most extreme.

A severe economic depression is thus likely to strain the American commitment to democratic, pluralistic values and to activate extremist tendencies within the public at large. Under such circumstances, Jews would undoubtedly be among those most susceptible to extremist attack. The tendency to single out Jews for recrimination, it would appear, would be most prevalent at lower-income levels. Less wealthy Americans would be most likely to focus their discontents upon elite power and elite economic manipulation. They would also be most predisposed toward political anti-Semitism as a result of their greater acceptance of anti-Semitic imagery. Jews, however, would not be the only minority to become more vulnerable during an economic crisis. Many middle-income Americans resent the governmental assistance given to blacks, Hispanics, and other poor minorities. If middle-income groups were to become harder pressed financially, it is likely that such resentments would grow and take on extremist forms. A severe depression would thus be likely to produce backlash reactions against poor minorities as well as against Jews or other elite groups.

A MIDDLE EAST CONFLICT

A second potential source of political anti-Semitism is the Middle East conflict between Israel and the Arab states. American Jews have been strong supporters of Israeli policies in the Middle East and effective lobbyists for this position in Washington. If these policies were to result in negative consequences for the United States, they might well produce a backlash reaction against American Jews. Two possibilities readily come to mind. First, the United States could be drawn into an unpopular war in support of Israel. Second, a pro-Israel policy might lead to an Arab oil embargo with disastrous effects upon the American economy.

The potential for conflict in the Middle East is so great that neither of these possibilities can be ruled out. Nevertheless, public opinion in the United States has been strongly supportive of Israel and of United States assistance to Israel (short of sending American troops into the Middle East). Further, no signs of a backlash against Israel or American Jews occurred during the Arab oil embargo of 1973.[7] A substantial change in public attitudes would thus be necessary for political anti-Semitism to develop from this source.

A JEWISH PRESIDENTIAL CANDIDATE

A third event that might trigger an anti-Semitic backlash is the nomination of a Jew for the presidency. Such a nomination would constitute a critical test of the American commitment to democratic norms of equality. Given the existing state of opinion in the country, it is uncertain how the test would be met.

On the positive side, it seems certain that the public reaction to a Jewish candidate would not be as hostile as once would have been the case. In the 1930s opinion polls indicated that more than half of all Americans would not support a qualified Jew for the presidency. By 1969, the last time the question was asked, only 8 percent said they would definitely not vote for a Jew, while another 6 percent were undecided. Public acceptance of other minority candidates—a black or a woman as president—has also increased during this period. Furthermore, the election of John F. Kennedy, a Catholic, would seem to have defused the religious issue in presidential politics. Kennedy won the 1960 election despite widespread opposition from Protestants.[8] Once in office, his Catholicism did not produce the dire consequences that had been predicted by his opponents.

Still, it appears likely that a Jewish presidential candidate would encounter strong political prejudices. In the first place, many Americans continue to accept various tenets of anti-Semitic ideology. Such anti-Jewish predispositions might easily be aroused during a presidential campaign, especially if reinforced by campaign oratory. Second, existing Jewish hate groups would operate in high gear during such a campaign. Their propaganda attacks might be too extreme for most voters, but they would inject anti-Semitic references into the election and make it easier for others to exploit the issue. Third, as history shows, the established political parties are not above appealing to popular prejudices when it suits their purposes. Thus it is likely that anti-Semitic appeals would be used by the opposition party or at least by some of its members. Finally, and most important, many Americans possess an imperfect understanding of and commitment to democratic principles. Their ability to detect and reject anti-Semitic appeals would thus be low.

For all these reasons, it seems likely that political anti-Semitism would be pronounced if a Jew were to run for the presidency. Whether such prejudices could carry the day would be a test of the American commitment to democracy and of the full acceptance of Jews in American society. At present, it is uncertain that it would be passed.

Summary

Extremist politics is a closing down of the democratic market place. It is the assertion that there is only one "truth" to be known and acted upon and that other positions are wrong and immoral. Extremist politics is legitimated by imputing evil motives to one's opponents or adversaries. It portrays the target groups as villains engaged in a conspiracy against the nation's interests and seeks to deny them democratic privileges on this ground.

Americans are drawn to extremist politics because of deeply held feelings of anxiety and frustration. They believe themselves to be losing out in contemporary society, whether in concrete terms of wealth and power or in some less tangible ways. Extremist politics provides an outlet for such individuals to express their feelings. It is a means to voice grievances that apparently cannot be satisfied through normal political channels. The rapidity of change in this country has left many Americans with feelings of anxiety and frustration and provides a large and almost continual base of potential support for extremist movements. Extremist groups, as a result, have gained strength and influence in America on a frequent basis. They have attracted millions of followers, have elected scores of candidates to office, and have had many of their ideas enacted into law.

Prejudice and bigotry play a large role in extremist politics. Extremist movements typically use prejudiced appeals as a means to consolidate their gains and to broaden their base of support. Prejudiced beliefs are not so much the cause or source of extremist politics as the glue that holds the various elements in an extremeist coalition together. Movements that have failed to focus upon a concrete villain have uniformly failed to gain much public support. Extremist movements, moreover, invent prejudicial beliefs as well as feed upon existing ones. Many of the negative stereotypes that Americans have held toward minorities were originally generated in this way. There were no native hostilities toward the Irish, for example, until extremist groups found it advantageous to attack Irish immigrants. Many elements of anti-Semitic ideology were similarly inspired for political reasons. Economic stereotypes may have been carried over from European culture, but the same cannot be said about alleged Jewish control of the news media, the motion picture industry, and cultural institutions generally.

Cognitive factors, finally, also play an instrumental role in extremist politics. Extremist beliefs are themselves a form of intellectual unenlightenment—a tendency to simplify and moralize political issues. They are also a violation of democratic norms of tolerance, fair play, civil rights, and civil liberties. Not surprisingly, then, extremist movements have often drawn support from the less-educated and cognitively less sophisticated elements in the population. It is when working-class Americans have aligned themselves with displaced elite groups that extremist movements have been the strongest.

The elements giving rise to extremist politics can readily be found in contemporary American society. This analysis suggests, furthermore, that extremist politics is likely to remain a recurring feature of political life in this country. Whether Jews will ever again become the principal targets of such extremism, as they were in the 1930s, is problematical. Anti-Semitic attitudes are not nearly as common now as they were in the 1930s and 1940s, and other groups, most notably blacks, have come to bear the main brunt of extremist attacks. Nevertheless, the prevalence of anti-Semitic imagery in the culture at large makes Jews vulnerable to extremist politics. The possibility of future political attacks upon Jews thus cannot be ruled out. The main defenses against political anti-Semitism are a firm cognitive commitment to democratic norms and principles and a rejection of prejudice and bigotry.

CHAPTER 10

Findings and Implications

THE PRECEDING CHAPTERS have covered considerable ground. Research findings from scores of studies, including the nine conducted as part of the Patterns of American Prejudice series, have been reviewed. The nature, extent, social location, and causes of anti-Semitic prejudice have been explored. Prejudice has been examined within the population at large as well as among urban blacks, adolescents, church members, Protestant ministers, and media users. Leading theories of prejudice have been presented and tested. Trends in anti-Semitic and racial prejudice have been delineated and compared. The linkages between prejudice and political extremism have been uncovered and commented upon.

The time has come to assess what these findings add up to. Four main questions, accordingly, are addressed in this final chapter. First, what have these studies discovered about the nature, extent, and social location of anti-Semitic prejudice in America? Second, what is the process through which anti-Semitic beliefs come to be accepted? Third, how is the persistence of anti-Semitism in America to be explained? Fourth, how, on the basis of these findings, might anti-Semitism best be resisted and controlled?

The complexities of prejudice—as well as the difficulties of studying it—are such that none of these questions can be answered as perfectly or as fully as might be desired ideally. Nevertheless, a great wealth of information has been collected in these studies, far more than has been available in the past. It is thus possible to be fairly definite in drawing conclusions about the nature, extent, and causes of contemporary anti-Semitism. It is also possible to offer some concrete suggestions as to how anti-Semitism might be combated effectively. Finally, while the findings and implications are applicable *directly* only to anti-Semitism, they illuminate understanding of other kinds of prejudice as well, especially racial prejudice.

184

The Findings

What, first of all, can now be concluded about the nature, social location, and sources of contemporary anti-Semitism? In this section the principal findings to emerge from the previous nine chapters are summarized. Subsequent sections deal with the causes of prejudice in greater depth and address the question of remedies as well.

THE NATURE OF CONTEMPORARY ANTI-SEMITISM

1. While anti-Semitism in America was once virulent and open, such is no longer the case today.

Anti-Semitism was rampant in America in the 1920s, 1930s, and early 1940s. Prominent spokesmen attacked Jews openly and viciously and millions of Americans expressed support for what was being said. Extreme hatred and loathing of Jews have all but disappeared in America today. Attitudes of this kind are sometimes found within political fringe groups, but they are rejected overwhelmingly by the public at large.

2. Very few non-Jews today favor discriminating against Jews in such public areas as employment, housing, college admissions, and hotels and resorts.

Public support for anti-Jewish discrimination was also once prevalent in this country. Many non-Jews thought it legitimate for Jews to be kept out of certain jobs or neighborhoods, admitted to colleges only under a strict quota system, and denied service in exclusive hotels and resorts. Such practices were common in many parts of the country. Discriminatory behavior of this type has virtually no support from the public today.

3. Public support for virulent "racism" and overt discrimination against other minorities has also generally and sharply declined over the past four decades.

To a considerable extent, the decline in extreme anti-Semitism has been accompanied by less public support for other extreme forms of prejudice and discrimination as well. A large majority of the public today accepts the principle that racial and other minorities should not be discriminated against in such public areas as employment, housing, schooling, and the use of public facilities. Non-Jewish white Americans have become less prejudiced toward black Americans as well as toward American Jews.

4. Anti-Semitic prejudice today is given major expression through the association of negative and objectionable traits with being Jewish.

As a general phenomenon, anti-Semitism today largely involves the harboring of negative images of Jews, more often secretly than openly. Such images are predominantly those traditional to anti-Semitism: that Jews are deceitful and dishonest in business, clannish in their behavior toward others, pushy and aggressive, vain and conceited, and that they control or have disproportionate influence over the media, motion picture, and banking industries. Some support is also found for such newer stereotypes as that Jews are more loyal to Israel than to the United States. Most American non-Jews hold some such stereotypic images of what Jews are like. About a third of the public thinks about Jews primarily in these terms and can thus be classified as anti-Semitic.

> 5. While support for discrimination against Jews in the public area has disappeared largely, discriminating against Jews in such private sectors as social club membership and intermarriage continues to be accepted by some non-Jews.

Non-Jews, in varying proportions, oppose interfaith marriages, support the right of social clubs to refuse membership to Jews, and reject the argument that Christmas carols should not be sung in public schools. Such attitudes, however, often derive from values other than prejudice, and Jews themselves often oppose intermarriage or favor the singing of Christmas carols in public schools. Americans holding such views are thus not always acting upon prejudiced feelings or motives.

> 6. Many non-Jews hold positive and sympathetic attitudes toward Jews.

Public attitudes toward Jews are by no means entirely negative or hostile; many non-Jews hold favorable images of what Jews are like and feel especially sympathetic or drawn to Jews. Indeed, considerably more Americans hold positive attitudes toward Jews than hold negative attitudes. They frequently describe Jews as warm and friendly, intelligent, ambitious, hardworking, successful, religious, and family-oriented. Anti-Semitism would undoubtedly be much more prevalent if such positive orientations did not exist. Blacks receive little such sympathy from whites and are far more often the object of prejudice and dislike. A primary cause of the difference seems to be the relative affluence of Jews and the relative poverty of blacks.

THE SOCIAL LOCATION OF ANTI-SEMITISM

> 7. Working-class Americans are more anti-Semitic than middle-class Americans, a result, largely, of the former's relative lack of education.

Anti-Semitism is found among all kinds of Americans, among the rich and poor as well as the young and old. In general, however, it is at lower socio-economic levels that prejudice toward Jews is most prevalent. The primary factor responsible for the greater anti-Semitism of working-class Americans is their relative lack of education. Americans who are equally educated vary little in prejudice, regardless of their incomes or occupations.

> 8. Older Americans are more anti-Semitic than younger Americans, a pattern again linked to education.

Older Americans are considerably more anti-Semitic than younger Americans and have been found to be so in the past as well. In part, this is because older Americans grew up during a period when anti-Semitism was more prevalent and more virulent. Primarily, however, it is because older Americans are less educated than younger Americans.

> 9. Black attitudes toward Jews differ somewhat from the attitudes held by non-Jewish whites—a reflection of the unique character of the relations that blacks commonly have with Jews.

In general, black Americans and white Americans think about Jews in the same stereotypic terms and are about equally anti-Semitic. By virtue of having certain unique kinds of economic and other relations with Jews, however, blacks are found to harbor some stereotypes more frequently than non-Jewish whites. Blacks more frequently express special economic animosities toward Jews as a result of the presence of Jews in black neighborhoods as store owners, landlords, employers, and creditors. Blacks also more frequently exhibit certain positive attitudes toward Jews, resulting from positive economic experiences with Jews, Jewish involvement in civil rights, and other factors. Because they share the condition of a minority subjected to discrimination, blacks are also less supportive than whites of anti-Jewish discrimination.

> 10. Prejudice toward Jews is distributed similarly to prejudice toward blacks.

Anti-Semitism and racial prejudice differ substantially in ideological content and acceptance. Racial prejudice portrays blacks in an especially derogatory manner and is more prevalent and pernicious in America. Despite these differences, anti-Semitism and racism are similarly distributed in the population at large. Both are more common in the working class, among the less-educated, among older Americans, in rural areas, and in the South (where racial prejudice is especially high still). These similarities suggest that the two kinds of prejudice share some common origins or causes.

THE SOURCES OF ANTI-SEMITISM

> 11. A lack of education is the main source of anti-Semitic prejudice in America. Education reduces prejudice through the teaching of cognitive skills and knowledge.

A lack of education is the most pronounced and consistent source of anti-Semitic prejudice in America. Greater exposure to the formal educational process is associated with lower levels of anti-Semitism among Americans of different incomes, occupations, ages, sexes, races, and religions. Education appears to reduce prejudice in many ways. Principally, it does so (a) by providing people with more knowledge about minorities and about the historical, social, and economic factors responsible for minority-group differences; (b) by teaching people to recognize prejudice and to understand its dangers; and (c) by providing cognitive skills, which increase people's capacity to detect prejudice and to reject it. Such factors also serve to reduce racial prejudice and, presumably, other kinds of prejudice as well.

12. Education also contributes to a reduction in anti-Semitic prejudice by teaching people norms of democracy, equality, civil rights, civil liberties, and cultural tolerance.

Education also contributes to a reduction in anti-Semitism by teaching people other values and norms which counteract prejudiced thinking. These include the beliefs that all people should be treated equally, that everyone has a right to express an opinion, and that cultural differences should be nourished and encouraged, among others. Such "ideal" norms often differ from the "common" norms prevalent in the culture. People accepting the ideal norms are likely to hold less prejudiced and more enlightened attitudes generally than those accepting the common norms.

13. No evidence is found that psychological theories of prejudice, including those which attribute prejudice to "authoritarian personality," contribute significantly to the explanation of contemporary anti-Semitism.

Anti-Semitism is sometimes explained in psychological terms, as a response to emotional needs or frustrations. The most prominent such theory is that linking prejudice to the existence of authoritarian personalities. No evidence is found that such psychological factors contribute significantly to contemporary anti-Semitism. They may do so indirectly by affecting the functioning of the cognitive process; or they may contribute to the maintenance of anti-Semitism if it becomes an element in an individual's personality. That anti-Semitism is a direct consequence of psychological malfunctioning is not confirmed. Psychological factors may have been more important in the 1930s and 1940s, when anti-Semitism was more virulent and extreme, and that is when such theories were first formulated.

14. Christianity fosters anti-Semitism when it teaches that there is no path to salvation except through Christ and where such teachings are interpreted as subjecting all nonbelievers to damnation.

Historically, Christianity has been an important source of anti-Semitism; Jews have repeatedly been reviled as religious heretics and "Christ-killers.'' Such attitudes have been less common in this country than elsewhere, and Jews and Christians have recently been engaged in a *rapprochement*. In many Christian churches, however, a particularistic theology continues to be taught, and, when internalized by clergy or laity, it remains a source of contemporary anti-Semitism. Jews are often seen by particularistic-minded Christians to be "unforgiven" for rejecting Jesus as Savior and to be collectively responsible even today for Jesus' crucifixion. Such attitudes generate not only religious hostility toward Jews but secular hostility as well.

> 15. The media can be an important interpreter of events pertaining to Jews, especially when people are otherwise uninformed.

How people interpret events pertaining to Jews and, ultimately, how they feel about Jews can be influenced significantly by the way such events are presented by the media. When knowledge is low, as it often is, the role of the media can be especially influential. During one recent event of particular importance to Jews, the Eichmann trial, the media played a generally positive role. While Israel sought to use the trial to remind the world about the horrors of the Holocaust, most Americans paid little attention to the trial or the facts it brought out. The media's generally sympathetic treatment of the issue, however, resulted in a favorable reception of the Jewish position. Indeed, Americans who were least knowledgeable about the trial—and who were the most anti-Semitic in their beliefs—most fully agreed with the case made against Eichmann.

The fact that the media acted in a positive fashion in this instance is no guarantee that it will on other issues. A comprehensive assessment of the media's role in prejudice formation or reduction has still to be made.

> 16. Prejudice is fostered through the political process in America, and Jews remain potential, if unlikely, targets of extremist politics today.

Politicians frequently appeal to public prejudices in an effort to win votes. While this sometimes occurs within the established parties, it is right-wing "extremist" movements that most fully and most dangerously exploit such prejudices. Extremist movements gain the bulk of their support among those who feel they are losing out by change. Such individuals displace their grievances upon minorities, blaming them for the social changes taking place. Extremist movements both feed upon existing prejudices and generate new ones. They are most successful when members of different social classes take out their grievances upon the same minority group.

The recurrence of extremist politics in America makes such political prejudice a continuing concern. Jews were a principal target of extremist groups in the 1920s and 1930s and remain potential extremist targets today. Among the conditions that might generate political anti-Semitism are a severe economic recession or a war in the Middle East. The nomination of a Jew as a presidential candidate would also be likely to produce increased political anti-Semitism.

How Anti-Semitic Beliefs Come to Be Accepted

These findings show that anti-Semitism has become less virulent, less overt, and to some degree less prevalent over the years. Psychological factors appear to have little if any role in promulgating anti-Semitism today, and Jews are in less danger of becoming political scapegoats. Americans generally are less prejudiced toward minorities than they were two or three decades ago.

Despite these changes, however, anti-Semitism remains fairly common in America, with about one in three Americans holding a substantial number of prejudiced attitudes toward Jews. How do such beliefs come to be accepted?

ON BEING AN ANTI-SEMITE

To answer this question, it is necessary first to consider what is involved in being an anti-Semite. As a contemporary phenomenon, anti-Semitism principally involves the harboring of negative beliefs or stereotypes about Jews. An anti-Semite is thus someone who thinks about Jews largely in stereotypic terms—who holds simplified, distorted, and negative conceptions about what Jews are like. These stereotypic beliefs serve, in effect, as an ideological belief system in relation to which Jews are perceived and evaluated. They cause people to associate derogatory characteristics with Jews and to dislike them for that reason.

Most non-Jews in America hold some such preconceived ideas or stereotypes about what Jews are like, thinking about Jews as being money-oriented, clannish, or in other stereotypic ways. All such stereotypes are by definition false in that not all Jews possess identical traits, nor are those characteristics associated with Jews wholly absent in other groups. In this sense, a majority of Americans can be said to possess anti-Semitic tendencies. They think of Jews as "different" from others and do so in traditional, centuries-old ways.

What distinguishes the anti-Semite from other people is the *scope* of the anti-Semitic imagery accepted and the *certainty* with which the stereotypes are believed. In the first respect, anti-Semites hold a number of stereotypic images of Jews which together form an integrated ideological perspective or world view. For the anti-Semite, such beliefs are mutually supportive and reinforcing. An anti-Semite, for example, might believe that Jews are bent on making money, that they engage in shady and underhanded practices to achieve this objective, and that they will especially take advantage of non-Jews in this pursuit. The central component of anti-Semitic ideology today appears to be economic. A few decades ago greater emphasis was placed upon the image of Jews as power-hungry—as surreptitiously seeking and obtaining political influence.

All of these anti-Semitic stereotypes are likely to have some "appeal" to non-Jews in that they will be thought about as potentially pertaining to Jews and not to some other minority group. This is true even for those who are unprejudiced or largely unprejudiced. Anti-Semites, however, differ from the less prejudiced in their unequivocal acceptance of these stereotypes as true descriptions of what Jews are like. They *believe* Jews to possess these traits and rarely entertain any notions to the contrary. There are, in this respect, few self-confessed bigots. Those classified as anti-Semitic in these studies seldom see themselves as prejudiced. While they acknowledge disliking Jews, they do not see this dislike as constituting anti-Semitism. They are convinced that Jews possess those egregious characteristics and that their dislike of Jews is therefore justified.

Two examples from actual interviews serve to illustrate how anti-Semites typically think about Jews and justify their positions:

> This questionnaire is apparently for the use of finding out if I am prejudiced against Negroes or Jews, which I can say I am not. I feel they should have a place in the community if they have earned the right. So far the Negroes are uneducated and unclean and haven't earned their place in the average community. The Jews are neither and they fit in most anyplace, but they are underhanded and sneaky. [A middle-aged housewife]

> Some of my replies in connection with races and faiths other than my own might seem prejudiced to some. But during my forty years of business life I have had a very good opportunity to observe the characteristics of the Negro and the Jew. . . . In my opinion, by far more than the majority of them retain the distinctive traits attributed to their race and/or faith. . . . Jews as a rule try almost every devious trick in the book to alleviate themselves from the fulfillment of their just obligations. [A retired business executive]

ON BECOMING AN ANTI-SEMITE

The very prevalence of anti-Semitic imagery in the culture makes its acceptance an option for everyone. Virtually all Americans are likely to come in contact with anti-Semitic stereotyping at one point or another in their lives. As a result, most Americans are placed in a position where they must consider the idea that Jews might be as they are depicted by anti-Semitic ideology, even if ultimately they reject such beliefs.

Given the anti-Semitism present in the culture, there are several routes through which Americans may be exposed to it and come to embrace it. Four are of particular importance: (1) exposure to authority figures who express anti-Semitic sentiments, (2) having predominantly anti-Semitic friends and associates, (3) reading or hearing negative things about Jews, and (4) having relations with Jews that are hostile or conflictual.

That the pronouncements of authority figures can unleash mass anti-Semitism was demonstrated most chillingly in Nazi Germany. Germany was one of the most civilized nations in Europe—in terms of its cultural and educational achievements—and by all appearances the German people were not rabidly or even unusually anti-Semitic. Under the conditions of the time, however, large numbers of Germans readily accepted Hitler's political denunciations of Jews and his policy of mass genocide. In this country, it was not too long ago that many Americans were attracted to the anti-Semitic diatribes of such figures as Henry Ford, Sr., Father Coughlin, Gerald Winrod, and Gerald L. K. Smith. Their allegations about Jews were widely accepted by Americans without any visible sign of concern regarding the accuracy of the charges made.

While it is less likely today that someone could gain a national following by denouncing Jews, authority figures can play a critical role in propagating prejudice among the young. The children of anti-Semitic parents, for example, will almost certainly be aware of their parents' negative feelings toward Jews and perhaps even be warned to stay away from Jews or to be extra careful in dealings with Jews. Such youngsters are unlikely to receive contrary information from other sources and, even when they do, to ignore their parents' prescriptions. Similarly, children whose Sunday school teacher portrays Jews as "Christ-killers" will have little reasons themselves to question such a characterization. Moreover, in most instances no other adult will be present to counter the allegation.

Associating with prejudiced people can also serve to bring attention to anti-Semitic imagery, reinforce existing anti-Semitic tendencies, and create social pressures to join in the stereotyping of Jews. Being around unprejudiced people will have the opposite effects, decreasing the likelihood of anti-Semitism. This is a general social tendency, of course—people tend to develop attitudes similar to those held by persons around them.

The most important of such social influences are those of the immediate family, followed by friends, co-workers, and neighbors. Anti-Semitic stereotyping frequently originates in the family setting, which is a primary transmitter of prejudice. It is often maintained by associating with friends and peers who dislike Jews and think ill of them. In a broad sense, such social influences serve to perpetuate prejudiced beliefs both over time and within certain social groups. They provide for the transmission of anti-Semitic imagery in ways that circumvent the "official" (and more tolerant) norms of the ideal culture. They also reinforce prejudiced tendencies found in different social groups (e.g., in lower socio-economic groups) or geographical locations (such as the rural South).

Still a third way by which anti-Semitic beliefs are brought out is through reading or hearing about Jews in the media or elsewhere. Many anti-Semites have no firsthand knowledge about what Jews are like; they have little personal contact with Jews and have never had a close Jewish friend. For such individuals, a primary source of information about Jews is that transmitted through newspapers, books, magazines, television, the radio, and the like. Most of what they know, or think they know, about Jews may have such origins.

Today these media sources rarely depict Jews in overtly negative ways and thus seldom directly promote anti-Semitism. They do, however, provide information which, for those so inclined, can be interpreted in prejudiced ways. For example, a news report to the effect that the "Jewish lobby" is influencing an important piece of legislation can be cited as evidence that Jews "have too much power in this country." Similarly, a story about a crooked businessman who happens to be Jewish might be taken as proof that Jews are dishonest and unethical in business. In such instances, it is not the message being communicated that is anti-Semitic but the ways in which it is received. For many Americans, this is the principal process by which "evidence" of Jewish behavior is obtained and anti- Semitic beliefs are fostered and maintained.

A final process involved in the acceptance of anti-Semitic beliefs is having personal contacts with Jews. As in the examples given above, anti-Semites often cite personal experiences with Jews as the basis for their anti-Semitic attitudes—as proof that Jews behave as depicted in anti-Semitic ideology. That personal contacts with Jews can, under certain circumstances, contribute to anti-Semitism was in fact found in these studies.

This finding, as noted, runs contrary both to the conventional viewpoint and to some previous research. Generally, it is believed, increasing the level of contact between different social groups will act to reduce prejudice, not increase it. It will do so by creating intergroup friendships where none previously existed and by providing evidence to contradict cultural stereotyping. The more that non-Jews come into contact with Jews, it follows, the more they should come to like Jews and to know that Jews do not possess those negative characteristics traditionally associated with them.

There are times, as these studies show, when this happens. However, as has also been demonstrated, personal contact can serve to exacerbate prejudice as well as to reduce it. Which effect will occur depends to a considerable extent upon the nature of that contact. If relations are hostile, abrasive, one-sided, or negative in other ways, they are likely to promote prejudiced feelings. Moreover, the prevalence of cultural stereotyping leads people to "look for" and find characteristics they may otherwise not have noticed. There are Jews, as there are non-Jews, who are money-oriented, pushy, clannish, or conceited. It is only when such attributes are found in Jews, however, that they are likely to be taken as an indication of group rather than individual behavior.

Two examples of contact leading to prejudice were found in these studies. Black Americans, first of all, have predominantly one-sided and oppressive relationships with Jews, as they do with non-Jewish whites. They interact with whites not as social equals but largely as customer to merchant, tenant to landlord, and employee to employer. Because Jews are often cast in such roles vis-à-vis blacks, economic hostilities toward Jews often develop, and as a group blacks hold more negative attitudes toward Jewish economic behavior than do non-Jewish whites. It is apparent even in this instance, however, that the prevalence of anti-Semitic imagery in the culture stands behind such stereotyping. Blacks in fact make far more negative assessments of the economic practices of other whites than of Jews. But it is Jews, not whites generally, who are thought of as engaging in devious and unethical economic behavior and are thus labeled in these ways.

The second example is from the study of adolescent prejudice. The Jewish students in this study were found to work harder in school to be better students and to be more motivated toward higher education— characteristics which, it was surmised, might lead to their having power in school, showing conceit, and appearing bossy as compared to the average student. In this sense, it is possible to see how the evidence acquired through personal contact might tend to validate anti-Semitic imagery. Non-Jewish teenagers knew Jews who presumably behaved in these ways. Once again, however, cultural stereotyping played a critical role in the acceptance of such beliefs. Were Episcopalian and Presbyterian youngsters, possessing identical academic characteristics, to exhibit similar traits, they would not be perceived in such negative terms simply because there is no similar anti-Episcopalian or anti-Presbyterian imagery in the culture to nourish such a perception.

While anti-Semitism can be reinforced and activated in many ways, then, it is the pervasiveness of anti-Semitic imagery in American culture which allows it to be accepted with such ease. Once the stereotypes enter a person's consciousness, they become filters through which any further information about Jews is processed. Jews are, in effect, placed on trial to prove themselves innocent of the charges made in the stereotypes. Such is the burden that prejudice places on its victims.

ON DISLIKING JEWS

One final aspect of anti-Semitism, a critical one, remains to be discussed. Anti-Semitic prejudice involves not only the harboring of negative beliefs about Jews but the disliking of Jews as well. To the anti-Semite, Jews possess characteristics that are despicable and odious. One typically dislikes those who are believed to be power-hungry, pushy, conceited, clannish, deceitful, and dishonest. Anti-Semites thus develop negative feelings toward Jews. Such feelings produce tendencies to shun Jews, to speak ill of them, and to support anti-Jewish discrimination. Those who dislike Jews intensely are also potential recruits for extremist groups using anti-Semitic appeals.

As these studies indicate, negative feelings about Jews are not always a consequence of negative stereotyping. Indeed, it is possible for someone to hold beliefs about Jews that by normal standards would be judged negative, to cite evidence to support these beliefs, and still to feel no hostility as a result. On some occasions, the result can even be feelings of sympathy toward Jews. An example might be someone who believes that Jews are overly clannish and stick together too much, but who believes that Jews behave in these ways because they are responding to the discrimination of others.

Which consequence follows from negative beliefs, as this example shows, depends upon how one accounts for the characterization of Jews contained in the belief. On the one hand a "racist" explanation may be given—one that conceives of the objectionable trait as resulting from genetically produced character deficiencies in Jews. Thinking in these ways is likely to produce negative feelings toward Jews. On the other hand, the same trait may be thought a result of historical, social, and economic conditions which Jews not only had no control over but were the victims of. In this instance, neutral and even positive feelings toward Jews can result.

The belief that Jews are clannish is thus responded to negatively when such behavior is interpreted as a sign of innate Jewish malevolence. It elicits a more favorable or sympathetic reaction when Jewish clannishness is viewed as a natural result of centuries of persecution and imposed segregation. Similarly, the belief that Jews were involved in Jesus' crucifixion can be interpreted in various ways. For some, it stigmatizes Jews forever and is the reason why Jews have suffered such persecution through the centuries. For others, it is a historical incident having no significance for the role of Jews in the world today.

Anti-Semitic stereotypes vary in the degree to which they can be subjected to alternative explanations. Some stereotypes are so inherently negative that their acceptance will almost always be attended by hostility. The beliefs that Jews are dishonest in business, "tricky," or "pushy" are difficult to accept in other than racist or racist-like terms. Other stereotypes, however, are amenable to numerous interpretations.

Anti-Semitic prejudice is thus a more complex phenomenon than is sometimes presumed. It involves, in the first place, the harboring of negative beliefs or stereotypes about Jews. An anti-Semite, by definition, is someone who thinks about Jews in terms of the ideological imagery of anti-Semitism. Additionally, however, anti-Semitism is characterized by holding negative feelings toward Jews and disliking them. Whether the stereotyping of Jews results in such negative feelings depends in large degree upon the nature of the stereotypes accepted and how they are explained. Some stereotypes inherently lend themselves to pejorative interpretations; others can be explained in neutral or positive terms. It is when stereotypes are explained in terms of innate, genetic differences that anti-Semitism can be judged to be most fully present.

Accounting for Anti-Semitism

Given these findings about contemporary anti-Semitism, any effort to account fully for its existence must deal with two additional questions. First, why is it that some people accept as true anti-Semitic stereotypes prevalent in American culture while others reject them? Second, why is it that some people come to hold racist explanations of Jewish–non-Jewish differences while others interpret these differences neutrally or even positively?

It is apparent from this research that anti-Semitism can be generated in a variety of ways. It can come about through the utterances of authority figures, certain interpretations of Christian faith, the economic presence of Jews in black neighborhoods, the opinions of family members or peers, or simply the reading or hearing of negative things about Jews. Regarding what is central to how anti-Semitism is generated, by whatever route, these studies are loud, clear, and consistent: Negative stereotypes of Jews and racist explanations of perceived differences between Jews and non-Jews are essentially products of a lack of knowledge on the one hand and faulty thinking on the other. This research thus supports the "cognitive" approach to conceptualizing and explaining prejudice. Prejudiced beliefs are simplifications and distortions of social reality. They are based upon misrepresentations, half-truths, and faulty logic. Americans with a high degree of intellectual ability, or "cognitive sophistication," will be sensitive to these facts and thus be able to resist thinking in prejudiced ways.

Being cognitively sophisticated means possessing a variety of skills and capabilities: factual knowledge about minority group behavior, an ability to reason and draw logical inferences, an awareness of social and economic history as it is relevant to minorities, an understanding of the dangers of prejudice, and an appreciation of the norms of tolerance and civil rights. The principal ways in which these cognitive skills decrease anti-Semitic prejudice are the following:

1. By providing factual knowledge with which to refute false generalizations about Jews. Some anti-Semitic stereotypes have no basis in existing factual knowledge. They have their origins in traditional anti-Semitic ideology, not in data derived from observations about the social world. For example, no evidence exists to show that Jews are more "dishonest" or "tricky" than other businessmen, nor is it known that Jews are "pushy and prone to show off." More cognitively sophisticated Americans are likely to know that such generalizations have no factual basis; the less cognitively sophisticated will not.

2. By reducing the tendency to use individual incidents or experiences as a basis for drawing broad generalizations about Jews. Anti-Semitic beliefs are sometimes formed around negative experiences or incidents involving

Jews. An individual feels that he or she has been treated poorly or wrongly by someone who is Jewish and cites this as a justification for holding anti-Semitic attitudes. For example, an individual may feel cheated by a Jewish store owner and conclude from this experience that Jews as a group are tricky and deceitful in business. The cognitively sophisticated person will know that such an incident, even if rightly perceived, provides no basis for drawing broad generalizations about all Jews. Less sophisticated individuals are more likely to ignore the rules of evidence and inference and to conclude that the behavior of a single Jew is characteristic of all Jews.

3. *By assisting people to detect prejudice when it is encountered and thus be in a position to reject it.* Anti-Semites are ignorant about what prejudice is. They seldom see themselves as prejudiced and will usually fail to recognize anti-Semitism in others. They are highly susceptible to picking up anti-Semitic sentiments from authority figures, their peers and associates, and the media. Cognitively sophisticated Americans have a better understanding of what anti-Semitism is and thus are better able to detect and reject anti-Semitic beliefs when they are encountered. Less sophisticated Americans have a weak resistance to the prejudices of others.

4. *By helping people avoid drawing false or invidious conclusions from "real" differences between Jews and non-Jews.* Some generalizations about Jews contain an element of truth in them. Jews in America are in fact more well-to-do than the average American, and it is also true that Jews "overwhelmingly reject Christ as the Savior." There is a grain of truth in the popular stereotypes concerning Jewish influence in the media, motion picture, and banking industries. Jews do not "control" these industries, but they are disproportionately active in them. There can also be particular contexts in which Jews do act in ways predicted in the stereotype. Under some conditions, Jews have sought to "stick together" to a greater extent than non-Jews.

Anti-Semites are unable to distinguish between the partial truths contained in these tendencies and the stereotyping involved in prejudice. More important, they falsely interpret the differences found between Jews and non-Jews in invidious and racist ways. For example, they conceive of Jewish wealth not as resulting from the occupational and educational characteristics of Jews, but as evidence that Jews are money-oriented and materialistic. Likewise, they explain the presence of Jews in the motion picture or media industries not in terms of career choice, and as a consequence of the historical exclusion of Jews from other industries, but as an indication of a Jewish attempt to control the communications media in America.

Cognitively sophisticated Americans are better able not only to distinguish between partial and absolute truths but also to avoid attaching invidious interpretations to those differences thought to exist betwen Jews and non-Jews. They do so primarily because of their greater understanding of the historical, social, and economic factors that have produced the distinctive traits found within different ethnic, religious, and racial groups. They are able to account for the difference of Jews, or other minorities, from others without resorting to essentially racist interpretations. They realize, for example, that the disproportionate presence of Jews in some occupations is a result of their exclusion from others. Americans without such knowledge and understanding will more easily succumb to the racist explanations of such "real" differences.

5. *By providing people with an understanding of the dangers of anti-Semitism and the effects of prejudice upon its victims.* Anti-Semites see nothing wrong with holding the beliefs they do. They are convinced that Jews possess the characteristics depicted in anti-Semitic ideology, and they accordingly feel justified in disliking Jews. They see no dangers in holding such prejudiced beliefs and no particular harm inflicted upon its victims.

Cognitively sophisticated Americans are more aware of the history of minority group prejudice and the effects of unchecked bigotry on both its victims and society at large. With respect to Jews, they are more likely to be aware particularly of the history of Jewish suffering and the past record of anti-Semitism in this country. For these reasons, they are able to resist anti-Semitic tendencies in themselves and to reject them in others. Cognitively unsophisticated Americans are without this extra shield against prejudice.

6. *By introducing individuals to the values of equality, democracy, tolerance, civil rights, and civil liberties.* Anti-Semitism is not an isolated set of beliefs for most Americans. Those who hold prejudiced beliefs toward Jews hold distorted, simplified, and unenlightened beliefs generally. They tend to see people as inherently unequal, to be intolerant of those who are culturally or socially different, to reject the right of political dissent, and to be prejudiced toward such other groups as blacks. It is no accident that anti-Semites think in these ways. Just as a lack of cognitive sophistication fosters prejudiced thinking, so it fosters the acceptance of other unenlightened beliefs and values as well. Moreover, thinking in intolerant and stereotypic ways generally makes the acceptance of anti-Semitic imagery much easier.

Cognitively sophisticated Americans more often possess those norms and values that counteract prejudiced thinking. They have a firmer intellectual grasp of and commitment to the virtues of democracy, the importance of civil liberties, the necessity of responsible and informed citizenship, and the need for diverse opinions to be heard and taken account of in the political arena. Commitment to such values by the cognitively sophisticated is an element in their being free of prejudice and, as importantly, a source of their advocacy that prejudice be combated in others. That there is a social taboo against prejudice in American society, despite its widespread practice, is largely the result of efforts by more intellectually enlightened, cognitively sophisticated citizens.

In sum, the intellectual skills and cognitive abilities discussed here militate against prejudiced thinking. They cause the anti-Semitic imagery that is so common in American culture to be rejected. They also foster opposition to prejudice in others. Alternatively, in the absence of the necessary intellectual skills and cognitive abilities, people are left highly susceptible to anti-Semitic stereotyping, to accepting the anti-Semitic statements of authority figures or close associates, to interpreting negatively what is read or heard about Jews in the media, and to bearing general resentments against Jews as a result of experiences with individual Jews.

PSYCHOLOGICAL THEORIES

In some writings on prejudice, anti-Semitism is explained in psychological terms. In general, these theories see anti-Semitism as a response to some emotional tension, need, or problem. Individuals in this emotive state are said to "take out" their frustrations and aggressive tendencies upon Jews. By disliking Jews—and associating objectionable traits with Jews—these people are allegedly better able to live with their own inner difficulties. From a psychological perspective, then, the anti-Semite is in some way emotionally impaired; he or she may have had a repressed childhood or be unable to cope with the demands of modern life. Anti-Semitism is thus seen as a basically irrational response to some inner problem or problems.

No evidence was found throughout these studies to support such psychological explanations of prejudice. As indicated, questions can be raised about the adequacy of existing measures of personality or the interpretations given to these measures. Furthermore, psychological theories may be important in those extreme cases where prejudice takes the form of a pathological condition. By and large, these studies did not address themselves to this type of anti-Semitism, which is more often found in political fringe groups than in the public at large. Finally, it is possible that anti-Semitic beliefs, once accepted, can serve psychological functions for some individuals. In this sense, psychological factors may play some role in the maintenance of prejudiced attitudes.

These qualifications aside, the evidence rules out psychological factors as an important source of contemporary anti-Semitism. That psychological factors play little, if any, role in contemporary anti-Semitism is an important finding. If it were otherwise, it is difficult to see how anti-Semitism could be reduced, since personalities are not subject readily to change. Contemporary anti-Semitism, however, cannot be dismissed as an irrational or pathological condition. It is primarily due to cognitive deficiencies in the individual—a condition, fortunately, that can be dealt with through concrete programs of amelioration.

How Anti-Semitism Can Be Resisted

A principal objective in initiating this research was to discover how anti-Semitic prejudice might be better understood and controlled. What kinds of actions, it was asked, might be undertaken to reduce the incidence of anti-Semitic prejudice in America? What specific strategies are likely to be most effective? What more might be done, especially, by the major socializing institutions of American society—the schools, the churches, and the media?

The findings provide grounds for both pessimism and optimism in formulating answers to these questions. On the one hand, the very pervasiveness of anti-Semitic prejudice means that it cannot be easily or quickly brought under control. On the other hand, these findings suggest that there are concrete steps that could be taken to strengthen people's resistance to prejudice. These involve the development and use of cognitive skills to contain anti-Semitic thinking.

TEACHING PEOPLE NOT TO BE PREJUDICED

The strategy suggested by this research, in short, is one of instruction. Anti-Semitism persists largely because people do not know enough not to be anti-Semitic—to reject anti-Semitic imagery when exposed to it or to situations conducive to anti-Semitic thinking. The findings contain several clues as to how people might be taught not to be prejudiced and how more effective programs to combat anti-Semitism might be devised.

First, instruction should not start and end, as it often does, with the simple proclamation that prejudice is wrong or evil. To teach no more than that anti-Semitism is bad is likely to have little or no effect upon personal beliefs. It is likely to have little relevance, most especially, to the confirmed anti-Semite. Moreover, simply proclaiming prejudice to be evil may create the dangerous illusion that it is enough merely to issue such a condemnation.

Second, instruction about prejudice should include instruction to those enlightened values and norms that are part of the "ideal" culture. These include the principles of equality, democracy, freedom of speech, freedom of religion, and the like. Values of this nature, once internalized, strengthen commitment to tolerance and provide reasons to avoid being prejudiced. They make it more difficult to accept different treatment of or discrimination against minorities.

Americans have a tendency, of course, to acknowledge ideal norms in principle and to disregard them in practice. Equality may be espoused, for example, by people who at the same time believe that a Jew should not be elected to the presidency or that it is all right that blacks be excluded from all-white neighborhoods. Simply teaching the ideal values of the culture is thus in itself an insufficient strategy to effect real attitudinal change. Nevertheless, it is important that prejudice not be treated as an isolated phenomenon and that the "syndrome of unenlightenment," which supports prejudiced thinking, be discredited. While a commitment to enlightened values is not a guarantee against prejudice, it can be, as these studies show, a factor in its reduction.

Third, instruction should deal with minority group stereotypes both openly and directly. That anti-Semitic beliefs exist should be acknowledged and the content of these beliefs discussed thoroughly and critically. This will not be difficult for those stereotypes which are blatant and obvious misrepresentations of reality. Pointing out the distortions in such beliefs will serve to expose factual errors associated with anti-Semitism and should expose the ideological character of anti-Semitic thinking. Some stereotypes, however, are not so easily analyzed in these terms. They may contain partial truths or be descriptive of Jews in particular settings. They may also be supported by the personal experiences of those being taught or by subjective evaluations of the relevant "evidence." The acceptance of these stereotypes is unlikely to be negated through reference to contrary evidence alone, however pertinent such evidence might seem. For the anti-Semite, there are other "facts" that refute or contradict those presented by the instructor.

The way to deal with the problem is not, as is frequently thought and practiced, to deny or ignore the existence of group differences, especially ones that reflect negatively on one group in comparison with another. It may seem wise to stay away from such discussions since acknowledging the existence of a negative feature about a minority may facilitate prejudiced thinking. A more likely result of such avoidance, however, is to compromise the instructor and impair his or her effectiveness. It may also produce a boomerang effect by making it seem that there may be some justification for prejudice after all.

The pedagogical strategy pointed to by this research, then, is a forthright acknowledgement of group differences and discussion of their nature, causes, and consequences. This is called for whether the differences have positive, negative, or neutral implications. It is especially important not to exclude discussions of negative attributes, so that those being instructed will not feel deceived.

Acknowledging that negative group differences exist is to risk providing validating evidence for those inclined to be prejudiced. To prevent this possibility, it is necessary to provide further instruction about the nature of group differences—instruction in how not to draw false conclusions from the differences or engage in racist explanations of them. The fourth suggestion for combating anti-Semitism, then, is to teach people how to use the rules of logic and inference and to understand what can or cannot be said about group differences. Instruction is needed on the distinction between relative and absolute group differences and between individual and group tendencies. Instruction is also needed to assist people to look beyond surface characteristics and easy explanations and to discover the more subtle and important reasons for human behavior. Just as students of chemistry learn to inspect a chemical solution to discover its properties, students of prejudice need to be able to examine human situations and decide what conclusions can or cannot be inferred from them.

Finally, special instruction is needed about how group differences come about. This involves instruction in the historical background of different religious, ethnic, and racial groups in America, the unique cultural heritages and values of these groups, and the social and economic positions they have come to occupy in society. More important, this involves instruction in how these factors affect minority group differences today. One might explain, for example, why it is that Jews are often employed in business or economic pursuits. Likewise one might discuss the historical circumstances through which blacks have ended up disproportionately poor and underemployed.

The purpose of such instruction is to teach people to avoid explaining group differences in genetic or racist terms. Jews, blacks, and others can exhibit tendencies toward different traits without having them ascribed to innate causes. People can be seen as different without being thought of in prejudiced terms.

Anti-Semitism, as noted, is so deeply implanted in American culture that its reduction can come about only slowly and with considerable effort. The same is even more true of racial prejudice. Nevertheless, instruction pursued along the lines suggested here would, if successful, make prejudice so indefensible intellectually as to render it inoperative even among those surrounded by prejudiced peers. Making prejudice inoperative would not necessarily result in the creation of friendly or approving attitudes toward those who are now the objects of dislike. Nor would it mean that traits which previously elicited a negative reaction will now be thought of positively. Such comprehension, however, does forestall an automatically hostile response and allows for group differences to be dealt with on their own terms. This in itself would constitute a significant change in human attitudes and behavior.

THE SCHOOLS AND PREJUDICE

It is apparent that the schools are the most appropriate and potentially effective agent to carry out the instructional strategy just outlined. To the schools has been delegated the task of educating the young. They are best equipped to provide the kind of comprehensive instruction necessary to combat prejudice, and they are committed, as one of their goals, to the teaching of enlightened, tolerant values.

By and large, however, the problem of prejudice has not had high priority on the agendas of the nation's educational institutions. Rarely, if ever, do school districts mobilize themselves in an all-out effort against prejudice. More significantly, perhaps, prejudice is not usually among the subjects thought to demand pedagogical attention. Courses on prejudice are not offered in the majority of schools, and there is no widely used textbook for such a course below the college level. Insofar as the subject is treated in more general social studies courses, it is dealt with briefly, and mostly in courses that are not required for all students.

The relative neglect of prejudice is surprising in light of the schools' enormous involvement with the problem of discrimination, especially its involvement in racial discrimination since the Supreme Court's historic ruling twenty-five years ago. A natural complement to efforts to bring about racial integration would seem to be a parallel effort to teach black and white youngsters how to get along with one another. Yet, except in more progressive school districts, no systematic effort has been made to deal with the human-relations side of integration. More often than not, youngsters were never prepared for desegregation, and in many instances teachers were not prepared either. To be sure, courses in black history and culture were introduced into school curricula. They were begun late in the game, however, and mostly as a result of pressure from black parents rather than as an analytically arrived-at strategy for dealing with prejudice. The policy followed, more by default than by design, has been to rely mostly on cultural contact to solve somehow the problem of prejudiced attitudes and to deal with overt instances of prejudiced behavior on an *ad hoc* basis.

The net effect is that racial harmony has not been a product of racial integration, and prejudice remains widespread in school populations. Judging from the results of the teenage study, this is true not only of racial prejudice but of anti-Semitism and a virulent but neglected form of class prejudice as well.

Just why the schools have dealt with the problem of prejudice mostly through a policy of benign neglect is not entirely clear. Implicit in the question is the assumption that educational institutions should be doing something more. Certainly there is precedent for looking to the schools as an instrument of social reform, and there is a belief in some quarters that this should be a primary goal. At the same time, the schools themselves are a creation of society and are thus under pressure to reflect social values rather than to change them. Such constraints are often exercised through local school boards and constituency control of the purse strings.

Another reason for the schools' failure to do much about prejudice is that prejudice often is not seen by school authorities as a serious problem. The prejudice of youngsters is made highly visible by research such as that reported here. But unless such research is undertaken, or unless prejudice is so severe as to lead to open conflict, it is not visible in the ordinary course of events. Prejudice is held in silence and, when displayed, is likely to be expressed privately rather than publicly, in hidden rather than open ways. Young people are especially inclined to conceal their prejudices from teachers and school officials.

A final and crucial reason for the schools' neglect of prejudice is that scholars dealing with the subject have been in sharp disagreement over the causes and remedies of prejudice. It has simply not been clear what could or should be done about combating anti-Semitism or other kinds of prejudice. Indeed, if the widely cited psychological approach is correct, there is not much the schools could contribute anyway. Thus it isn't as if blueprints for prejudice control were available but not being used. A school district with the conviction that prejudice control is a school responsibility would have to start almost from scratch to develop a comprehensive program. Since no school district has the resources to do that, it is not surprising that little is currently being done.

The pedagogical strategy outlined here, it is suggested, should provide schools with an effective set of guidelines for formulating such programs. It remains, however, for school authorities and scholars to find the best ways to implement these strategies. Some experimental work would be required, for example, to decide at what age levels such instruction should be provided and whether it would be better offered in a single course devoted exclusively to prejudice or at appropriate points throughout the school curriculum. These obstacles notwithstanding, the promise that such an instruction program would effect a substantial reduction in prejudice seems to be sufficiently compelling to justify some effort on the part of the nation's educational institutions to try it out.

THE CHURCHES

The churches in this country are likewise in a position to affect the prejudices of Americans. They, more than other institutions, claim to serve as moral guides for the nation. They also have large and diverse memberships, which can be approached directly on the issue.

By and large, however, the churches have not been vigorous opponents of prejudice in America. They have tended more to accommodate to existing prejudices than to resist them, and have sometimes themselves been a source of bigotry. Not long ago the Sunday morning worship period was aptly described as the most segregated hour of the week. In recent years the churches have become more attentive to the problem of prejudice, both within their own ranks and in the society at large. Efforts to combat prejudice, however, have been limited in scope and have met with little apparent success among the rank-and-file membership. A majority of laypersons have opposed church involvement in racial issues, and there is no evidence that Christians are any less prejudiced than non-Christians.

As with the schools, then, a greater commitment is required if the churches are to be more effective in combating prejudice. There would seem to be strong reasons for making such a commitment, given the churches' moral teachings on love and brotherhood and their own contributions to prejudiced beliefs and behavior.

What the churches might do is suggested by several of these research findings. An obvious first step is for the churches to re-examine their own teachings about prejudice, especially about Jews and Judaism. Are Jews depicted in hostile or stereotypic ways in church literature? Do church doctrines, however unintentionally, appear to promote negative beliefs or feelings toward Jews? In particular, it is imperative for the churches to inspect their teachings about the crucifixion and the Jews' role in it. Efforts should be made to eliminate any suggestion that modern-day Jews are implicated in the death of Jesus two thousand years ago.

Merely eliminating negative references to Jews, of course, is not enough, nor is issuing a formal repudiation of the doctrine of Jewish culpability. Few laypersons pay attention to their churchs' official pronouncements, and fewer still seem to be influenced by them. What is also needed is a direct, forthright examination of the issue of prejudice from a religious perspective. This should involve, at a minimum, presenting the churches' position on the issues of prejudice and discrimination in as specific and straightforward terms as possible. Such broad principles as "loving thy neighbor" and "treating people as equals" are not seen by most laypersons as statements on prejudice. They are accepted without considering how they might apply to anti-Semitic stereotyping, racial discrimination, and problems of prejudice generally. To be effective, the churches must make these connections in clear and concrete terms. This should be done not only at the national level in official church pronouncements and policy statements but also, and most especially, at the local parish level in terms that are relevant to issues in the local community.

It is also important for the churches to deal squarely and honestly with prejudice within organized religion itself. It is hypocritical, as well as counterproductive, to condemn prejudice elsewhere while ignoring its religious elements. Highly useful would be a discussion of the findings reported in Chapter 5 showing how religious beliefs promote anti-Semitism. Orthodox Christians should be made aware of the relation between religious particularism and secular anti-Semitism. They should have it shown to them that it is possible to maintain such religious convictions without holding hostile attitudes toward Jews. Evidence might be presented on segregation practices within the churches. It can be shown how separate black and white churches developed and how efforts have been or could be made to promote greater integration within organized religion.

Not everyone will agree on such matters, and some church members are likely to reject any suggestion that the churches have been prejudiced. Pointing out such patterns will shock and disturb some churchgoers. Nevertheless, attacking prejudice within organized religion will help not only to rectify the problem but also to educate the laity. It will promote a personal understanding of and grappling with the problems of prejudice.

Finally, an effective church strategy against prejudice would include some of the elements of the pedagogical strategy discussed earlier in this chapter. Church members must be assisted in understanding what prejudice is, how it comes about, and why it should be rejected. Christians are anti-

Semitic not only because a particular vision of their faith promotes such attitudes but also because they are cognitively unprepared to think about prejudice and its relation to religion. The same is true of racism and other kinds of prejudice against minority groups.

No systematic effort has been made to review for present purposes the parish educational materials which the churches of America distribute on the subject of prejudice. Scrutiny of the output of several denominations, however, suggests that not much attention is being given to the topic. Age-graded materials sometimes touch on prejudice and sometimes do not. Where they do, the subject does not appear to be treated at a level of sophistication that is likely to make children or adults more capable to deal cognitively with prejudices when they confront them. Still, those engaged in composing these materials appear genuinely concerned with making a contribution to prejudice reduction among the churches' constituency. If they are to succeed, higher priority must be given to prejudice as a subject for pedagogical attention, and the quality and quantity of educational material on prejudice being produced by the churches need to be improved substantially. In this regard, the pedagogical strategy outlined earlier as appropriate for the nation's schools also recommends itself for consideration by religious educators, especially those responsible for the substantial investment the churches now make in the production and distribution of materials for parish education.

THE MEDIA

A third socializing institution that has an important part to play in determining the extent to which prejudice remains an element in American culture is the media. The media in America are a primary source of information about what minorities are like, what they do, and how others respond to them. They are thus in a crucial position to reinforce existing cultural stereotypes or to educate the public against them. The influence of the media, moreover, appears to be growing in America. This is in part because of a broadening in the media's audience, but mainly because of the declining role of other socializing institutions.

Relatively little is known about how the media actually affect racial and religious attitudes in America. Examples can be cited where the media have pandered to popular prejudices on the one hand and have dealt with prejudice in enlightened and informative ways on the other. In general, the media's treatment of minorities probably has not been much different from that of other institutions in American society. They have been a principal conveyer of stereotypes during more prejudiced periods in American history but, because of the changing climate of public opinion, have become more sensitive in recent years to how prejudices against minorities are portrayed.

The media's responsibilities, however, are in many ways unique and entail special problems. This is especially true of the reporting of the news. News accounts provide the raw data in relation to which Americans can test minority group stereotypes, finding evidence either to confirm or invalidate them. The accepted norm in news reporting is "objectivity"—presenting all sides of a story fully and without bias. What constitutes objectivity, however, can be difficult to determine and put into practice. Is this norm satisfied, for example, when a reporter presents all of the immediate "facts" surrounding a story about a particular minority or minority group member? Or does it require providing additional background information and interpretative materials so that the audience can more fully comprehend minority group behavior? Most news reporting about minorities does not go beyond the bare facts or surface characteristics of the story.

It is possible, moreover, for the news media to be impartial in *how* they report the news but to be selective and biased in *what* they report. Newspapers, for example, may exhibit the strictest standards of objectivity in reporting about crimes in which blacks are involved, but may systematically underreport more positive news about blacks. This may be a conscious policy designed to appeal to the majority of the readership or a largely unconscious one, reflecting a lack of awareness of events in the black community. In either case, the result is to publish more negative than positive stories about blacks.

The imbalance in reporting is often reinforced by another feature of news coverage, the tendency to stress the lurid, sensational, and unusual over the ordinary, commonplace, and benign. Stories about crime and rape, for example, are more likely to make their way into the news than reports about community meetings or ordinary acts of kindness. The result is to present a rather bleak picture of the overall human condition. For minorities, however, this emphasis upon the deviant and unusual can further distort their media image. News coverage of poor minorities, such as blacks, is likely to focus upon crime, drug use, neighborhood disturbances, protests, and other such behavior more characteristic of the deprived. News reports featuring Jews will often focus upon such distinctive issues as conflicts over religious practices, Jewish lobbying activities in Washington, and Jewish support for the state of Israel. The overall impression conveyed is that blacks and Jews are as they are depicted in traditional stereotypes.

Similar problems exist in media presentations that are primarily for entertainment. Minorities have often been excluded from such programing or portrayed in stereotypic and prejudiced ways. In the past, for example, blacks were typically shown as servants or comedians—as superstitious, cowardly, servile, good-natured, and inferior. White writers, producers, and directors constructed black roles to conform with white stereotypes— "black boys" carrying the white man's luggage, black natives sneaking around in the jungle, black tap dancers doing a buck-and-wing.

Such stereotypic portrayals, of course, are no longer tolerated today. Black Americans have become principal characters in television series, serious documentaries, motion pictures, plays, novels, and advertising. A remarkable change has occurred over the past two decades. At the same time, the culture has changed over this period as well, and it is not clear whether the media's presentation is any farther "ahead" of the culture than in the past. The dominant portrait of blacks, for example, has often been simpleminded; blacks are shown as fine as long as they can be seen to hold traditional white middle-class values. On other minorities—Mexican-Americans, Puerto Ricans, and American Indians—the media have largely remained silent or tended toward stereotypic treatments.

While some progress has been made, then, the media clearly could become a more effective agent against prejudice. Given the media's critical role in confirming and passing on cultural stereotypes, those involved in the various media would seem to have a special obligation to deal more directly and forcefully with minority group problems. Prejudice control should be viewed as a principal responsibility for the media, as much as it is for the schools and the churches.

A minimal effort in this direction would be to extend the norm of objectivity to news selection as well as news reporting. Concrete steps could be undertaken to ensure that the media do not convey overly negative or false impressions about what minorities are like. This would entail a rethinking of standards of newsworthiness so that they do not primarily reflect the values and interests of the dominant majority. Greater coverage should be given to the day-to-day affairs of minority group communities and an attempt made to balance negative news stories with more positive ones. A concerted effort, finally, should be made to recruit and train larger numbers of minority group members for news staffs. No matter how well intentioned, white reporters will not have the same storage of information, insights, and sensitivity to events occurring in minority neighborhoods.

Additionally, the media would seem to have some responsibility to move beyond reasoned objectivity and to enter the struggle against prejudice openly and unabashedly. They might involve themselves in efforts to educate their audiences about the nature and prevalence of bigotry in America; to inform them about minority group culture and the unique socioeconomic history of different minorities; and to nurture the kind of sophistication and consciousness that would make them want to do something about prejudice. This might also involve giving priority to the "positive ordinary" rather than the "negative extraordinary" in minority group life and treating minorities in more complex and sophisticated ways in entertainment programing.

The media can rightly claim that they have moved in all or most of these directions in recent years. Particularly outstanding have been such television programs as *Of Black America*, *Roots*, and *Holocaust*. These and other presentations have shown that complex materials can be dealt with sensitively and informatively. Still, much remains to be done in both news and entertainment areas. An occasional documentary or serious feature is not enough to offset the pervasive cultural stereotyping of minorities or the message conveyed in other media programs. The media must find ways to transcend the culture and educate the public if they are to play a more positive and effective role in prejudice control.

THE ROLE OF INDIVIDUALS

There is little likelihood that the schools, the churches, or the media are going to take up or even consider the suggestions offered here as a result of this book's publication. It would be the height of wishful thinking to anticipate such results. Institutions are not moved to change simply because they are exhorted to do so.

At the same time, if such dramatic results are not anticipated, some expectations are harbored in advancing these suggestions that there will be individuals who might take them up, and that through individual effort some added leverage might be gained in efforts to combat prejudice in the society. One such expectation is that there will be school administrators, teachers, and school board members who will be persuaded that the schools can do more in the struggle against prejudice and, thus persuaded, will take the initiative to see that their schools accept the challenge. What really is needed is for a few schools, or even one, to lead the way—to build model programs for dealing with prejudice and to demonstrate their effectiveness. Part of the reason the schools are not doing more is that there are no role models to be emulated.

Individual clergy, church members, and media executives and staff have leverage that they might exert on their institutions to cause greater and more creative attention to be paid to the problem of prejudice. As with the schools, good examples of churches acting creatively to deal with the widespread prejudice exhibited by church members are virtually nonexistent. The media have attempted more and have had some "one-shot"successes. Missing still, however, is an example of any medium seriously exploring what it might be capable of accomplishing if the subject of prejudice were to be given sustained and comprehensive attention.

In sum, in all three institutions there is a need for a demonstration that they can make a creative contribution to prejudice reduction in the society. More than anything else, successful demonstrations, where they can be emulated, afford the most promise of engaging the schools, the churches, and the media in the struggle against prejudice. Where this book can possibly make a contribution is in stimulating the kind of individual initiative necessary for such demonstrations to be attempted.

Anti-Semites and persons who are otherwise prejudiced are unlikely to read this book, so it cannot be expected to have much direct effect in reducing prejudice. It is hoped, however, that those individuals who do read it will feel themselves informed, more effectively armed to deal with the prejudice they encounter in their everyday lives, and better able to foster the kinds of institutional efforts that will be necessary to make prejudice a vestige of America's past rather than, as now, a still pervasive element of America's culture.

Notes

Preface (pp. ix–xiv)

1. The full results of the study of anti-Semitism in the national American population were published originally in Gertrude J. Selznick and Stephen Steinberg, *The Tenacity of Prejudice: Anti-Semitism in Contemporary America* (New York: Harper & Row, 1969).

2. The full report on the study of anti-Semitism among black Americans is contained in Gary T. Marx, *Protest and Prejudice: A Study of Belief in the Black Community* (New York: Harper & Row, 1967).

3. The full report is in Seymour M. Lipset and Earl Rabb, *The Politics of Unreason: Right-Wing Extremism in America, 1790–1970* (New York: Harper & Row, 1970), revised edition Chicago: University of Chicago Press, 1978.

4. The full report on this study is contained in Charles Y. Glock and Rodney Stark, *Christian Beliefs and Anti-Semitism* (New York: Harper & Row, 1966).

5. The full report on this study is also contained in *ibid.*

6. For the full report on the study of clergy, see Rodney Stark, Bruce Foster, Charles Y. Glock, and Harold Quinley, *Wayward Shepherds: Prejudice and the Protestant Clergy* (New York: Harper & Row, 1971).

7. For the full report, see Charles Y. Glock, Robert Wuthnow, Jane Allyn Piliavin, and Metta Spencer, *Adolescent Prejudice* (New York: Harper & Row, 1975).

8. The full report is in Charles Y. Glock, Gertrude J. Selznick, and Joe L. Spaeth, *The Apathetic Majority: A Study Based on Public Responses to the Eichmann Trial* (New York: Harper & Row, 1966).

Chapter 1. Anti-Semitism in Contemporary America (pp. 1–20)

1. Charles Herbert Stember et al., Jews in the Mind of America (New York: Basic Books, 1966).

2. See, for example, Arnold Foster and Benjamin R. Epstein, The New Anti-Semitism (New York: McGraw-Hill, 1974).

3. Gertrude J. Selznick and Stephen Steinberg, The Tenacity of Prejudice: Anti-Semitism in Contemporary America (New York: Harper & Row, 1969).

4. Some of the respondents scoring low on this index, it should be noted, did so because of their tendency to answer "don't know" on one or more items. That such Americans don't accept the stereotypes distinguishes them from the anti-Semitic. Yet "don't-knowism" indicates at least a susceptibility to anti-Semitism, and it is useful to separate this group from those consistently rejecting negative stereotypes. When this is done, only 20 percent of the American public emerges as completely unprejudiced. This standard is stringent, but it takes into account the extent of self-conscious and principled opposition to anti-Semitism. It is used, on occasion, in some of the subsequent discussion of the findings of this study.

5. Stember, et al., Jews in the Mind of America, p. 121.

6. Ibid.

7. Polls conducted in 1974, 1975, and 1976 by Yankelovich, Skelly, and White, Inc.

8. Stember, et al., Jews in the Mind of America, pp. 54, 65.

9. NORC results cited in Rita James Simon, Public Opinion in America: 1936–1970 (Chicago: Rand McNally, 1974), p. 87. See also Stember et al., Jews in the Mind of America, p. 69. Similar changes were recorded in two poll items asked over a shorter time span. In 1952 and again in 1966 national samples were asked: "Do you think the Jews stick together too much, or not?" In 1952, 47 percent replied in the affirmative; in 1966, 39 percent—a drop of 8 percentage points. Catholic Digest, April 1967, p. 116. Likewise in 1952 and again in 1966 the question was asked: "Compared with most people of your religious beliefs, would you say most Jews are about the same, better, or not as good in being fair in business?" The proportion replying "not as good" declined 11 percentage points, from 37 to 26 percent. Catholic Digest, August 1967, p. 118.

10. Stember et al., Jews in the Mind of America, pp. 56, 65.

11. 1975 national survey conducted by Louis Harris and Associates.

12. Reported in Gallup news releases for August 22, 1965, and June 3, 1967, and in George H. Gallup, The Gallup Poll: Public Opinion 1935–1971 (New York: Random House, 1972), pp. 1575, 1985, 2190. Opposition to a Catholic or black as President has declined during this period as well.

13. Attitudes appear to have "softened" toward intermarriage since the 1930s. A review of earlier survey results is found in Stember et al., Jews in the Mind of America, pp. 104–106.

14. Polls throughout this period showed that about a third of the American public blamed Jews for their situation or saw the Nazi persecutions as rooted in Jewish faults. In 1938 a national sample was asked: "Do you think the persecution of the Jews in Europe has been their own fault?" Ten percent said "entirely the Jews' fault," and 48 percent "partly their own fault." Hadley Cantril, *Public Opinion 1935–1946* (Princeton, N.J.: Princeton University Press, 1951). At three separate times in 1938 and 1939, the question was asked: "Do you think the persecution of Jews in Europe has been chiefly due to unreasoning prejudice, or do you think it has been largely their own fault?" The proportion saying it was largely the Jews' own fault ranged from 27 percent to 32 percent. Stember *et al., Jews in the Mind of America,* p. 138. A 1942 poll, finally, asked specifically why Hitler took away the power of the Jews in Germany. Forty-six percent said either that Jews were too powerful or that the Jews were running the economy. Cantril, *Public Opinion.*

Chapter 2. The Social Location of Anti-Semitism (pp. 21–32)

1. Thomas F. Pettigrew, "Parallel and Distinctive Changes in Anti-Semitic and Anti-Negro Attitudes," on Charles Herbert Stember *et al., Jews in the Mind of America* (New York: Basic Books, 1966), p. 388

2. T. W. Adorno, Else Frenkel-Brunswik, D. J. Levinson, and R. N. Sanford, *The Authoritarian Personality* (New York: John Wiley & Sons, 1964), and Bruno Bettelheim and Morris Janowitz, *Social Change and Prejudice* (New York: Free Press, 1964).

3. Donald T. Campbell, "Stereotypes and Perception of Group Differences," *American Psychologist* 22 (1962): 817–829; John Harding, Harold Pvoshansky, Bernard Kutner, and Isador Chein, "Prejudice and Ethnic Americans," in Gardner Lindzey, ed., *Handbook of Social Psychology,* 2d ed. (Reading, Mass.: Addison-Wesley, 1969), pp. 1–76; and Bernard Kramer, "Dimensions of Prejudice," *Journal of Psychology* 27–28: 389–451.

4. A 1975 survey conducted by Louis Harris and Associates.

5. Charles Herbert Stember, "The Recent History of Public Attitudes," in Stember *et al., Jews in the Mind of America,* p. 227.

6. *Ibid.,* pp. 228–229, and Charles Y. Glock and Rodney Stark, *Christian Beliefs and Anti-Semitism* (New York: Harper & Row, 1966).

7. Jewish respondents in a national survey in 1966 were asked whether they thought Protestant and Catholic employers would discriminate against them because of their religion. Twenty-six percent named Protestants, 37 percent named Catholics. *Catholic Digest,* August 1967, pp. 113–116. In another 1966 national survey, Jewish respondents were asked: "Do you think most (Protestants, Catholics) look down on people of your beliefs or not?" Forty-four percent of Jews agreed for Catholics, only 16 percent for Protestants. Another question was, "Do you think that (Protestants, Catholics) as a group try to interfere in any way with your religious beliefs or personal liberties, or not?" Nineteen percent of Jews said

Catholics try to interfere, while 9 percent said this of Protestants. *Catholic Digest*, November 1966, p. 59.

8. It was estimated that, if the elderly were as educated as the young, their rate of anti-Semitism would be 49 percent instead of the 59 percent that actually was in the data. This adjusted figure was arrived at by applying the rate of anti-Semitism exhibited by the elderly at each educational level to the educational distribution of the young.

9. Stember, "Recent History of Public Attitudes," p. 222.

10. *Ibid.,* pp. 224–225.

11. Similar residential differences are reported in *ibid.,* pp. 225–226.

12. 1975 Harris Survey.

Chapter 3. Education and Anti-Semitism (pp. 33–53)

1. See Gertrude J. Selznick and Stephen Steinberg, *The Tenacity of Prejudice: Anti-Semitism in Contemporary America* (New York: Harper & Row, 1969), esp. pp. 135–169; Robin M. Williams, Jr., *Strangers Next Door* (Englewood Cliffs, N.J.: Prentice-Hall, 1964); and Gunnar Myrdal, *An American Dilemma* (New York: Harper & Row, 1944).

2. Bruno Bettelheim and Morris Janowitz, *Social Change and Prejudice* (New York: Free Press, 1964).

3. T. W. Adorno *et al., The Authoritarian Personality* (New York: Harper & Row, 1950). See also Nevitt Sanford, "Authoritarian Personality in Contemporary Perspective," in J. N. Knutson, ed., *Handbook of Political Psychology* (San Francisco: Jossey-Bass, 1973), pp. 139–170.

4. Bettelheim and Janowitz, *Social Change and Prejudice.*

5. The index was developed using statements numbered 1, 2, 7, 8, and 9 from Table 3-1. Respondents were scored according to how many of these five items they answered in a simplistic way. Those scoring 4 and 5 on this index were judged to be "high" in simplism, those scoring 2 and 3 "medium" and those scoring 0 and 1 "low."

6. Richard Christie and Marie Jahoda, eds., *Studies in the Scope and Method of "The Authoritarian Personality"* (New York: Free Press, 1954).

7. The questions were worded as follows: "Would you be in favor of a law saying that groups who disagree with our form of government could not hold public meetings or make speeches, or opposed to it?" "Would you be in favor of a law saying that the President must be a man who believes in God, or opposed to it?"

8. The politicians were Hubert Humphrey, William E. Miller, Dean Rusk, and C. Douglas Dillon.

9. The sports figures were Roger Maris, Y. A. Tittle, and Arnold Palmer. The

entertainers were William Holden, Paul Newman, Vince Edwards, and Frank Fontaine.

10. Recent Gallup polls consistently report the proportion of Americans who profess a belief in God to exceed 90 percent.

11. See Samuel S. Stouffer, *Communism, Conformity, and Civil Liberties* (Gloucester, Mass.: Peter Smith, 1963).

12. The five items are the two described earlier to measure support of the Constitution and items 1, 6, and 8 on Table 3-2; scores of 3 or more are designated as high.

Chapter 4. Anti-Semitism Among Black Americans (pp. 54–72)

1. James Baldwin, *Notes of a Native Son* (Boston: Beacon Press, 1962), p. 28.

2. For blacks without work contact, the rate of economic anti-Semitism was 47 percent; for those with work contact, it was 61 percent. Figures such as these must be treated with some caution, however, since a tendency exists for survey respondents to overreport their contacts with Jews or other such groups.

3. For the full report, see Gary T. Marx, *Protest and Prejudice: A Study of Belief in the Black Community* (New York: Harper & Row, 1967).

4. In the 1975 Harris poll, 43 percent of the black respondents agreed that "Jews have to work harder because they are discriminated against in so many places"; only 27 percent disagreed. Among whites, 33 percent agreed and 52 percent disagreed.

5. In the 1975 Harris poll, 40 percent of the black respondents agreed that "Jews have supported rights for minority groups more than other white people"; 20 percent disagreed. Among whites, 35 percent agreed and 33 percent disagreed.

6. David Caplovitz, *The Poor Pay More* (New York: Free Press, 1965).

7. The same may also hold for black merchants. Merchants in low income areas, regardless of race, must deal with greater theft, maintenance costs, and the like. Consequently, they are more tempted to take advantage of customers.

8. Caplovitz, *The Poor Pay More.*

9. The cutoff point used to estimate the degree of anti-Semitism differed in this study from the national survey. Thus percentage-by-percentage comparisons cannot be made with the white respondents examined above.

10. Dick Gregory, *Nigger* (New York: Dutton [Cardinal], 1965), p. 35.

11. One recent survey suggests that these age differences in black militancy have smoothed out in the middle-to-late 1970s. *New York Times,* February 26, 27, 28, 29, 1978.

12. It might also be considered that in some instances black businessmen may consciously utilize anti-Semitism as a means of gaining support.

Chapter 5. Anti-Semitism Among the Young
(pp. 73-93)

1. C. A. Renninger and J. E. Williams, "Black-white Color Connotations and Racial Awareness in Preschool Children," *Perceptual and Motor Skills* 22 (1966): 771-785; J. K. Morland, "Racial Recognition by Nursery School Children in Lynchburg, Virginia," *Social Forces* 37 (1958): 132-137.

2. For the full report of the study, see Charles Y. Glock, Robert Wuthnow, Jane Allyn Piliavin, and Metta Spencer, *Adolescent Prejudice* (New York: Harper & Row, 1975).

3. It was felt that students might react differently to statements about adult Jews and teenage Jews, since their contacts were largely with the latter. As a result, half the subjects in this study were asked their beliefs about "Jews in general" and half about "Jewish teenagers." No significant differences were found in the responses to these two wordings, however, and only the beliefs about Jewish teenagers are reported here.

4. Richard D. Lambert and Marvin Bressler, "The Sensitive-Area Complex: A Contribution to the Theory of Guided Culture Contact," *American Journal of Sociology* 60 (1955): 583-592; Irwin Katz, *Conflict and Harmony in an Adolescent Interracial Group* (New York: New York University Press, 1955); Barbara K. MacKenzie, "The Importance of Contact in Determining Attitudes Toward Negroes," *Journal of Abnormal Psychology* 43 (1948): 4, 417-441; John Mann, "The Effects of Interracial Contact on Sociometric Choices and Perceptions," *Journal of Social Psychology* 50 (1959): 143-152; Muzafer Sherif, *Intergroup Conflict and Cooperation: The Robber's Cave Experiment* (Norman: Oklahoma University Press, 1961); and Gary T. Marx, *Protest and Prejudice* (New York: Harper & Row, 1967), pp. 154-159.

5. E. S. Bogardus, "Measuring Social Distances," *Journal of Applied Sociology* 9 (1925): 299-308, and *idem, Social Distance* (Los Angeles: the author, 1959).

6. See the discussion of the Nicholls Homophily-Heterophily Index in Glock *et al., Adolescent Prejudice*, pp. 181-182.

7. See *ibid.,* pp. 183-184.

8. One of the early works in which this theory gained clearest expression, albeit with regard to racial prejudice rather than anti-Semitism, is John Dollard's *Caste and Class in a Southern Town* (Garden City, N.Y.: Doubleday, 1937). This theory was then formalized in John Dollard, Neal Miller, Leonard Doob *et al., Frustration and Aggression* (New Haven: Yale University Press, 1939). The major statement of this theory is found in T. W. Adorno, Else Frenkel-Brunswik, D. J. Levinson, and R. N. Sanford, *The Authoritarian Personality* (New York: Harper & Row, 1959).

9. For a review of the literature on intergroup contact and prejudice, see Y. Amir, "Contact Hypothesis in Ethnic Relations," *Psychological Bulletin* 71 (1969): 319-342. See also J. J. Preiss and H. F. Ehrlich, *An Examination of Role*

Theory (Lincoln: University of Nebraska Press, 1966), and Robin M. Williams, Jr., *Strangers Next Door* (Englewood Cliffs, N.J.: Prentice-Hall, 1964).

10. Probably the best-known exposition of this thesis remains that of Gunner Myrdal, *An American Dilemma* (New York: Harper & Row, 1944). See also Gertrude J. Selznick and Stephen Steinberg, *The Tenacity of Prejudice: Anti-Semitism in Contemporary America* (New York: Harper & Row, 1969), ch. 8.

11. See Selznick and Steinberg, *Tenacity of Prejudice*, ch. 8, and Donald T. Campbell, "Stereotypes and the Perception of Group Differences," *American Psychologist* 22 (1967): 817–829, as well as the discussion and notes in Chapter 3 above.

12. See Adorno *et al., Authoritarian Personality*, and R. Christie, J. Havel, and B. Seidenberg, "Is the F Scale Irreversible?" *Journal of Abnormal Social Psychology* 56 (1958): 143–159.

13. The items for this scale were taken from the California Personality Inventory, specific items being selected with the advice of Prof. H. G. Gough. Ten of the original twenty-six items were selected.

14. Morris Rosenberg, *Society and the Adolescent Self-Image* (Princeton, N.J.: Princeton University Press, 1965).

15. H. G. Gough, *California Psychological Inventory Manual* (Palo Alto, Cal.: Consulting Psychologists Press, 1957).

Chapter 6. Christian Sources of Anti-Semitism (pp. 94–109)

1. The full report of these studies is contained in Charles Y. Glock and Rodney Stark, *Christian Beliefs and Anti-Semitism* (New York: Harper & Row, 1966).

2. The report of this study is in Rodney Stark, Bruce D. Foster, Charles Y. Glock, and Harold E. Quinley, *Wayward Shepherds: Prejudice and the Protestant Clergy* (New York: Harper & Row, 1971).

3. Pastoral letter of January 30, 1939, *Amtsblatt fürdie Erzdiözese Freiburg*, February 8, 1939, quoted in Guenter Lewy, "Pius XII, the Jews, and the German Catholic Church," *Commentary*, February 1964, pp. 23–35.

4. Quoted in Lewy, "Pius XII."

5. Charles Y. Glock, Benjamin B. Ringer, and Earl R. Babbie, *To Comfort and to Challenge* (Berkeley: University of California Press, 1967), and Andrew M. Greeley, *The Denominational Society* (Glenview, Ill.: Scott, Foresman, 1972).

6. Wayne Dehoney, letter to the editors of *Newsweek*, May 23, 1966, in response to a story on "Christian Beliefs and Anti-Semitism."

7. Catholics have often been the objects of religious prejudice themselves, and this apparently contributes to their somewhat lower levels of anti-Semitism. Catholics, however, do not appear to be any more tolerant than Protestants or

atheists. About a third of each religious group, for example, would not allow an atheist to teach in a public high school.

8. These two studies were based upon slightly different samples, of course, and the two estimates are thus not drawn from comparable populations. If anything, however, the lay sample (based upon the San Francisco Bay Area) should comprise more disproportionately unprejudiced respondents than the clergy sample (based upon the state of California as a whole).

Chapter 7. Anti-Semitism in the News (pp. 110-129)

1. For the report on the full study, see Charles Y. Glock, Gertrude J. Selznick, and Joe L. Spaeth, *The Apathetic Majority: A Study Based on Public Responses to the Eichmann Trial* (New York: Harper & Row, 1966). As noted in the Preface this study is based upon a representative sample of residents of Oakland, California.

2. These figures for Oakland are almost identical with the national figures. In a Gallup poll conducted in April 1961, 87 percent of the public indicated that they were aware that the trial was going on.

3. For a discussion of how these two measures are constructed, see Glock, Selznick, and Spaeth, *Apathetic Majority*, pp. 187-188.

4. This was true of white respondents, but not of blacks. Since the number of black respondents in this survey was small, this and subsequent discussions of knowledgeability will be limited to the white sample.

5. Yosal Rogat, *The Eichmann Trial and the Rule of Law* (Santa Barbara, Calif.: Center for the Study of Democratic Institutions, Fund for the Republic, November 1961), p. 32.

6. *New York Times Magazine*, December 18, 1960.

Chapter 8. Anti-Semitism and Racial Prejudice (pp.130-157)

1. Prior to the late 1960s, opinion surveys used the term "Negro" rather than "black." For purposes of consistency, however, the latter designation is used throughout the chapter.

2. The 1942 survey was conducted by the National Opinion Research Center (NORC), as were additional polls asking this question in 1944, 1946, 1956, and 1963. See Herbert H. Hyman and Paul B. Sheatsley, "Attitudes Toward Desegregation—Seven Years Later," *Scientific American* 211 (July 1964): 16-23, and Rita James Simon, *Public Opinion in America: 1936-1970* (Chicago: Rand McNally, 1974), pp. 56-58.

3. Gertrude J. Selznick and Stephen Steinberg, *The Tenacity of Prejudice: Anti-Semitism in Contemporary America* (New York: Harper & Row, 1969), p. 171.

4. The Harris Survey, October 4, 1971.

5. These statistics are found in National Opinion Research Center, *Cumulative Codebook for the 1972-1977 General Surveys*, University of Chicago, 1977.

6. For figures for 1970 and earlier, see Herbert H. Hyman and Paul B. Sheatsley, "Attitudes Toward Desegration," *Scientific American* 195 (December 1956): 35-39; Hyman and Sheatsley, "Attitudes—Seven Years Later"; and Andrew M. Greeley and Sheatsley, "Attitudes Toward Racial Integration," *Scientific American* 225 (December 1971): 13-19. The 1977 figures are in NORC, *Cumulative Codebook*, 1977.

7. Gallup Poll Release, October 12, 1975. The National Opinion Research Center has asked a similarly worded question with identical results. See NORC, *Cumulative Codebook*, 1977.

8. See, for example, the Harris Survey, October 2, 1975, and July 8, 1976, and the Gallup Poll, October 2, 1975. Similar results have been obtained in surveys conducted at the University of Michigan's Center for Political Research (formerly Survey Research Center).

9. *Ibid.*, especially the Harris Survey, July 8, 1976.

10. In a 1942 poll 84 percent of whites agreed that there should be "separate sections in towns and cities for blacks to live in." In another poll that same year, whites were asked whether they thought "(a) there should be laws compelling blacks to live in certain districts; or (b) there should be no laws, but there should be an unwritten understanding, backed up by social pressure, to keep blacks out of the neighborhoods where white people live; or (c) blacks should be allowed to live wherever they want to live, and there should be no laws or social pressures to keep them from it." The proportions favoring these options were 41, 42, and 13 percent respectively. NORC and *Fortune* polls cited in Hazel Erskine, "The Polls: Negro Housing," *Public Opinion Quarterly* 31 (Fall 1967): 488.

11. Data for 1942, 1956, and 1963 are found in Hyman and Sheatsley, "Attitudes—Seven Years Later"; data for 1972 in NORC, *Cumulative Codebook*, 1977. The 1972 figure includes 1 percent of respondents who said they would "like it" if a black person were to move into their block.

12. Data from the Center for Political Studies, cited in Seymour Martin Lipset and William Schneider, "The Bakke Case: How Would It Be Decided at the Bar of Public Opinion?" *Public Opinion* 1 (March–April 1978): 39.

13. Data for 1963 and 1970 are found in Greeley and Sheatsley, "Attitudes Toward Racial Integration"; data for 1977 in NORC, *Cumulative Codebook*, 1977.

14. NORC, *Cumulative Codebook*, 1977; CPS surveys.

15. NORC, *Cumulative Codebook*, 1977.

16. See Simon, *Public Opinion in America*, pp. 64–65. The responses in Table 8-2 are from NORC surveys reported in Hyman and Sheatsley, "Attitudes— Seven Years Later," and NORC, *Cumulative Codebook*, 1977.

17. Simon, *Public Opinion in America*, p. 65.

18. See, for example, the Harris Survey, July 18, 1977; *New York Times*/CBS News Survey, July 1977; and NORC, *Cumulative Codebook*, 1977.

19. See Lipset and Schneider, "Bakke Case," for a review of several polls dealing with this subject.

20. See Greeley and Sheatsley, "Attitudes Toward Racial Integration."

21. It should be noted, however, that somewhat different wording was used on these two inquiries. For data on anti-Jewish discrimination, see Chapter 1.

22. Data for these three years are provided in, respectively, Hyman and Sheatsley, "Attitudes—Seven Years Later"; Greeley and Sheatsley, "Attitudes Toward Racial Integration"; and NORC, *Cumulative Codebook*, 1977.

23. Gallup surveys cited in Hazel Erskine, "The Polls: Interracial Socializing," *Public Opinion Quarterly* 37 (Summer 1973): 290, 292.

24. NORC, *Cumulative Codebook*, 1977.

25. *Ibid.*

26. Data on social club discrimination against Jews are provided in Chapter 1. It should be noted that, whereas the question on antiblack discrimination was asked in 1977, that on anti-Jewish discrimination was asked in 1964—when discriminatory attitudes in general were more common.

27. Data for 1963 and 1970 are found in Greeley and Sheatsley, "Attitudes Toward Racial Integration"; data for 1977 in NORC, *Cumulative Codebook*, 1977.

28. Data for 1958, 1961, and 1973 are Gallup Survey figures, cited in *The Gallup Opinion Index*, October 1973, and in Hazel Erskine, "The Polls: Race Relations," *Public Opinion Quarterly* 26 (Spring 1962): 148. The 1977 figure is from NORC, *Cumulative Codebook*, 1977.

29. Hyman and Sheatsley, "Attitudes Toward Desegregation."

30. Cited in Simon, *Public Opinion in America*, p. 74.

31. Harris Survey releases, September 1, 1969; January 15, 1973; and September 12, 1977. In general, there was a slight increase in perception of discrimination between 1969 and 1972 and a larger drop between 1972 and 1977. White responses to these questions are demonstrated in the following: agreeing that discrimination existed in getting decent housing—46 percent in 1969, 51 percent in 1972, 34 percent in 1977; agreeing that discrimination exists in getting white-collar jobs—38 percent, 40 percent, and 34 percent, respectively; agreeing that discrimination exists in getting quality education—23 percent, 29 percent, and 19 percent; agreeing that blacks are discriminated against in getting "full equality"—43 percent, 40 percent, and 33 percent. A similar trend is found in questions asked a metropolitan sample of whites in 1968 and again in 1978. For 1968, see Angus Campbell, *White Attitudes Toward Black People* (Ann Arbor, Mich.: Institute for Social Research, 1971), p. 13. The 1978 figures are from a *New York Times*/CBS News survey, reported in *New York Times*, February 26, 27, 28, and 29, 1978.

Harris also asked white respondents in 1966 and again in 1969 whether they thought "in general" that black people were being discriminated against. In 1966, 61 percent said yes, 28 percent no, and 11 percent were unsure. In 1969, 46 percent said yes, 43 percent no, with 11 percent undecided. Harris Survey release, September 1, 1969.

32. Harris Survey release, July 8, 1976.

33. See Campbell, *White Attitudes*, p. 136, and CPS codebooks for 1972 and 1976.

34. Harris Survey releases, January 15, 1973, and September 12, 1977.

35. For the 1964 and 1968 figures, see Campbell, *White Attitudes*, p. 138; the 1976 figure is cited in Lipset and Schneider, "Bakke Case."

36. Data for 1963 and 1970 are found in Greeley and Sheatsley, "Attitudes Toward Racial Integration," data for 1972 and 1977 in NORC, *Cumulative Codebook*.

37. White respondents repeatedly told pollsters during this period that the civil rights movement was, in their opinion, hurting the cause of blacks. The following question, for example, was included in the national study: "I'd like to ask you to compare your feelings about blacks now with your feelings a year or so ago. Would you say that you are much less sympathetic to blacks now, somewhat less sympathetic, somewhat more sympathetic, or much more sympathetic?" Thirty-seven percent said somewhat or much less sympathetic, 15 percent somewhat or much more sympathetic, and 48 percent about the same. On another question, 47 percent of whites agreed that "blacks today are demanding more than they have a right to." Selznick and Steinberg, *Tenacity of Prejudice,* p. 171. Consistent with these patterns, whites also largely blamed blacks themselves for the circumstances in which they lived. In 1968, for example, Gallup asked whites: "Who is more to blame for the present conditions in which blacks find themselves—white people or blacks themselves?" Fifty-eight percent said blacks, 22 percent whites, with 20 percent having no opinion. Cited in Simon, *Public Opinion in America*, p. 74.

38. That is, when the educational factor was controlled, the relationship between racial prejudice and occupation and income largely disappeared. This was the same pattern found for anti-Semitism.

39. See, for example, Hyman and Sheatsley, "Attitudes Toward Desegregation"; Hyman and Sheatsley, "Attitudes—Seven Years Later"; Greeley and Sheatsley, "Attitudes Toward Racial Integration"; and especially Campbell, *White Attitudes*, pp. 54–67.

40. U.S. Bureau of the Census, *Statistical Abstract of the United States: 1977*, 98th Ed. (Washington, D.C., 1977,) p. 136.

41. Hyman and Sheatsley, "Attitudes Toward Desegregation" and "Attitudes—Seven Years Later"; Greeley and Sheatsley, "Attitudes Toward Racial Integration"; and Campbell, *White Attitudes*, pp. 54–67.

42. This was found in the national study, as well as in Campbell, *White Attitudes,* pp. 54–67.

43. Greeley and Sheatsley, "Attitudes Toward Racial Integration," p. 16.

44. *Ibid.*

45. *Ibid.*

46. Hyman and Sheatsley, "Attitudes Toward Desegregation."

47. Selznick and Steinberg, *Tenacity of Prejudice*, p. 176; Greeley and Sheatsley, "Attitudes Toward Racial Integration," p. 16.

48. For the ethnic breakdown of racial prejudice, see Greeley and Sheatsley, "Attitudes Toward Racial Integration," p. 17. Information on anti-Semitism is from a Harris survey cited in Chapter 1.

49. Charles Y. Glock and Rodney Stark, *Christian Beliefs and Anti-Semitism* (New York: Harper & Row, 1966).

50. The only exception was the greater discriminatory attitudes of Southern Baptists on three of these questions. It turned out that a large number of the Southern Baptist respondents were originally from the South, which would account for this difference.

51. The full results of this study are found in Charles Y. Glock, Robert Wuthnow, Jane Allyn Piliavin, and Metta Spencer, *Adolescent Prejudice* (New York: Harper & Row, 1975)

52. As in studying teenage anti-Semitism, half of this sample of adolescents was asked to respond to these items as they applied to "black teenagers" and half as they applied to "blacks in general." As with anti-Semitism, no differences were found in these responses, and the figures here are in reference to black teenagers.

Chapter 9. Politics and Prejudice (pp. 158–183)

1. The full report of this study is found in Seymour Martin Lipset and Earl Raab, *The Politics of Unreason: Right Wing Extremism in America, 1790–1970* (New York: Harper & Row, 1970; revised edition, Chicago: University of Chicago Press, 1978).

2. As one extremist supporter has written, "I'd lay my money any day on the hick pharmacist in Podunk Corner having a somewhat firmer grasp of the economic, social and moral facts of life than just about any one Congressman picked at random." Elizabeth Linington, *Come to Think of It* (Boston: Western Islands, 1965), p. 78.

3. Actually, this was a reemergence. The Ku Klux Klan had existed for a brief period following the Civil War as an organization to keep the newly emancipated black population in check. It was a smaller, more localized phenomenon at the time and faded away as whites reasserted their power in the South.

4. Robert Welch, *The Truth in Time* (pamphlet published by the John Birch Society).

5. Wallace actually began his career as a liberal populist. However, he lost his first race for the governorship of Alabama in 1958 and attributed his defeat to the racist tactics of his opponent. Afterward he declared: "John Patterson out-niggered me. And boys, I'm not going to be out-niggered again."

6. Rodney Stark and Stephen Steinberg, *It Did Happen Here* (Berkeley: Survey Research Center, University of California at Berkeley, 1967).

7. See Louis Harris, "Oil or Israel?" *New York Times Magazine*, April 6, 1975.

8. See Philip E. Converse, "Religion and Politics: The 1960 Election," in Angus Campbell, Philip E. Converse, Warren E. Miller, and Donald E. Stokes, eds., *Elections and the Political Order* (New York: John Wiley & Sons, 1966), pp. 96–124.

Index

Age
  aging process as responsible for anti-Semitism, 27–28, 32, 187
  and difference in education by generation, 27, 28, 31, 32, 157, 187
  and first appearance of anti-Semitism, 73
  political anti-Semitism correlated to, 27
  and racism, 143–144, 146, 149–152, 153–155, 157
  social club discrimination correlated to, 27
  See also Education; Schools; Youth and anti-Semitism
American Independent Party, 171
American Protective Association, 166
"un-American," as political extremist slur, 161
Anomie
  and anti-Semitism, 50, 51–52
  defined, 49–50
  and education, 50–51
  and extremist politics, 178
  and norms, 50–52
  and simplism, 38
  See also Cognitive theories, abilities; Education; Social strains, changes; Socio-economic status
Anti-Defamation League, xi–xii, xvii
Anti-Semitism
  extent of, xii–xv, 1–2, 5–7
  public vs. private, 15–16, 19–20, 186
  virulence of, 106, 185
  See also Age; Blacks, anti-Semitism among; Black–Jewish relations; Christianity and anti-Semitism; Churches; Class and racism; Cognitive theories, abilities; Discrimination; Education; Emotive theories; Extremism, political; Intellectual factors; Jews perceived as . . .; Jews, presence of; Media; Mi-

norities; Politics; Prejudice; Psychological factors; Racism; Schools; Simplism; Socio-economic status; Stereotypes; Tolerance; Urban–rural differences; Youth and anti-Semitism
Atheists, tolerance of, 45
Authoritarian personality
  characteristics of, 36–37, 188
  and exposure to anti-Semitic authority figures, 191–192, 196, 197, 198
  and F scale, 48–49
  influenced by level of parents' education, 49
  and level of education, 37
  and syndrome of unenlightenment, 47–49
  See also Cognitive theories, abilities; Emotive theories; Germany, Nazi; Hitler
Authoritarian Personality, The
  emotive theory as discussed in, 36, 37, 47, 216
  F scale, use of in, 39–41, 48–49, 87

Baldwin, James, 54
Banking, perception of Jewish control of, 5, 8, 9, 186
  acceptance of, by sex, 28
  age and, 28
  black attitudes toward, 56, 61
  reality of, 197
Ben-Gurion, David, 111, 119
Biological traits, taught as cause of social difference, 27
Black–Jewish relations
  ambivalent nature of, 67–69
  assessing, xii
  contact, type and degree of, 63, 64, 67–68, 71, 187
  cooperation on mutually beneficial legislation, 63

225

Christmas carols, singing of in school, 12, 16, 186

"Christ-killer," Jews labeled as. *See*: Christ

Churches
congregations and clergy studied, xiv-xv
efforts of, to fight anti-Semitism and prejudice, xii-xiii, 204–206, 209
segregation in, 204–205
as source of anti-Semitism, 1, 192
See also Catholics; Christianity and anti-Semitism; Orthodoxy; Particularism; Protestants

Church members
awareness of official church pro-nouncements, 101, 205
particularist vs. clerical anti-Semitism, 108
and religious tolerance, 95
See also Clergy; Orthodoxy; Par-ticularism

Civil rights
adolescent attitude and anti-Semitism, 88–89
attitude toward, related to anti-Semitism, 47, 144–145
and education, 47
Jewish participation in, 55, 58, 62–63, 69, 71, 144, 187
and John Birch Society, 170
and the media, 43
movement from South to North, 144–145
violated by extremism, 183
white attitude toward, 138–139, 140–141, 142, 144–145
See also Black-Jewish relations; Discrimina-tion; Education; Extremism; Minori-ties; Norms, common; Norms, ideal

Class and anti-Semitism, 22–25, 26, 141–142, 186–187
among youth, 78–81
See also Cognitive theories, ability; Discrimination; Education; Extremist politics; Middle class; Norms, com-mon; Norms, ideal; Social changes, strains; Socio-economic status; Tolerance

Class and racism, 141–142, 152–153
See also Cognitive theories, ability; Discrimination; Education; Extremist politics; Middle class; Norms, com-mon; Norms, ideal; Social changes, strains; Socio-economic status; Tolerance

Clergy, attitudes of
blame on Jews for Crucifixion, 102–103, 104, 189
Particularist, vs. lay and anti-Semitism, 108, 109

Protestants, and orthodoxy, 98–99, 104, 108
Protestants, and salvation, 100, 108, 189
on religious tolerance, 95, 108
survey conducted, xv
See also Catholics; Churches; Particularists; Protestants; Orthodoxy

Clubs, social discrimination by
acceptance of, by age, 27
adolescent attitude toward, 79, 80
ambiguity of "public" nature of, 15–16, 186
black vs. Jewish, 138
black opposition to, 58, 64
against blacks, 138, 156, 220
against Jews, xi, 11, 12, 15–16, 19–20, 186, 220
as middle-class phenomenon, 22, 24, 25

Cognitive theories, abilities
and adolescents, 73–74, 88–90, 154–155,
dominated by emotive elements, 37, 188
education, lack of, and intellectual unenlightenment, 38, 44–45, 52, 53, 86–87
and Eichmann trial, 118–119
and F scale, 38–41, 43, 48, 49
and ideal norms, 35, 41–42, 88–89, 159, 169, 170, 171, 174, 180, 196
intellectual sophistication and prejudice, 34–35, 88–90, 91–92, 93, 187–189
and orthodox religion, 104–105, 109
simplism, 38–41
and syndrome of unenlightened beliefs, 47–49, 200–201
and tolerance of outgroups, 45–47
See also Education; Emotive theories; Ex-tremist politics; Tolerance

Communists, as target of political ex-tremism, 159, 168, 169–170, 171, 174, 175, 177

Colleges, discrimination against Jews, 11, 12–13, 185
as middle-class phenomenon, 22

Committee of One Million, 168

Congregationalists, 164

Conspiracy theories (espoused by extremist politics)
as bridge between different social classes, 162, 165, 166, 167, 169, 172, 173, 175, 176, 177, 182, 183, 189
against Catholics, 166–167
against communists, 168, 169–170
against Jews, 167, 168, 170
as manipulated by intellectuals, 162
used to gain votes by extremists, 164, 165–168
See also Cognitive theories, abilities; Edu-cation; Extremist politics; Prejudice;

Radical Rightists, 176
Rednecks, 176–177
Region
  anti-Semitism distributed by, 29–30, 145
  differences caused by urban–rural
    dispersal, 30, 32
  importance of, and racism, 144–145
  racism distributed by, 131–132, 142–143,
    144–145
  Rednecks, 176–177
  See also Education; Urban–rural
    differences
Republican Party, and political extremism,
  xiv, 166, 174, 176
  anti-Catholic elements in, 166
  support for McCarthyism, 170
Revech, Itzhak, 112
Rogat, Yosal, 119
Roper Public Opinion Library, xiv
Rosenberg's scale of self-esteem, 87

Schools
  discrimination against Jews, xi
  and exposure to cultural diversity, 24
  integration, and busing, 133–135, 137,
    140, 145, 155, 156, 203
  as reflection of social values, 203
  as source of anti-Semitism, 1, 204–205
  and struggle against prejudice, xii–xiii, 74,
    86, 202–204, 209
  See also Busing; Cognitive theories, abili-
    ty; Education
Segregation
  American attitudes about, 11–12
  Christianity and, 94,
  in church, 204–205
  Jewish, contemporary vs. historic, 3–4,
    94, 195
  See also Civil rights; Discrimination;
    Education; Housing; Integration
Self-acceptance
  and venting frustration on others, 87, 91
  See also Cognitive theories, ability;
    Emotive theories
Servatius, Robert, 112
Sex, acceptance of anti-Semitism by, 28–29,
  145
Silver Shirts, 168
Simplism
  and anomie, 38
  and anti-Semitism, 38, 39, 47, 71
  attitude toward education, 38–39
  current events, knowledge of, 38
  and degree of education, 39, 40, 43,
    44–45, 47
  democratic norms, support of, 38
  and extremist politics, 162–163, 165, 166,
    171, 178, 183

See also Cognitive theories, ability;
  Education; Prejudice
Smith, Alfred, 167
Smith, Gerald L. K., 101, 168, 192
Social distance
  and anti-Semitism among adults, 156
  and anti-Semitism among adolescents,
    78–81, 92, 152, 153
  and racism, 151–152, 153, 156
  See also Class and racism; Friendship;
    Socio-economic status
Social Distance Scale, 78
Social sensitivity, insensitivity, as function
  of intellectual sophistication, 22, 24, 25
  See also Cognitive theories, ability; Edu-
    cation; History; minorities; Norms,
    ideal; Prejudice; Tolerance
Socio-economic status
  and anti-Semitism, 23, 31, 186–87, 192
  and anti-Semitism among youth, 84–85,
    157, 192
  education as determinant of, 27
  lowering of, and extremist politics, 160,
    161, 164–165, 166, 169–170, 171, 173,
    174, 180
  and racism, 142–143, 146, 152–153, 154,
    156, 157
  See also Class and racism; Conspiracy
    theories; Extremist politics; Social
    distance; Youth
South
  acceptance of antiblack stereotypes in,
    131–132
  anti-Semitism in, 29–30, 146, 187
  anti-Semitism compared to racism in, 146
  busing in, 133–135, 145
  effect of education on racism in,
    142–143, 145
  political anti-Semitism in, 29, 30
  rural anti-Semitism in, 30, 32, 145, 156,
    192
  See also Busing; Christianity; Education;
    Extremist politics; Integration; Or-
    thodoxy; Particularism; Urban–rural
    differences
Stereotypes
  acceptance, degree of, 7–11, 19, 20,
    28–29, 47, 75–77, 78, 81, 149–151,
    190–192, 193–193
  acceptance of, as index of anti-Semitism,
    2, 6–7, 19, 20, 185–186
  anti-Semitic compared to racist, 149–151,
    191
  black acceptance of, 56, 57, 60, 61, 62,
    63, 71, 72, 187, 193–194
  and dislike of Jews, 194–195, 198
  logic of, 2–3, 4, 5, 34, 93, 175, 183, 186,
    191, 195

SEP 27 1979

5-12-94